RAVE REVIEWS FOR
FREE AGENT NATION

"A book with interesting facts . . . appealing interviews, friendly prose, and a provocative point of view."
—*New York Times*

"Funny . . . compelling and thoughtful . . . Pink is a good writer, quite a good one . . . entertaining . . . fine prose."
—**CNN.com**

"Excellent . . . Pink astutely summarizes what this major shift in employment means to millions of Americans. . . . Highly recommended."
—*Library Journal*

"That rare business book—both substantial and enjoyable to read."
—*The Economist*

"A nice surprise . . . punchy prose . . . prescient prognostications . . . Pink has done his homework, demonstrating most ably that the movement toward free agency is a symptom of much greater socioeconomic changes."
—*Miami Herald*

"Helps open the way for a national dialogue about the future meaning of career and community."
—*Orange County Register*

"The most important business book you will read this year."
—*Washington Business Forward*

more . . .

"Pink's key points ring true."
—*MBA Jungle*

"Pink writes more eloquently and with more humor than virtually all of his shelf-mates in the business section."
—**Monster.com**

"The most thoroughly researched, engagingly written examination of the self-employed phenomenon to date."
—*American Way*

"Astute observations . . . intriguing predictions. . . . It is our great good fortune to have the current political/economic map drawn by such an astute, articulate, and downright droll cartographer."
—*Times of Trenton*

"[Pink is] willing to challenge the status quo. . . . FREE AGENT NATION will shake up corporate America."
—*BookPage*

"Enlightening and insightful."
—*Harvard Business School Working Knowledge*

"Few books have depicted exactly how work and life have been transformed more accurately."
—*Financial Advisor*

FREE AGENT NATION

The Future of Working for Yourself

DANIEL H. PINK

WARNER
BUSINESS
BOOKS™

NEW YORK   BOSTON

Warner Business Books
Warner Books

Time Warner Book Group
1271 Avenue of the Americas, New York, NY 10020
Visit our Web site at www.twbookmark.com.

The Warner Business Books logo is a trademark of Warner Books.

Printed in the United States of America

Originally published in hardcover by Warner Books.
First Trade Edition: May 2002
10 9 8 7 6 5 4

The Library of Congress has cataloged the hardcover edition as follows:

Pink, Daniel H.
    Free agent nation : how America's new independent workers are transforming the way we live / Daniel H. Pink.
        p. cm.
    Includes index.
    ISBN 0-446-52523-5
        1. Self-employed—United States. 2. Entrepreneurship—United States.
    I. Title.

HD8037.U5 P56 2001
331.25—dc21

                                                                00-066257

Cover design by Roger Black
ISBN 0-446-67879-1 (pbk.)

For Jessica, of course

Contents

Author's Note

This book is a ground-level view of a revolution in how Americans work and live. It is the product of more than a year on the road and face-to-face interviews with several hundred independent workers. Except where noted in the text or endnotes, all quotations in the pages that follow (including the epigraphs that open each of the first thirteen chapters) come from interviews I conducted, and recorded on audiotape, during my journey through Free Agent Nation. In nearly all cases, I use people's real names. In the few instances where, at the subject's request, I use a pseudonym or disguise the person's identity, I note that in the text.

Among the many things I learned in my travels was how time-starved most Americans feel. And among the many things I've learned from reading nonfiction books is how little authors do to accommodate this reality of their readers' lives. That's why, at the end of every chapter of this book, I've included what I call "The Box." The Box contains the chapter's key information and arguments. It consists of four small entries: "The Crux," which summarizes the chapter in 150 words or less; "The Factoid," one particularly revealing statistic from the chapter; "The Quote," which pulls from the chapter one representative quotation; and "The Word," a novel term or phrase from the new vocabulary of free agency. Read only "The Box" and you'll miss the chapter's narrative and nuance—but not, I hope, its point.

Prologue

I suppose I realized that I ought to consider another line of work when I nearly puked on the Vice President of the United States.

It was a sweltering June day in Washington, D.C.—the kind of day that drenches your shirt and sours your mood. I was completing my second year as then Vice President Al Gore's chief speechwriter. And I was doing it hunched in front of my computer, banging on the keyboard, hoping that when my fingers stopped I'd have produced another sentence, and that this new sentence would move me closer to completing one of two speeches that were due that afternoon.

Seated at nearby desks were two other, only slightly less beleaguered, speechwriters with whom I shared a large and mangy office. Even on this most oppressive of days, we wore the mandatory uniform for White House men: suit pants, a starched shirt, and a tie cinched to the Adam's apple. Room 267 always smelled vaguely like a junior high locker room, but today was especially rank. As a climatological sauna baked the nation's capital, here in our own mini–seat of power, the air-conditioning had gone kaput. But away I typed, skittering ever nearer to finishing each speech, even as I melted into my cheap, gray chair.

At 5:45 that evening, I pulled both speeches from my printer, and scooted to the Vice President's West Wing office, about sixty paces down the hall from the Oval Office. At 6:00 P.M. the schedule called for "speech prep," a peculiar meeting, wherein the Vice President reads your speech and explains what he likes—or, more often, what he doesn't—as you sit there, mostly silent, absorbing the critique. This particular speech prep, however, was better than most. Gore was lighthearted and jokey (his office, let history record, had air-conditioning that day), and mostly satisfied with the texts. When the meeting began breaking up after about forty-five minutes, I lifted myself out of my chair—and immediately felt nauseated and light-headed.

I walked out of the Vice President's office, shut his imposing mahogany door behind us, and lingered in his waiting room, where still more aides answered phones, screened visitors, and guarded the inner sanctum. Noticing that I was wobbly, one of my colleagues said, "Dan, you look green."

"Yeah," I responded. "I don't feel so good."

The next thing I remember I was regaining consciousness, seated in a waiting room chair. And I was vomiting—steadily, calmly, like a seasoned pro. Not onto the plush vice presidential carpet fortunately, but into a ceremonial bowl that was a gift, I think, from the Queen of Denmark. (I've since learned that under certain interpretations of international treaties, my regurgitation could be construed as an act of war against the Nordic nation.) I looked up and blinked away the haze to reveal the horrified faces of my colleagues, unaccustomed to such displays in the West Wing. My first thought: "Oh no, this is how they're going to remember me. After all the blood I've sweated, the great lines I've written, the indignities I've endured, I'm going to be known as the guy who upchucked in the Veep's office."

Before long, Gore emerged from behind his office door, surveyed the scene, squared his heels to look at me, and drawled, "But Daaaaann. I said I *liiiiiked* the speech." Then after being assured by the ever-present Secret Service agent that I was a threat to neither his safety nor the U.S. Constitution, he returned to his office. A White House doctor arrived shortly thereafter. He spirited me to a West Wing examination room, checked my vitals, and issued the following diagnosis: exhaustion.

Three weeks later, on Independence Day, I left that job. Indeed, I left *all* jobs for good. I became a free agent.

I forged an office out of the attic of my Washington, D.C., home, and tried to parlay my skills and contacts into something resembling a living for my young family. I secured a contract with *Fast Company* magazine, and jumped on the phones to see if somebody would pay me for prose. Soon, they did—and I began working for myself, writing speeches and articles for just about anybody whose check would clear.

Now, truth be told, this move from the White House to the Pink House was something I'd been contemplating for a long time. My job had its charms at first—trips aboard *Air Force Two*, meetings at the vice presidential mansion, chance encounters with Wolf Blitzer. But before long, the hypoxia of having reached the heights of my profession gave way to a dull sadness. I missed my wife. I missed our daughter. I missed my life. And perhaps strangely for someone normally in "public service," I missed making a difference.

And I wasn't alone. At least that's what I sensed. Several of my friends and neighbors were making similar moves. They were abandoning traditional jobs to strike out on their own. Some, of course, were keen on building the next great company. But most were thinking smaller. Like me, they were tired and dissatisfied. They just wanted to be in charge of their lives.

Following this hunch, I asked my editors at *Fast Company* if I could look into this phenomenon—and what I found astonished me. It wasn't simply that legions of people were declaring independence—becoming self-employed, independent contractors, and micropreneurs. It was *why* they were doing it, and *how.* I wrote a cover story for the magazine about these "free agents," and within a day of publication my e-mail in box was bulging with messages, many of them downright gleeful. Each day, dozens of electronic epistles arrived thanking me for writing the article, and for identifying and legitimizing this new way to work.

At the same time, many commentators and pundits took aim at free agency. First, they said it couldn't *be:* a *Washington Post* columnist suggested that I ought to start taking Thorazine to curb my obvious hallucinations. Then they said it couldn't be *good: The New Yorker* called the article the "most eloquent manifesto" for the end of loyalty in America.

Regular people were cheering me on. Elites were shouting me down. I knew I was on to something.

The trouble was, that's about all I knew. The more I investigated free agency, the more I realized that our knowledge of this emerging workforce was at best scant—at worst, pathetic. Even with corporate downsizing an established practice, and computers and the Internet becoming more powerful every day, nobody could tell me much about people who work on their own or who have formed very small enterprises. The most likely sources of such information, the government's statistical agencies, didn't have the answers. Not the Bureau of Labor Statistics, which generates the influential monthly unemployment figures. Not the Commerce Department, even though one of its bureaus proclaims itself America's "national factfinder." And not the Treasury Department, which printed money but didn't much know how people earned it.

Then I hit upon an idea. How does any nation endeavor to understand itself? It takes a census. It talks to people, asks them a series of questions, and tries to paint a portrait of the country at that moment. Since we don't know much about free agents, why not conduct a census of Free Agent Nation?

On the day before my thirty-fourth birthday, the authorities chose to celebrate by issuing an urban heat advisory. The temperature had cracked three figures, the humidity had turned thermonuclear. I don't do well in heat (see above), but I had work to do. I was heading to Suitland, Maryland, a dreary little town three miles outside Washington. There, across the street from a strip mall, whose tenants include the A-1 Pawn Shop and the Christ Did It All Beauty Salon, is a four-acre plot of government land rimmed by a barbed wire fence—headquarters of the United States Census Bureau. And on the second floor of one of the complex's five buildings—a three-story box of beige bricks that resembles a Brezhnev era elementary school—sat the man I was after, James F. Holmes.

Holmes was acting director of the U.S. Census Bureau, a talented thirty-year bureau veteran thrust into the top job when the previous director abruptly resigned. In the space of a week, he'd gone from a post as director of the Census Bureau's Atlanta office to temporarily running the entire 2000 Census. Relying on some contacts I'd made at the White House, I'd arranged a meeting with Holmes, though I kept my exact purpose murky.

Holmes proved to be an exceptionally nice man from the moment he opened his door and welcomed me into his office. He wore an ecru shirt, a brown tie with a dizzying pattern, and a constant but sincere smile. Wisps of white hair crawled through his black mustache. His alert eyes gleamed behind square glasses. Holmes chatted amiably about the census as I summoned the courage to ask him the question that had brought me to his office.

I told him how impressed I was that the Census Bureau could manage a task as awesome as enumerating some 280 million people—and how useful the resulting data would be to the country. But, introducing the subject as gently as I could, I added that the government hadn't done a great job of counting free agents, describing their lives, or charting their future. What he needed—jeez, what America needed—was a census of Free Agent Nation. Then I offered to help. "If you'll deputize me," I said, "I'll go out and do the job myself."

His cheery disposition evaporated. He looked at his conference table, then up at me, then back down, and then up at me again.

I explained to Holmes that my census would be much like the 1790 census, the first census of the United States. Back then, Secretary of State Thomas Jefferson handled the job with the aid of only seventeen federal marshals. It wasn't perfect, but it was revealing. Jefferson admitted as much when he delivered his results to President George Washington. He sent Washington a letter in which the known returns were written in black and the conjectures in red. But those general impressions, Jefferson assured the President, were results "very near the truth." That would be my standard, too. If he deputized me to take a census of Free Agent Nation, I promised Holmes, I'd deliver results "very near the truth."

"I see you've done your homework," the acting census director sighed. "But it's not the sort of thing we ordinarily do. I'm afraid the answer is no." He agreed the country needed to learn more about microbusinesses, solo workers, and independent professionals—and he seemed somewhat interested in the project. Then when I turned my head, he excused himself, sprang from the table, and left his office. He said he wanted to ask his secretary Carol for something, though I suspect he also directed her to keep one finger on the button that speed-dialed security.

When Holmes returned, he handed me a slip of paper with the name of the Census Bureau staffer who specialized in the self-employed.

"I'm sure she'll be helpful," I told him. "But I'd like to do this myself. And I'll do it for free."

"Well, that's very nice of you," he said, remaining standing and subtly edging me out of his office.

"So there's no chance, huh?"

He shook his head.

"Okay," I said as I left the office. "I'll let you know how it goes."

He smiled, shook his head again, and returned to his conference table, where he would greet the next special pleaders who had already massed outside his office.

I called my wife from the Suitland parking lot. "He wouldn't deputize me," I told her. "I guess we'll have to do it ourselves."

"Cool," Jessica said. "Let's go."

And we did. For the next year, she and I, our young daughter—and before long, a second daughter—traveled America in search of Free Agent Nation. In countless cities in a few dozen states—in coffee shops, libraries, lobbies, and bookstores, in living rooms, kitchens, basements, and backyards—I talked with free agents of all varieties about their work, their lives, their dreams, their troubles, and their future. Like Jefferson, I was seeking results "very near the truth."

This is what I found.

PART ONE

Welcome to Free Agent Nation

1

Bye, Bye,
Organization Guy

"I'm not an organization woman. I'm not good at protecting the organization."

—Lisa Werner Carr (Dallas, Texas)

At 7:45 on an April morning, I find myself doing something I've never done before and likely will never do again: I'm standing outside a 7-Eleven in Bayside, Queens, scoping for a sixty-eight-year-old woman. Ah, there she is. Betty Fox . . . aka Grandma Betty . . . aka GrandmaBetty.com. She's pocketbook-clutching confirmation that the free agent ethic is seeping into almost every corner of American life.

Betty's story begins in the early 1960s. Her husband, David, dies at the age of thirty-three, leaving her to raise their two sons. The women's movement is dawning. *The Feminine Mystique* is flavoring the zeitgeist. But while one Jewish housewife named Betty is encouraging women to seize the workplace, this Jewish housewife named Betty finds the workplace seizing her. Forced to earn a living for her family, she becomes a bank teller. After that, she takes a clerical job at a boys shirt company, where she works for sixteen years. Then the company goes under—and Betty goes on unemployment. Through a Queens neighbor, she eventually finds a job as an office manager for a small billing company.

Until the company moves too far away for Betty to commute. She's sixty-seven. She doesn't have a job. She doesn't have a pension. But she's got a son who's a bank technology officer—and he hooks her up with WebTV, a service that lets people surf the Internet using their television sets.

Within a year, Betty becomes a citizen of Free Agent Nation.

Her Web site is called GrandmaBetty.com, "The Starting Point for Active Seniors." When she first experimented with WebTV, she always found too much material and never what she wanted. ("I'd search for 'peaches,' and I'd get all these pornographic sites!") So she started organizing material herself—and her son put the collection on her own Web site. Unbeknownst to her, she'd created what the venture capitalists and Internet gurus call a "portal." And through that portal came tides of e-mail. People asked Grandma Betty how to make yeast rolls, what to do about "severe constipation," where to buy support stockings. Betty surfed for answers, zapped replies, and added new links to her site. Today, she's got about fifty categories. Her entertainment section is *the* place to go for links to Ed Sullivan sites. Her "Humor Center" includes dillies like: "Old accountants never die. They just lose their balance."

As for the organizing principle, "It's all alphabetical," she told me proudly and repeatedly at the Queens diner where we talked. She's also an affiliate with a few online retailers, which produces a small revenue stream to accompany the writing and consulting gigs she's landed because of her Internet presence. Some large companies have even tried to buy her out.

"This is so much better than working for a boss," she says. "My son calls my site sticky. That's what I am. I'm sticky."

She is also the future. Although she may not know it, Betty Fox represents a fundamental change in the form, function, and ethic of American work. She's working solo, operating from her home, using the Internet as her platform, living by her wits rather than the benevolence of a large institution, and crafting an enterprise that's simultaneously independent and connected to others. Betty Fox is a free agent.

Over the past decade, in nearly every industry and region, work has been undergoing perhaps its most significant transformation since Americans left the farm for the factory a century ago. Legions of Americans, and increasingly citizens of other countries as well, are abandoning one of the Industrial Revolution's most enduring legacies—the "job"—and forging new ways to work. They're becoming self-employed knowledge workers, proprietors of home-based businesses, temps and permatemps, freelancers and e-lancers, independent contractors and independent professionals, micropreneurs and infopreneurs, part-time consultants, interim executives, on-call troubleshooters, and full-time soloists. And many others who hold what are still nominally "jobs" are doing so under terms closer in spirit to free agency than to traditional employment. They're telecommuting. They're hopping from company to company. They're forming ventures that are legally their employers, but whose prospects depend largely on their own individual efforts. And they're swapping, or being forced to swap, steady salaries for pay-for-performance agreements that compensate them in commissions, stock options, and bonuses.

Beneath the radar of the political and media establishment, tens of millions of Americans have become free agents. Some—fed up with bad bosses, dysfunctional workplaces, and the false promise of instant riches—have leapt. Others—clobbered by layoffs, mergers, and downturns—have been pushed. But they've all ended up in the same place, with many more on their heels. Understanding these new independent workers will be crucial to making sense of your own career, your own business, and the nation's social and economic future. Grasping Silicon Valley's latest hot technology or charting the trajectory of the Dow Jones Industrial Average may be interesting. But to truly understand where the economy is heading, you need to get to know free agents—who they are, what they do, how they work, and why they've made this choice.

THE WHYTE STUFF

For several generations, the American economy had a very different human emblem. In 1956 William H. Whyte, Jr., an editor at *Fortune*, began a now legendary work of nonfiction with these two sentences: "This book is about the organization man. If the term is vague, it is because I can think of no other way to describe the people I am talking about."[1]

The Organization Man. The title marched into our national vocabulary. The label described what was then the quintessence of work in America: an individual, almost always male, who ignored or buried his own identity and goals in the service of a large organization, which rewarded his self-denial with a regular paycheck, the promise of job security, and a fixed place in the world. "They are the dominant members of our society . . ." Whyte wrote of the Organization Men, "and it is their values which will set the American temper."[2] Whyte's book became a surprise hit—occupying the best-seller list for seven months and corporate and college reading lists for several decades.

The Organization Men often preached rugged individualism. But instead of living by it, they had lowered "their sights to achieve a good job with adequate pay and proper pension and a nice house in a pleasant community populated with people as nearly like themselves as possible," Whyte wrote. They abided by what he called a Social Ethic, a secular theology that placed the organization at the center of belief—an all-knowing being that was master, servant, and benefactor. In the catechism of work, you were loyal to the organization so that the organization would be loyal to you. Belongingness mattered more than idiosyncrasy, group harmony more than individual expression. And you pledged fealty to a large institution, and accepted the demands of its theology, not merely because it was a shrewd way to achieve financial stability—but because it was a proper and honorable way to live. "When a young man says that to make a living these days you must do what somebody else wants you to do," Whyte wrote, "he states it not only as a fact of life that must be accepted but as an inherently good proposition."[3]

Indeed, Whyte discovered that much of America's long-standing reverence for self-made men and pioneer spirits had dissolved and hardened into pity. "The entrepreneur, as many see him, is a selfish type motivated by greed, and he is, furthermore, unhappy."[4] Not the Organization Man. So long as he resisted the temptations of independence and conformed to the accepted behavioral code, he would lead a satisfying life: "The man of the future, as junior executives see him, is not the individualist but the man who works through others for others."[5]

Whyte wrote *The Organization Man* in the midst of an extended economic boom. And for much of the remainder of the twentieth century, the Organization Man was the passkey to understanding the American economy. Whether you were a manager, a housewife, a journalist, or a student, if you understood the Organization Man—his constellation of values, his form of employment, his place in the broader society—you understood almost everything you needed to know about work in America at that time. But Whyte discovered that this new ethic also reached beyond the corporate hive. It infiltrated universities and laboratories. It became the animating idea of the suburbs. Gradually, it established the very premises of our national life. If you understood the Organization Man during those postwar decades, you understood America itself at that time—what assumptions girded our present, what aspirations guided our future.

It's easy to forget how tightly Organization Man thinking gripped our lives. The Fortune 500 list, launched within two years of Whyte's book, became a central indicator of national well-being—those giant companies a measure of economic might and a testament to our capacity to produce millions of jobs. And corporate paternalism, so obviously an anachronism today, was not only prevalent, it was *explicit*. My grandfather, for example, worked forty years for the phone company—an enterprise known universally as "*Ma* Bell." Metropolitan Life Insurance, another large and respected employer, prided itself on being "*Mother* Met." And Kodak, which until a decade ago accounted for one third of the Rochester, New York, economy, was known locally as the "Great Yellow *Father*." (Kodak sometimes even edged from parenthood to divinity. The day the company issued its yearly bonuses was known around town as St. Kodak's Day.) Like faithful parents, organizations would take care of their own.

But beginning in the 1980s, and reaching a crescendo in the 1990s, conditions and attitudes changed. Between 1984 and

1994, Ma Bell winnowed its workforce by 120,000 people.[6] Mother Met laid off ten thousand workers. The Great Yellow Father cut more than twenty thousand jobs. Companies sometimes still called themselves families. But they kept finding themselves explaining that some members of the family would, uh, be leaving home. Meanwhile, new technologies simultaneously reconfigured corporate structures and equipped individuals with the computing and communications firepower once reserved for large companies. As the twenty-first century unfolded, it had become clear that the Organization Man had lost much of his power as the decoder ring of the American economy. What was much less clear was what figure would replace him.

Until now.

This book is about the free agent. If the term is vague, it is because I can think of no other way to describe the people I am talking about. They are free from the bonds of a large institution, and agents of their own futures. They are the new archetypes of work in America. Today, in the shadow of another economic boom, America's new economic emblem is the footloose, independent worker—the tech-savvy, self-reliant, path-charting micropreneur.

Consider this: Fewer than one in ten Americans now works for a Fortune 500 company. The largest private employer in the U.S. is not Detroit's General Motors or Ford, or even Seattle's Microsoft or Amazon.com, but Milwaukee's Manpower Inc., a temp agency with more than 1,100 offices in the U.S.[7] The dream of America's young people? Not to climb through an organization, or even to accept a job at one, but to create their own gig on their own terms—often on the World Wide Web.

This transition from one icon to another is embodied in the Fitzgerald family, a spirited clan from upstate New York. Walt Fitzgerald moved up the organization chart—until he was eased out, at age fifty-five, after thirty years of service. His daughter, Theresa Fitzgerald, climbed the corporate ladder—until at age thirty-five, having achieved the senior position in her department, she quit to become a free agent.

For Walt Fitzgerald, the large organization was General Electric, the multinational mammoth whose manufacturing operations allowed his hometown of Utica, New York, to proclaim itself the "Radio Capital of the World." Walt joined GE in 1958. He'd stay for the next three decades. After a first job drawing and designing radio cabinets, he moved into package design, which led him to the marketing department—which eventually resulted in an almost twenty-year stint managing trade shows for the company. All the while, he lived the life of an Organization Man—even though he never considered himself one ("I never thought too much about it," he told me) and even though he was something of a renegade inside the operation. (Well before the advent of business casual, Walt often went to work without a necktie, to the horror of many colleagues.) He commuted fifty miles each day, leaving the Fitzgerald home before Theresa and her four siblings woke up, eating breakfast at a diner, then driving to his office in Syracuse.

It was a good life, he said, but not necessarily the life he wanted. When Walt won a $500 bonus for an improvement idea he'd dropped in the office suggestion box, he used the money to enroll in a correspondence course at the Famous Artists School, founded by Norman Rockwell. "I used to get up every morning at 4:30 or 5:00 and do my assignments before I'd go to work," he says. His talent was obvious. Rockwell himself told him so. But Walt never had the time to pursue his dream of becoming an artist. When he began managing trade shows, "That kind of just went away. I was not doing any art at all, and it became very frustrating to try to do any." Walt may have led a Norman Rockwell life—but what he wanted was the life of Norman Rockwell.

In 1985, at a conference in South Carolina, Walt clicked on a hotel television and learned that his company was acquiring another behemoth, RCA. That $6.3 billion acquisition soon prompted layoffs in the merged company and a new attitude internally. "Until then, you always pretty much knew where you stood," he told me one morning over huevos rancheros in Santa Fe, New Mexico, where he now lives. "It was the first time in my career that politics seemed to get in the way of doing my job." Not much later, sensing that once-loyal Organization Men like him were no longer highly prized, he took a buyout. At age fifty-five, he had a full pension, a broken marriage, and no job.

Around the same time, his daughter entered the workforce. Armed with a degree in graphic art, Theresa landed a job at United Media, a large company that, among other things, syndicates and licenses comic strips. This Organization Daughter rose quickly—from someone else's flunky to someone with flunkies of her own. She began as a junior designer, won a promotion to senior designer, and within a decade became creative director, the big kahuna of her department. In her father's day, that constituted success.

But Theresa's rise—always accompanied by more money and greater responsibility—moved her further and further from what she loved. Like her father, her passion was art. But instead of doing art, she was managing people who did art. "I'd come into the studio, and say, 'You guys are having all the fun,'" Theresa says. Stuck at meetings and drained by corporate politics, she left her job when she'd reached its very heights—a career move she calls a "reverse commute." But rather than get another job, she became a free agent. She now works out of her computer-equipped Brooklyn apartment designing logos, packages, and other materials for an assortment of clients instead of a single boss. She earns more money, attends fewer meetings, and does the work she loves. "It's very pure," she told me one afternoon at a coffee joint on Manhattan's Upper West Side. "I'm really more of a craftsperson than a manager."

So, it turned out, was her dad. A few months after Walt left GE, executives there hired him back as an independent consultant to oversee several projects. He did well—so well they offered him a full-time job. But Walt declined. This Organization Man decided to stay a free agent, a craftsperson plying his trade. Like daughter, like father.

Hollywood, USA

The transition from Organization Man to free agent is both a cause and a consequence of another profound economic and social change: Power is devolving from the organization to the individual. The individual, not the organization, has become the economy's fundamental unit. Put more simply, we're all going Hollywood.[8]

During the first half of the twentieth century, large studios run by commanding figures like Jack Warner and Louis B. Mayer dominated the movie business. The studios controlled much of the technology, most of the distribution, and nearly all the talent needed to make a film. Actors, directors, writers, and technicians usually were their permanent employees, glamorous wage slaves. But in the 1950s, due to the rise of television and a U.S. Supreme Court anti-trust decision that forced studios to divest themselves of their theaters, the studio-centered system crumbled and power shifted. The individual became preeminent, and the industry adapted itself to the individual's rise. Today, the movie business works on a different model. Talented people (actors, directors, writers, animators, key grips, and so on) and very small firms come together for a particular, finite project. When they complete the project, they disband, each participant having learned new skills, forged new connections, deepened existing relationships, enhanced their reputations within the industry, and earned a credit they can add to their résumé. Some portion of these people may gather again—along with a new crop of people—for another project. And when that project wraps, the free agents again will head their separate ways. Over and over it goes. Talent assembles in a specific place for a specific purpose—and when the mission is complete, this makeshift organization disassembles and its individual units move to the next gig.

The Hollywood model is the free agent model. Large permanent organizations with fixed rosters of individuals are giving way to small, flexible networks with ever-changing collections of talent. Increasingly, this is a common arrangement for producing new Web sites, new electronic goods, new magazines, new buildings, new ad campaigns, new pharmaceuticals, and just about any other product or service whose key ingredients are the brainpower, creativity, skill, and commitment of the people involved. To craft a new piece of software, high-tech companies enlist platoons of free agent programmers and code jockeys, who work on teams with a few traditional employees under tight deadlines and intense pressure. When the product ships, the free agents ship out—their wallets fatter, their résumés longer. Orchestras that don't have a permanent slate of musicians—for instance, the New York Chamber Symphony, the Brooklyn Philharmonic, the American Symphony Orchestra—assemble free agent musicians for performances.[9] And a public relations firm—say, Smith & Jones P.R.—often consists now of only Smith and Jones, whose major skill is collecting the right group of other professionals for a particular project. "Work today," says business über-guru Tom Peters, "is about two things: talent and projects."[10]

This broad shift in power from the organization to the individual has provided the individual with enormous flexibility, producing a corresponding and equally profound change on the personal level. In the era of the Organization Man, work was a one-size-fits-all proposition. You wore a blue collar or a white one, slipped on your work boots or buttoned up your gray flannel suit. People generally arrived at work at the same time as their colleagues—and left in unison as well. Try to picture work in that era and you'll likely conjure one of two images: a regiment of identically dressed assembly line workers exiting the factory gates at the sound of the whistle—or a herd of gray-flanneled middle managers boarding a commuter train in lockstep at precisely 7:31 A.M. Uniform work required uniformed workers.

Today, thanks to a host of factors—among them, technology, prosperity, the Hollywood model of organizing production—work is no longer confined to a single size. It has transformed from mass-produced to handcrafted, from off-the-rack to tailor-made. Theresa Fitzgerald, like other free agents, begins work when she must and ends it when she can. Some days, that's a regular nine-to-five arrangement, other days it's eleven to eight. Still other days, she might not work at all. So long as she's serving clients and making money, it's up to her. If she wants to grow her operation larger, she can. If she doesn't, she doesn't have to. It's up to her. If she can afford it, she can accept certain assignments and decline others. It's up to her. Even though he bristled against it, Walt Fitzgerald mostly adapted himself to the One Size Fits All Ethic. His daughter's credo is My Size Fits Me.

The mass production economy flourished through the assembly line techniques of Frederick Winslow Taylor, whose Scientific Management theory preached repetition, rote routines, standardization, and "One Best Way"—a practice that came to be known as Taylorism. The free agent economy flourishes through a different approach—personalized, customized, fashioned to the individual—what we might call "Tailorism."

The turn from Taylorism to Tailorism is a key reason why most free agents enjoy working this way. It is likely the reason that, given a choice between being an employee and being self-employed, more than seven out of ten Americans choose self-employment.[11] For both the doers and the dreamers, free agency is not just a style of work. It's a way of life. And—here's the point—it's usually a *better* way of life. This insight, borne out in hundreds of interviews and in the stories I'll tell later in this book—and confirmed by academic research and public opinion data—surprises some, who expect rampant fear and loathing in Free Agent Nation. To be sure, the positive sentiments are not universal. The Bureau of Labor Statistics reports that well over half of what it calls "contingent workers" said in a survey that they'd rather be working at full-time, traditional jobs.[12] And one trip to Seattle, where permatemps without benefits work alongside Microsoft employees with lucrative stock options—sometimes for years—is enough to understand the dark side of the temping of America.

Yet the fiercest resistance to the rise of free agency comes not from independent workers themselves, but from those whose current position derives in part from deftly playing by the old rules. "No matter how much we dream about it, most of us prefer the security of a job and paycheck," grumbled *Fortune*, the old economy journalistic baron in whose pages Whyte's landmark ideas first appeared. "No amount of entrepreneurship propaganda will change human nature. High levels of self-employment aren't so much proof of a creative and courageous workforce as evidence that a desperate population doesn't have job opportunities."[13] For this delegation of doomsayers, free agency is a threat—both to their status and, perhaps more important, to their cherished notions about how people should behave, how companies must operate, and how economies can flourish. But like it or not, celebrate it or excoriate it, Free Agent Nation isn't going away. As science fiction writer William Gibson once said, "the future is here; it's just not evenly distributed." And as this future distributes itself more evenly, it is upending several long-held assumptions about work and life in America.

PREMISES, PREMISES

If actions are the architecture of our lives, premises are the plumbing. You can't see them—but like the pipes or wiring that snake invisibly through a home, they determine the capabilities of the structure and the efficiency of its performance. Stick with me on this analogy, because it's about to get slightly weird. Imagine that a few strange people crept into your home while you were on vacation, and replaced your electrical system with solar power. Then suppose they removed the concrete foundation and substituted wheels. And say they also decided that your second bathroom ought to be a mini basketball court—so they redid the plumbing and added a hardwood floor and a hoop. When you returned from vacation, your house might look outwardly like the three-bedroom, two-bath colonial you departed two weeks before. But what you've really got is a solar-powered, mobile home with an indoor arena. And that will affect both the possibilities and limits of the family manse.

Free agency is like those odd architectural interlopers. Quietly, it has rewired the circuitry and remodeled the structures on which our social, cultural, and economic house is built. It's here—deep in the realm of premises and first principles—that free agency is having its greatest impact. It has already begun overturning a dozen central assumptions about contemporary American work and life.

MISTAKEN PREMISES

1. Loyalty is dead. Last decade's blaze of downsizing, this decade's dot-com layoffs, and the end of lifetime job security have eroded loyalty in the workplace, right? Not quite. In Free Agent Nation, loyalty isn't dead. It's different. Instead of the up-and-down loyalty that runs from an individual to an institution, free agents practice a new side-to-side loyalty—a fierce allegiance to clients, colleagues, ex-colleagues, teams, professions, projects, and industries. In some ways, loyalty is stronger than ever.

2. The workforce is adrift, operating without a broad social contract. True, the implicit employment deal that reigned in the Organization Man's day has disappeared. But a new one has emerged, the animating bargain of free agency in which individuals trade talent for opportunity.

3. The best measure of economic success is growth. The traditional view is that a larger company with higher profits is more successful than a smaller company with lower profits. But these economics don't necessarily apply to free agents. Bigger isn't better. *Better* is better. As millions of free agents decide that staying small is preferable to growing big, they are redefining the very notion of success.

4. The free agent economy makes workers less secure. Sometimes. But as many free agents fashion a diversified portfolio of multiple clients, customers, and projects, they often find themselves *more* secure than traditional employees.

5. Parents must try to balance work and family. For much of the past two decades, middle-class Americans have struggled to balance work and family. Corporations have responded with so-called family-friendly initiatives and governments have passed laws mandating family leave. But these well-intentioned efforts haven't alleviated the anxiety. Why? They offer One Size Fits All solutions for a My Size Fits Me workforce. That's why many free agents have taken a different approach and scrapped the balancing act altogether. For them, the solution is mostly to *erase* the boundary between work and family. Blending, not balance, is often their answer.

6. *Small entrepreneurs and solo workers, missing that fabled water cooler, are isolated and lonely.* Isolation is a genuine risk of working this new way, but free agents have formed an array of ingenious small groups to rebuild workplace social life and redefine community.

7. *Americans should—or even want to—retire.* Retirement is, in many ways, a twentieth-century aberration. Why should it be a twenty-first-century fixture—especially when the notion is increasingly less necessary, not to mention less desirable, for many older Americans? Instead of going gently into the retirement night, free agents are inventing a new old age. Just ask Grandma Betty.

8. *Public education is in a crisis that can be repaired with better testing, higher standards, and more rigorous discipline.* The main crisis in schools today is irrelevance. And the main problem with most education solutions is that they incrementally improve Taylorist solutions for a Tailorist workforce. Of all the institutions in America, schools have least adapted themselves to the free agent economy. Watch for more middle-class families opting to home-school their children on their own terms and consistent with their own values. And expect more Americans to begin questioning whether formal schooling should be compulsory and whether a college degree is necessary.

9. *"Empowering" workers and trying to "retain" them is a wise strategy for corporate managers at talent-starved companies.* As more employees head for the exits, more organizations are redoubling their efforts to keep them in their cubicles. But these tactics tend to fail because they rest on flawed assumptions. "Empowerment" implies that the organization holds the power, and is generously granting some of it to the individual. But in a free agent economy, organizations need individuals more than individuals need organizations. ("Hey, I think I'll empower GM today by showing up for work.") Corporate attempts at empowerment, consequently, are both laughable and patronizing. Ditto for "retention." With a free agent workforce, you can inspire people and challenge people, but you can't "retain" them.

10. *Americans ought to get their health insurance through an employer.* This is the standard arrangement for most Americans under sixty-five who have health insurance. The trouble is, it's an arrangement built on a historic accident and underpinned by almost no economic or moral logic. Why should employer-based health insurance continue—especially when fewer of us will *have* employers?

11. *Men are overrepresented in the workforce and in the top positions of the economy.* Women still earn less than men for similar work. And women still face a stubborn glass ceiling. Those aren't good things, but they might end up mattering far less than some think. Women are a driving force behind free agency, and could possibly dominate the free agent economy.

12. *Rampant individualism is fraying our social fabric.* Critics on both the left and the right agree on one thing: Our common culture is corroding. And they argue that a hypercharged free agent economy, with its fleeting rela-

tionships and temporary commitments, only speeds the corrosion. However, free agency may have the opposite effect. Instead of fraying bonds, it will mend them. Instead of eroding community, it will repair it. Instead of promoting a race to the bottom, it will trigger a scramble to the high ground. The "art of association"—genuine community forged by ones "own interest rightly understood"—that Alexis de Tocqueville noted on his visit to America two centuries ago is alive and well in Free Agent Nation.

Free agency is reconfiguring the basic assumptions of American work and life. And as these tectonic plates slide into new positions, what appears on the surface will begin to change as well. Existing arrangements will topple. New ones will arise in their place. For all the talk about paradigm shifts and digital revolutions, for each climb in the S&P 500 and collapse in the NAS-DAQ, for every panting account of this Internet millionaire and every scornful chronicle of that dot-com implosion, we have been missing the larger story.

Free agency is the *real* new economy.

THE BOX

CHAPTER 1

THE CRUX: In the second half of the twentieth century, the key to understanding America's social and economic life was the Organization Man. In the first half of the twenty-first century, the new emblematic figure is the free agent—the independent worker who operates on his or her own terms, untethered to a large organization, serving multiple clients and customers instead of a single boss. The rise of free agency shatters many ironclad premises about work, life, and business in America— from how companies should operate, to how we structure our health care, retirement, and education systems, to which values guide our lives. To truly understand the new economy, you must first understand the free agent.

THE FACTOID: The largest private employer in the U.S. is not Detroit's General Motors or Ford, or even Seattle's Microsoft or Amazon.com, but Milwaukee's Manpower Inc., a temp agency.

THE QUOTE: "This book is about the free agent. If the term is vague, it is because I can think of no other way to describe the people I am talking about. They are free from the bonds of a large institution, and agents of their own futures. They are the new archetypes of work in America."

THE WORD: *Tailorism.* The free agent's approach to work; descendant of Taylorism, Frederick Winslow Taylor's One Best Way method of mass production. Under Tailorism, free agents fashion their work lives to suit their own needs and desires— instead of accepting the uniform values, rules, and structure of a traditional job. Opposite of the One Size Fits All ethic of the Organization Man era. (Synonym: *My Size Fits Me*)

2

How Many Are There?
The Numbers and
Nuances of Free Agency

"I have no idea how many free agents there are. But everywhere I look, I have friends who have gone off on their own."

—Leigh Gott (Milwaukee, Wisconsin)

For a few years during the 1990s, I was a peripheral player in one of the federal government's most important secret rituals. On the first Friday of every month, the U.S. Bureau of Labor Statistics releases a data-drenched document called the *Monthly Employment Report*. The innocuously wonky title belies the report's massive influence. Within its pages are rivers of numbers that can buoy or bury global financial markets with a single up or down movement—so the figures are carefully guarded, lest they trickle out and equip somebody with lucrative inside information.

At 8:00 A.M. on the appointed Friday, the commissioner of the Bureau of Labor Statistics, along with an aide, meets with the U.S. secretary of labor in the secretary's cavernous office overlooking the U.S. Capitol. The commissioner tells the labor secretary (and usually one of his or her own top staffers) about the previous month's employment data: how many Americans had jobs, how many couldn't find work, and what the nation's unemployment rate was. The foursome discuss what that month's numbers mean for the economy—in particular, how the ever-irritable financial markets may react. Then at 8:30, the BLS reveals the data to the rest of the world. For a half hour, the four people in that office know what at that moment is perhaps the most valuable information on the planet. And for five minutes, they used to let me in on the secret.

I worked as an aide and speechwriter to Robert B. Reich, who headed the U.S. Labor Department during President Clinton's first term. Each "numbers day," I'd camp outside his office, station myself before a computer, and await my signal. Then at 8:25, somebody would invite me into the sanctum where I would learn the numbers, talk to Secretary Reich about his views on the figures, and depart to craft a press statement on his behalf. It was a heady moment. During those three hundred glorious seconds, I knew something that Bill Gates, George W. Bush, even Oprah Winfrey could not know: the U.S. unemployment rate. (Federal Reserve Chairman Alan Greenspan knew, of course. He gets the numbers Thursday afternoon.) And as I wrote the statement, which inevitably concluded that the month's figures confirmed the wisdom of Clinton administration economic policies, I'd periodically toggle to some online newswire or listen for a nearby TV. Because by 8:31, markets around the world were reacting to this news—sometimes swooning in despair, other times swing-dancing in delight. And by the time the U.S. stock exchanges opened an hour later, billions of dollars were changing hands—entire fortunes were being made and lost—in response to the numbers that emerged from that nearby room.

But for all the peculiarly nerdy thrill of being privy to this information before anyone else, I was always a little concerned. Back then, and still today, the BLS seemed a bit behind the times. Here in the early dawn of the twenty-first century—when desktop computers and handheld PDAs grow unrelentingly more powerful and preposterously more compact, when an electronic information skin sheathes the globe, when new developments in genetics and biotechnology shake our notions of life itself, and when the form, function, and location of work is in upheaval—the Bureau of Labor Statistics divides all American workers into two categories:

"Farm" and "Nonfarm."

As a card-carrying member of the nonfarm economy, I found this a bit insulting. As an investor, I found this a tad worrisome. (Most of my investments are parked in the "nonfarm" sector.) And later, when I tried using the BLS figures to determine the size of the free agent workforce, I found it downright frustrating.

Indeed, as I investigated further, I discovered that the BLS didn't really understand what free agents are—let alone how many they number. The agency does compile some figures for temps, self-employed Americans, and independent contractors—but all are likely undercounts and those three categories are but subsets of free agents.

Even the surveys that the government uses to gather data are geared to a way of work that is fast becoming the exception rather than the norm. To collect the underlying information for the unemployment rate, the government relies on what's called The "Current Population Survey," a monthly telephone and door-to-door sample of about fifty thousand households. Think about the previous week, the government surveyor directs his subject. "Were you employed by government, by a private company, a nonprofit organization, or were you self-employed?" Now imagine someone like Theresa Fitzgerald, the Organization Daughter we met in Chapter 1, answering that question. Suppose that this week she was on a two-month design project for Amalgamated Wireless. She'd probably say that she was "employed" by Amalgamated Wireless—even if when the project ends, she'll be off to a new gig at Industrial Carpet Supply, Inc. But she's not an employee—not Amalgamated Wireless's, not Industrial Carpet's, not anyone's. She's a free agent. For workers like her, a snapshot of what somebody's doing in a given week may conceal more about that person's broader work life than it reveals.

Now suppose Theresa thought a bit and said, "You know, strike that. I'm not employed by anyone. I'm really self-employed." The surveyor would then ask Theresa if she had incorporated her one-woman operation. (Many free agents incorporate to limit their legal liability.) If Theresa said yes, she'd be marked as a paid employee and would be tallied as a wage and salary worker—a *nonfarm* wage and salary worker, no doubt—and not a free agent. In the eyes of the numbers police, she'd be an employee of a corporation (albeit her own), much like the wage and salary types over at Industrial Carpet.

What's more, the other survey the feds use—which purports to measure employment *growth*—surveys only "business establishments" and therefore ignores the *unincorporated* self-employed. Since these Americans don't hold "jobs"—that is, they aren't an employee of an establishment—tallies of whether employment is growing or shrinking don't include them.

Here's the problem: Free agents, and ever more working people generally, do not nestle comfortably into the categories "employer" and "employee." Free agents are *neither* employers nor employees; free agents are *both* employers and employees. That may sound like a Zen koan, but it's a key feature of this new economy.

In a sense, the government has become adept at separating apples and oranges, tossing them in their proper piles, and methodically counting the fruit in each stack. That's a valuable exercise. But it becomes less illuminating when vast numbers of us become, say, papayas. The federal fruit counters call reddish papayas apples and orangish papayas oranges. It's better than not counting at all, but it's still not quite right.

To be fair, getting the tally right is extremely difficult. After all, the essence of data collection is grouping like things together. But the essence of free agency is to distinguish one's self from the group—to craft one's own unique style of work rather than adapt to a standardized form. Tailorism, rather than Taylorism. And tracking free agents isn't easy. Regular employees are like flowers. Rooted in the ground, they may sway in the breeze a bit, but they move only when some external force uproots them, ending or threatening their very lives. Free agents are more like bees. They flit from place to place—doing their business and moving on. Just as it's easier to count flowers than bees, it's easier to count "employees" than free agents.

Twice, in 1995 and 1997, the BLS tried to count what it calls "contingent" workers—an effort that managed to be both underinclusive and overinclusive. Underinclusive because it relied on the same narrow categories it had always used. Overinclusive because it also said that contingent means "basically those jobs that are not expected to last."[1] Isn't that *every* job nowadays? Many people can't be sure their company, or even their industry, will be around in ten years or even five. Most workers, in fact, will outlive just about any organization for which they work, as we'll see in the next chapter. How can anybody expect his current job to "last"?

Note to Uncle Sam: We're all contingent now.

Neither the BLS nor any other government statistical agency is at fault here. The BLS in particular has many extremely dedicated and talented people, and the agency is actually one of the federal government's most effective. But with an annual budget of $399 million, it simply lacks the resources to do the job right. More taxpayer dollars go to subsidizing peanut production than to collecting and analyzing the labor statistics that roil the stock market and shape government policy.[2] And free agency isn't the only creek where our measuring sticks are becoming less accurate. In many other realms, the economy has raced faster than our ability to measure it. For instance, productivity—how many widgets somebody cranks out in a given unit of time—has traditionally been a crucial measure of economic performance. But how do you measure productivity in an economy in which one good idea is more valuable than a thousand identical things? Or take the problem vexing many accounting firms and auditors: How do you construct a balance sheet for a company with few hard assets—buildings, equipment, cars, and other easily countable things—but with many extremely valuable *intangible* assets such as brands, patents, and people? Or consider inflation, the Darth Vader of the old economy. If a computer costs a little more than it did last year, but it's twice as powerful, is that inflation? Or is it really deflation? Accurately measuring who works how is merely the latest in a series of statistical challenges that the changing economy poses.

Still, coming up with some reliable numbers on the size and shape of Free Agent Nation is important for understanding this new way of work—even if those numbers are only, in Jefferson's phrase, "very near the truth." And a way to begin is by grouping these new workers into some broad categories.

THREE FREE AGENT SPECIES

Unlike Organization Men, free agents don't fit into neat taxonomic compartments. "There are very few universals with this group," says America's premier demographics journal. "They're builders, salesmen, and Mary Kay reps. It makes for a demographic debacle."[3] But using the several hundred interviews I conducted around the country, and drawing on a range of private data sources, public opinion surveys, and economic research, I've found that most free agents are at least approximations of one of three basic free agent species: soloists, temps, and microbusinesses.

Soloists

The most common variety of free agent is the soloist—someone who works for herself, generally alone, moving from project to project selling her services. Theresa Fitzgerald is a good example.

Soloists, though, are not exactly a twenty-first-century innovation. Writers, artists, and photographers have worked this way for decades—usually calling themselves freelancers. And both the idea of freelancing and the term itself are even older, dating back to the Middle Ages and the bands of Italian and French mercenaries who roamed Europe looking for a war. These so-called free companions would fight for any sovereign and march under any banner—if the price were right and the battle worthy. When this notion migrated to England, some British subjects began calling these rent-a-knights "free lances." They weren't free of charge, but they were free of loyalty. Have lance, will travel. The term became commonplace thanks to Scottish poet and novelist Sir Walter Scott, whose 1819 work *Ivanhoe* included these semifamous lines:

> "I offered Richard the service of my Free Lances. . . . Thanks to bustling times, a man of action will always find employment."

And while "freelance" often connoted merely alternative employment, the term has frequently carried the faint whiff of dishonor. Late-nineteenth-century British newspapers often branded members of Parliament "freelancers" when those legislators criticized their own party or voted with the opposition. During the same era, some used the term to describe a persistent adulteress. And for a time in the 1960s, "freelancer" was slang for a prostitute who didn't have a pimp.[4]

Today's freelancers are a less vilified portion of the workforce. Hundreds of professional associations contain the word "freelance" or "freelancers" in their names. And this category has even spawned its own subcategory: workers MIT professor Tom Malone has dubbed e-lancers. E-lancers find gigs through the Internet, team up online for particular projects, and then go their merry way into cyberspace when the project ends.

While Europe in the Middle Ages produced a knightly label for soloists, America in the twentieth century produced—what else?—a legal term: independent contractor. Just as "freelancer" is ingrained in the vernacular, "independent contractor" is defined in the law. It's a term that defines what a soloist is by what she is *not*. An independent contractor is *not* an "employee." She *doesn't* have a single, enduring, more or less permanent relationship with one employer. This distinction matters a great deal under the law. Most wage-earning employees, especially those employed by larger companies, are covered by a quilt of labor laws—statutes and regulations that guard their pensions, give them the right to unionize, require time-and-a-half for working more than forty hours in a week, protect them against race and sex discrimination, and mandate minimum safety levels at their workplaces. Independent contractors, by contrast, lack the protections of almost all of these laws.

Self-employed soloists also go by a variety of nonlegal terms that are useful in describing their work if not counting their numbers. Among the terms: *consultant*, once a euphemism for an unemployed white-collar worker, now a common label for independent workers; *permalancer*, someone who begins as a contract worker and decides to maintain that status even when offered a traditional job; *techno-cowboy, hired gun, lone ranger*, and other labels from the Wild West; *gurus, nomads, gypsies*, and other labels from the Ancient East; *cab driver* and *information backpacker*, often used to describe new media freelancers; *lone eagles*, coined by the think tank Center for the New West; and terms based on tax status such as *sole proprietor* and *1099er*. One of the best in this collection is British management philosopher Charles Handy's *portfolio worker*. Soloists have a portfolio of clients, assignments, and roles—rather than a single function, narrow task, and sole employer.

However we label this first species of free agents, we know that the U.S. has plenty of them. They are plumbers, management consultants, independent truckers, graphic designers, carpet installers, and computer programmers—just about any occupation in which a person can work for a series of clients. According to one study, the percentage of workers who described themselves as self-employed jumped from 22 percent in 1998 to 26 percent in 2000. More than 40 percent of American men have had a period of such self-employment at some point during their careers. Tax returns reporting self-employment income *doubled* between 1970 and 1993.[5] And several large industries depend on vast numbers of solo workers. For example, according to a Harvard study, in the $175 billion home remodeling industry, 70 percent of the labor force is self-employed.[6]

Aquent Partners, a temporary staffing firm, and many others use the term "independent professional" or IP, to describe the high-end version of this workforce. While the BLS counts nine million independent contractors, the Aquent Index (a yearly survey of the independent workforce) says IPs number 33 million, or nearly one fourth of the total workforce.[7] Link Resources, a market research firm, projects that the number of such independent workers will reach 36.5 million within two years.[8]

Most research on the subject indicates that soloists enjoy this life and relish its opportunities:

- A 1996 study found that "more than 4 out of 5 independent contractors . . . preferred working as independent contractors, as opposed to being someone else's employee." Even among those who'd been *pushed* into this way of working—people who'd been downsized or fired—66 percent said they'd now rather be soloists than wage slaves.[9]

- Full-time independent contractors earn an average of 15 percent more than their employee counterparts.[10]

- Independent professionals are twice as likely as W-2 workers to have personal incomes above $75,000 per year.[11]

What does this quick survey tell us about how many people are soloists, our first free agent species? According to the BLS figures, which we know are undercounts, there are about 10 million unincorporated self-employed Americans, four million self-employed who have incorporated their solo operations, and about two million people who are self-employed in addition to holding a regular job, an endeavor that's frequently a diving board into the waters of free agency.[12] All told, that amounts to 16 million people. The U.S. Senate Small Business Committee puts the figure higher—between 22 and 25 million. And as we saw above, both Aquent Partners and private research operations place the number of independent professionals at more than double the BLS figure. For this bee-counting exercise, I'll err on the conservative side. Let's halve Aquent's estimate and edge toward the BLS undercount: *Working in America today are about 16.5 million soloists.*

Temps

If soloists are free agents by design, temps are often free agents by default. Many would rather have a "permanent" job—but coldly efficient corporations, slimy temp agencies, and the temps' own lack of ambition or ability conspire to pin them to the bottom of the economic ladder. Movies like *Clockwatchers*, samizdat 'zines like *Temp Slave!*, and acidly funny Web sites like Temp 24-7 (all of which I'll discuss in Chapter 13) chronicle temps' demeaning treatment, and reinforce their status as disposable workers, not much different from paper towels and toner cartridges. This popular perception has roots in reality. Only 45 percent of temps have health insurance, usually because their spouse is covered, and only 2.5 percent have a retirement plan.[13] According to one economist's survey, only 27 percent of temps said they preferred their current work arrangement; 63 percent said they wanted a regular job.[14] Says another economist, "The majority of temporary help agency workers would choose another work arrangement if labor market conditions or their personal situations were different."[15]

Yet temps seem to be a fixture of the modern economy, especially at large companies. The Conference Board found that as many as 90 percent of major multinational companies "make regular use of temporary workers, either hired directly or supplied by agencies."[16] A Coopers & Lybrand survey of the 392 fastest-growing U.S. businesses found that nearly two thirds outsourced work to temps—and that those businesses produced revenues 22 percent higher than other firms.[17] Companies such as Xerox have scrapped the term "temp"—a four-letter word—and begun calling their temporary workers "special assignment representatives" to avoid stigmatizing them with an unwelcome label. Other companies have established in-house temporary departments to manage the constant influx of interim workers. Temps—er, special assignment representatives—have gone from being a short-term corporate cost saver for business downturns to a long-term corporate strategy for business survival.

The evidence abounds:

- In the first half of the 1990s, the temporary personnel business created more net new jobs than any industry in America. Since 1995, temporary employment has grown three times faster than traditional employment.[18]

- On a typical day in 1982, 415,000 Americans were working as temps.[19] By 1999, that number had increased more than 600 percent—to three million temps going to work on a typical weekday.

- Twenty-five years ago, the temporary staffing industry had revenues less than $1 billion. By 1990, total revenues had climbed to $20 billion. Today, temporary staffing is a nearly $80 billion industry.[20]

- California's leading job producer during the last half of the 1990s was the temporary help industry, whose 180,000 new jobs were more than software and electronics manufacturing combined.[21] In Silicon Valley, temp workers are twice as prevalent as in the rest of the country.[22]

By some measures, pay for temps is rising faster than pay for other workers. This is especially true of white-collar, high-skill temps, who tend to make more than their counterparts in traditional salaried jobs. Large cities like Washington and Houston have thriving temporary lawyer industries. As health maintenance organizations grab a larger share of both the medical system and the health care dollar, temporary doctors and free agent nurses are becoming more common. And yesterday's Kelly Girl is often today's interim biochemist. Annual revenues of Kelly Scientific Resources, a division of the venerable staffing giant Kelly Services launched in 1995, already top $100 million. However, less-skilled temps don't have it as good. Clerical temps, for example, tend to earn less than clerical workers who are employees.[23]

This division of temp fortunes is deep and wide. On one edge of the divide are interim executives—men and women who parachute into a company for six months to save it from disaster, temporary CEOs who can coax a tender start-up out of the nest, and corporate samurai who can turn around a flailing operation. These high-end temps can earn as much as $5,000 per day, and work with considerable freedom, not the least of which is the ability to float above corporate politics. There are even agencies (which I'll look at in Chapter 10) that specialize in such carry-out business leaders: large staffing firms like IMCOR and Executive Interim Management; boutique firms that specialize, for example, in interim college presidents; and Silicon Valley companies like iCEO and CFOs2Go. Consider Randy Komisar, a self-described "virtual CEO" in Portola Valley, California, who's shepherded a half-dozen high-tech companies through muddy pastures. He has opportunities disgruntled pencil-pushing temps can't imagine. "I'm an equity slave," he says. "I never accept a check."[24]

Meanwhile, 850 miles away—and on the opposite shore of the temp worker gulf—sits Sybil Lundy. She has a check, but no equity. She worked at Microsoft for three years. But despite her tenure, she was always a temp—that is, a Seattle temp agency was her nominal employer even though she did all of her work at Microsoft's office, for Microsoft products, and alongside Microsoft employees. Full-fledged Microsoft employees wore blue badges; Lundy wore an orange badge. Blue badges got paychecks and stock options; orange badges got paychecks and no options— neither the financial nor professional variety. Some of the people she worked with became millionaires; Lundy, who never had the opportunity to "go blue," remained a permatemp.

The social bottom line: The temp population is cleaved into two halves; both halves are growing, but only one half is growing prosperous. The statistical bottom line: *Working in America today are about 3.5 million temps.*

Microbusinesses

The federal government defines "small business" as an enterprise that has fewer than five hundred—or sometimes fewer than one hundred—employees. Many federal laws don't apply to firms whose workforce numbers less than fifty. But erupting across Free Agent Nation is a blaze of enterprises that are exceptionally small, sometimes consisting of only two or three people. Call them microbusinesses. And call them a growing force. Between 1994 and 1998, enterprises with fewer than twenty employees created four out of every five new jobs in the economy—nine million new positions in all. Some of these small operations no doubt failed and thus eliminated many jobs as well. But the fact remains: More than half of American companies today have fewer than five employees.[25]

For example, Lindsay Frucci operates a one-person New Hampshire–based company called No Pudge! Foods, Inc., which makes a no-fat brownie mix that it sells to grocery stores and directly to consumers via an Internet storefront. Frucci works mostly alone, but her enterprise is closer in form and spirit to a bakery company than to a soloist Web designer who services clients and moves on.

The Internet is helping spawn Frucci's microenterprise and many others. Over the last ten years, economists have found that as an industry uses more information technology, the average size of firms within that industry shrinks.[26] Ninety percent of all engineering firms, for instance, are now small shops—with an average of four employees each.[27] Digital networks have become so powerful that a single individual or a tiny cluster of people can attain the power, scope, and access of a large corporation without sacrificing the independence, flexibility, and joy of being small. Already the U.S. has an average of about one company for every seven workers. But with business incorporations today growing five times faster than the population, some predict that in twenty years the number of enterprises may double—creating an economy that averages about one company for every three workers.[28] The combination of limited barriers to entry, robust and inexpensive information networks, and the wider availability of both formal and informal capital is making starting a business not much harder than buying a home or getting a driver's license.

The folklore of Silicon Valley would have you believe that the launching pad for most businesses is the family garage. And that mythology turns out to be just a few feet from reality. Millions of microenterprises begin—and often remain—in the home itself. A Wells Fargo study found that 69 percent of all new businesses are located in the owner's place of residence.[29] The headquarters of Frucci's international venture is *over* the garage of the four-bedroom Elkins, New Hampshire, house she shares with her husband, two teenage sons, two dogs, and one very fat black cat who sleeps on her desk. The location is convenient, and it reflects how personal her microbusiness is. "I live this company," Frucci says. "Whether I'm grocery shopping or driving in the car, I live this company. This is not what I do. This is who I am."

Home-based businesses, like all free agent varieties, are difficult to count. Some may be less than full-time operations, side ventures of a working parent. Others operate in the cash economy, and therefore elude government enumerators. In Southern California, officials estimate that Los Angeles County may have as many as 45,000 home-based businesses that are unaccounted for in the government's tax, property, or zoning records.[30] "Official government statistics don't come close to capturing the surging significance of small and midsize businesses," writes former *Wall Street Journal* columnist Tom Petzinger, one of the new economy's most astute observers, adding, "Surveys of households reveal that businesses are forming at three times the rate expressed in tax records."[31] And private data, collected by a range of sources, suggest that the neighborhood is alive with the sounds of free agent commerce:

- Two business school professors, writing in the *Wall Street Journal*, put "the number of home-based businesses at more than 12 million and rising."[32]

- The Michigan Small Business Development Center estimates that in the U.S., a new home-based business starts every eleven seconds.[33]

- The American Association of Home-Based Businesses counts more than 24 million home businesses. The

Home Based Business Owners Association, another trade association and self-described chamber of commerce for homegrown microenterprises, says they total 27 million.[34]

• Business research group IDC predicts that the number of home-based businesses will surpass 37 million by 2002.[35]

Indeed, the home itself is being reconfigured as a place that's not a respite from work, but the central location for it. One third of American households have a home office.[36] And the number of home office households will grow six times faster than general U.S. households.[37] One reason for this commercial migration home, of course, is technology. The average household today spends more on computer technology than on major appliances, lawn and gardening, or housewares.[38] That's the *average* household, not just those with a free agent in the basement.

So who's down in that subterranean space trying to build a microbusiness? It's not the stock image of "home knitters and quilt-makers who fit their work around child care and household responsibilities," according to Kathryn Stafford, an Ohio State University professor who has studied this free agent breed. Instead, "most home-based workers are men performing traditional work in fields like sales and construction." Her study of 899 home-based workers in nine states found that more than half were male. The average home-based worker was forty-four years old, married, had some education beyond high school, and had been involved in work at home for nearly a decade.[39] Half of home-based ventures fall into two business categories: maintenance (cleaning, construction, home repair, and so on) and business services (such as data processing, graphic arts, and accounting).[40] But while men now outnumber women in the home-based business arena, as they do in the total labor force, the explosion of groups such as Home-Based Working Moms, Mompreneurs, and the National Association of Entrepreneurial Parents again suggests that women increasingly are powering the microbusiness trend.

One intriguing variety in the broad fields of microbusiness is what entrepreneurial free agents Jim Salmons and Timlynn Babitsky of Raleigh, North Carolina, call the "nanocorp." That's an enterprise that is, in their marvelous phrase, "ruthlessly small." They say, "That doesn't imply that we roam around beating up on folks. It means that a nanocorp is committed, ruthlessly committed, to a 'no-growth' policy. The 'ruthless' of 'ruthlessly small' is a reminder to ourselves that we are using size as a competitive weapon."

In Free Agent Nation, small isn't just beautiful. It's better. And it's big. Take the largest estimate for home-based businesses (which, again, is a subset of microbusinesses). Subtract the four million incorporated self-employed so we don't double count. Eliminate another 10 million to be conservative. We end up with the figure I'll use: *Operating in America today are roughly 13 million microbusinesses.*

Free Agent Employees

As I traveled the country interviewing the new workforce, several people asked me whether an employee could be a free agent within a large corporation. Is that even possible? Or is "free agent employee" an oxymoron, ready to take its place alongside "jumbo shrimp," "civil lawyer," and "healthy tan"? If you hop from project to project inside a company, always looking for the next cool assignment, navigating your career like a Hollywood star even though you're the W-2 employee, you are indeed working in the free agent style. And if you change jobs every two years, find yourself regularly out of work because of a churning job market, or consider each work episode an engagement rather than employment, you definitely share considerable common ground with the soloist, the temp, and the microbusiness. Plenty of evidence indicates that people who are official employees are working like free agents. For example:

- About 11.1 million Americans are telecommuters—that is, they work for an organization, but do so from a remote site, usually their home. Other estimates place the figure slightly higher—closer to 14 or 15 million Americans.[41] Often, telecommuting is the marijuana of the workforce: a gateway to the harder drug of pure, uncut free agency.

- According to the *New York Times*, "among some types of information technology professionals . . . the generally accepted turnover rate hovers around 50 percent. That means the average worker switches jobs every six months."[42]

- In 1998, 45 percent of California's adult population had worked at their current main job less than two years. Median job tenure in the state was only three years—less than the average tenure for the original free agents, major league baseball players.[43] The average Californian changes teams more often than a millionaire shortstop.

- In 1999, according to *U.S. News & World Report*, approximately 17 million workers quit to take other jobs, up six million from five years earlier.[44]

While these workers may be free agents in spirit, they don't quite qualify as free agents in statistics. The emergence of free agent employees certainly affirms a deep change in the underlying ethic of work, but I won't include them in my tally.

BEE COUNTING

So where do these three free agent species leave us? Conservative subtotals inevitably produce a conservative final figure. With 16.5 million soloists, 3.5 million temps, and 13 million microbusinesses, our "very near the truth" total is 33 million free agents. By comparison, in 1999 the Ford Foundation estimated 37 million "freelancers, office temps, and independent contractors."[45] Working Today, a New York–based advocacy group for independent professionals that I'll discuss in Chapter 13, puts the free agent figure at about 30 percent of the American work-force. That's the same portion that both the General Accounting Office and the Economic Policy Institute say are in "nontraditional work."[46] Thirty percent of the workforce equals about 41 million Americans. *Business Week* basically concurs, going with an estimate of 43 million "contingent" workers.[47]

Yet even if we use my more modest total, the number is staggering: 33 million people represents about one out of four American workers. One out of four. Without a single order being issued or a single memo sent from headquarters, one fourth of the American workforce has declared its independence from traditional work. And as we'll see in subsequent chapters, that portion will inevitably swell in the next ten years—due to several demographic, cultural, technological, and financial forces. (One market research firm, for instance, predicts that by 2010, 41 percent of the workforce will be free agents.[48])

Compare this figure with other sectors of the workforce, and its significance sharpens into focus. Take manufacturing—the sorts of jobs whose disappearance politicians lament and whose presence, even to this day, is considered a measure of national well-being. The economy now has nearly 15 million more free agents than it has manufacturing workers. Or take the 20 million government employees, whose ranks actually have been larger than manufacturing workers for nearly a decade. Thirty-three million free agents means that these new independent workers outnumber all the Americans who work for federal, state, and local governments combined—including police officers and public school teachers. The population of Free Agent Nation exceeds the populations of the entire manufacturing sector and the entire public sector.

Or consider this politically tinged comparison: The American economy has twice as many free agents as it has members of labor unions. Even as the total workforce has grown, union membership has slowly dropped—to 16.5 million people. Separate out the roughly seven million union members who work for governments, and the figures are even more striking. Fewer than one in ten workers in America's $7 trillion private economy belongs to a labor union.[49] Put it more starkly: Today, America Online has about 10 million more members than all the nation's labor unions combined.[50] And Free Agent Nation, 33 million strong, has more members than both.

Of course, not everybody has declared free agency. If we know that about one out of four Americans has become a free agent, further calculation reveals that about three out of four of us have *not* taken the plunge. (At least not yet.) And some data do show countercurrents to the tide of free agency. For instance, in 1998, according to the Labor Department, 33 percent of men over age twenty-five had been with the same company for more than ten years. That's a 13 percent drop from five years earlier, but still a respectable portion and certainly a sign that job tenure isn't shrinking in every office and factory.[51] Another study found that average tenure at fifty-one large companies, and the percentage of workers with more than ten years of service, has actually increased.[52]

And yet even data not precisely about free agency confirm that something powerful is rippling through the workforce. Wrap your mind around this startling statistic from California, the state where nearly every economic and workforce trend of the last century—the rise of Silicon Valley, the commercial power of Hollywood, the spread of public higher education, the tax revolt of the late 1970s, the expanding influence of Latino and Asian immigrants—has begun: In 1999, only one third of California's workforce held a traditional job—that is, a single, full-time, year-round, permanent position with one employer, leaving for work in the morning and returning at night. Two thirds of the state's workers held so-called nontraditional positions—independent contractors, self-employed professionals, part-timers, and so on.[53] *In other words, two out of three California workers did not have the employment arrangement on which nearly all American laws, taxes, and social assumptions are based.*

As goes California, so goes America. And California is going free agent.

THE BOX

CHAPTER 2

THE CRUX: Work has changed so swiftly and so profoundly in recent years that traditional methods of measuring it are proving at best weak—at worst, misleading. (The federal government, for instance, still groups workers into two categories: "farm" and "nonfarm.") While categorizing such an individualistic breed is difficult, free agents usually approximate three general species: soloists, temps, and microbusinesses. And using official figures, private studies, and academic research, we can fashion conservative estimates of the size of each group: 16.5 million soloists, 3.5 million temps, and 13 million microbusinesses. In all, at work in America today are 33 million free agents—about one in four American workers. (And that doesn't include telecommuters, inveterate job-hoppers, and other quasi–free agents.) Even this conservative 33 million figure means that free agents easily outnumber all manufacturing workers and all government workers—and may be the largest single cluster of workers in the economy.

THE FACTOID: Two out of three workers in California do not hold traditional jobs—the permanent, year-round, full-time, outside-the-home employment arrangement that is the basis of nearly all American labor laws and social assumptions.

THE QUOTE: "Free agents, and ever more working people generally, do not nestle comfortably into the categories 'employer' and 'employee.' Free agents are *neither* employers nor employees; free agents are *both* employers and employees. That may sound like a Zen koan, but it's a key feature of this new economy."

THE WORD: *Nanocorp.* A microbusiness that remains "ruthlessly small"—as both a personal preference and a competitive strategy.

How Did It Happen?
The Four Ingredients
of Free Agency

"We're moving back to the butcher, the baker, the candlestick maker."

—*Norm Stoehr (Minneapolis, Minnesota)*

To understand how free agency happened, it helps to think less in the mechanical terms of cause and effect—and more in the culinary terms of ingredients and tastes. In a chocolate cake, it's hard to tell where the flour stops and the sugar begins, or which part of the cake is egg and which is cocoa. Is flour a *cause* of the chocolate cake? Not really. Is flour crucial to the chocolate cake's existence? Of course. Does the flour need the egg and sugar and cocoa to create the final product? Absolutely.

Free agency is like that chocolate cake. It has no single cause. But it does have a bunch of ingredients, four of which have been essential in its rise.

THE END OF AMERICA'S ECONOMIC ADOLESCENCE

The first ingredient is the changed relationship between individuals and organizations. During the decades after World War II, a simple bargain glued that relationship together. Workers offered a company loyalty; in return, the company offered security. Workers did what they were told, seldom questioned corporate policies, and rarely skipped from job to job. Companies more or less assured employees a job for life, issued a regular paycheck, and offered a predictable pension upon retirement.

This loyalty-for-security compact formed the foundation of corporate paternalism, and few companies worshipped it more reverently than IBM. For fifty years, across its far-flung operations, IBM maintained a "full-employment" policy. The company guaranteed its workers that it would never lay them off. Never. No matter how much business dropped or the economy drooped, their jobs were safe. "[The policy] was a religion," one manager told *Fortune*. "Every personnel director who came in lived and died on defending that practice. I tell you, this was like virginity."[1] But by the early 1990s, IBM lifted its corporate window shades and saw a world more starkly challenging than it ever imagined. Upstart computer companies were gobbling market share. Globalization had opened new markets and let loose still more competitors. And a series of internal woes—strategic blunders and a slow-footed bureaucracy—made these external challenges even tougher. Faced with few alternatives, IBM abandoned its no-layoff policy, and in 1992 and 1993, whacked its payroll by 120,000 employees.[2] The event was the workplace equivalent of the tumbling of the Berlin Wall just a few years earlier: Everybody knew something monumental had just occurred, but nobody had a clue what would happen next.

Boeing, the world's largest aerospace company and the Northwest's biggest job producer, followed a similar path away from paternalism. From the company's inception in 1916, Boeing cast itself as a protective parent. The company called itself a family, helped establish suburbs in Seattle for its workers, and paid in full for employee health insurance. But slowly—at first, imperceptibly—the wider world changed. And by the mid-1990s, those changes had reached a crescendo—a slump in Asia, a rocky merger with McDonnell Douglas, and fierce competition within the aircraft industry. So in 1998, the company's top seventy-five officers held a weekend retreat to figure out how to respond. The following Monday, they returned to the company's Seattle head-quarters to make an important announcement. Boeing was no longer a "family." It was a "team." That soon became the company mantra: "More team, less family."

At Boeing, IBM, and elsewhere, the notion that corporations were families turned out to be, at best, an outdated promise, at worst, an outright charade. It was almost as if Ma and Pa Corporation—their mortgage payments increasing, their own futures bleak—looked around one day and saw a bunch of nineteen-year-olds flopped on the family couch watching reruns and munching corn chips. "This hurts us a lot more than it hurts you," they said. "Now get out of the house!" To which the kids, chastened into candor, replied, "Fine. I've always thought this place sucked anyway." For the American worker, adolescence was over. Adulthood—and free agency—had begun.

CHEAP, HOUSEABLE MEANS OF PRODUCTION

The next ingredient in the free agent mix is technology. If you climbed into a time machine and journeyed back to America when Thomas Jefferson was conducting his 1790 census, the workers you'd encounter would look a lot like free agents. You'd see plenty of craftspeople, lots of farmers, and all kinds of small merchants. But you'd come across rather few people who hold what today we call a "job." And except perhaps for the occasional soldier or minister, you'd see almost nobody employed by a large organization. For most workers, big institutions weren't necessary. Before the Industrial Revolution, most of the things people needed to earn their living they could buy easily and keep at home.

It was only when these things—the means of production, to use Karl Marx's famous phrase—became extremely expensive, and impossible to house and maintain, that large organizations began to dominate. In the industrial economy, the tools required to earn a living were too costly for an individual to purchase, too complicated for one person to operate, and too cumbersome to store at home. (A man could hammer out horseshoes by himself in a tiny backyard workshop, but manufacturing a Model T there was a bit more challenging.) This increase in the size, scale, cost, and complexity of technology turned the workplace, in one sense, into a gigantic toolshed. The boss opened the shed for a prescribed set of hours, made sure the workers used the tools properly and together, and then closed the shed and sent the workers home. Capital and labor, once so intertwined the distinction scarcely mattered, became separate entities. Capitalists owned the equipment. Laborers earned their money by receiving a sliver of the enormous rewards those giant machines produced.

Today, the means of production once again have gone preindustrial. The tools of the idea economy are widespread, cheap, houseable, and operable by one person. In 1965, there was one computer for every 100,000 Americans; today, the ratio is three computers for every five Americans.[3] The microchip in a $1.29 drugstore greeting card packs as much computing power as the room-sized mainframe computers of the 1950s. My home office, with two phone lines and hardware worth less than $3,000, contains as much computing power as *Apollo 11*. Even IBM, nearly toppled a decade ago by cheap and plentiful computing, has converted to this new religion. In ads for its $1,200 PC, targeted at soloists and microbusinesses, the company touts the possibilities of "You, inc.,"—and promises, "It might not make you a giant conglomerate, but it sure could help you scare one."

At the same time, and perhaps with even greater consequences, getting online has become easier and cheaper. In 1996, 25 percent of home offices were connected to the Internet; by 1998, it was 65 percent. The consulting firm Arthur Andersen predicts that by 2004, 91 percent of Americans will be online.[4] Meanwhile, high-speed broadband connections are widespread. And as wireless technology quickly becomes inexpensive and reliable, more of these tools will become portable, making the means of production like a turtle's shell—something knowledge workers tote with them wherever they go.

People still work for large organizations, of course. But fewer *must*. And many have concluded that if they can afford the tools themselves, they ought to buy them and reap all the profits those tools and their brainpower create—rather than simply the fraction some employer decides to share. Tell the thirty-something in the art department she can't have the afternoon off to visit her elderly mother, and she may just pack up her PageMaker software, iMac, and T-1 line—and open her own home-based design shop. "Digital technology is the first infinitely scalable economizing tool," writes Tom Petzinger in his outstanding 1999 book, *The New Pioneers.* "It is driving marginal costs toward zero. It reduces or eliminates barriers to entry. . . . Technology is taking the capital out of capitalism."[5] And in the process, it's taking the organization out of the Organization Man.

For proof, I needed to look no further than Leesburg, Virginia, where Sandy Kleppinger established a thriving software sales business from her home—thanks solely to the online auction Web site eBay. With the Web, she faced few barriers to entry and minimal start-up costs. Almost instantly, she had a storefront open twenty-four hours a day, seven days a week to anybody on the planet with an Internet connection. eBay calls this phenomenon "capitalism for the rest of us."[6] I call it Digital Marxism: In an age of inexpensive computers, wireless handheld devices, and ubiquitous low-cost connections to a global communications network, workers can now own the means of production.

PROSPERITY

Free agency's third ingredient is prosperity—not the stock option wealth of the roaring 1990s, but the astonishingly high standard of living that has reached deep into the middle class. Measured against our own history or the current condition of the rest of the world, twenty-first century middle-class Americans are extraordinarily prosperous. Consider:

- Two thirds of American households own the homes they live in, the highest rate in American history.[7] (Compare that to 1940, when most Americans rented their dwellings, most homes didn't have heating and air-conditioning, 30 percent of homes lacked running water, and more than 15 percent of households had no flush toilets.[8])

- In 1957, one year before John Kenneth Galbraith dubbed America "The Affluent Society," per capita income was $8,700 (measured in today's dollars). Today, we're a *doubly affluent* society. Per capita income has increased to $20,000.[9]

- "By 1993, more than 90 percent of *officially poor* families had a color television, a little more than 70 percent had their own washing machines, and 60 percent had VCRs and microwaves. Poor families in the United States are more likely to have these modern amenities than is the average resident of most Western European nations today or the typical U.S. resident twenty-five years ago," according to author David Whitman.[10]

These remarkable achievements have not simply improved lives. They have altered national expectations. In the space of two generations, the default assumption of American life has shifted from the fear of privation to the expectation of comfort.

The Great Depression profoundly and permanently affected the attitudes of the people who lived through it. These Americans remembered destitution—and they feared its return. That's one reason why the Depression-era parents of baby boomers recoiled when their children tried to "find themselves," or disdained them as dilettantes when they sought work that was "meaningful." But haunting economic fear—and the public attitudes it engendered—is no longer seared in the American consciousness. After all, about 85 percent of Americans today were not even *alive* during the Great Depression.[11] Sure, people endured a flat stock market in the 1960s, winding gas lines in the 1970s, occasional recessions during the 1980s and 1990s, and the stock market plunge and dot-com shakeout of 2000. But for most middle-class Americans, hope-flattening, life-altering despair on the order of the Great Depression is simply not part of their memory.

When the expectation of comfort displaces the fear of privation, work begins serving an expanded purpose—something beyond simply earning money to survive. It becomes a way not just to make money, but also to make meaning. If you're not worried about food, shelter, and other basics, then you might as well do something you enjoy, something that satisfies some higher needs. With many corporate environments still so stultifying, free agency is the answer for more and more workers—and prosperity allows it now more than at any other time in our history.

THE SHRINKING HALF-LIFE OF ORGANIZATIONS

The final ingredient is the radical change organizations have undergone in their structure and operation. Start-up companies can form in a matter of weeks, get financed in a few months, and go public within a year. And they can disappear just as quickly. In other words, the half-life of nearly every organization is shrinking.

Think of the economy as a body and a company as a prescription drug. In the past, companies had a nearly permanent half-life—that is, they stayed in the body for a long time, sometimes seemingly forever. Today, the hypercharged economy metabolizes companies with astonishing speed, flushing them out of the system when they cease being effective or start becoming toxic.

Recall the story of Netscape, once the darling of the New Economy. Netscape was formed in 1994. It went public in 1995. And by 1999, it was gone, purchased by America Online and subsumed into AOL's operation. Life span: four years. Half-life: two years. Was Netscape a company—or was it really a project? Does the distinction even matter? What matters most is that this short-lived entity put several products on the market, prompted established companies (notably Microsoft) to shift strategies, and equipped a few thousand individuals with experience, wealth, and connections that they could bring to their next project.

And Netscape is not alone. A University of Texas study found that between 1970 and 1992, the half-life of Texas businesses shrank by 50 percent.[12] Likewise, a Federal Reserve analysis of New York companies found that the type of firm that created the most new jobs (microbusinesses with fewer than ten employees) often had the shortest life span.[13] The life cycle of companies has been compressed into Internet time. And one result has been that jobs, too, have diminishing half-lives. Ten years ago, nobody ever heard of a Web developer. Ten years from now, nobody may remember Web developers.

Most important, at the very moment the longevity of companies is shrinking, the longevity of *individuals* is expanding. Unlike Americans in the twentieth century, most of us today can expect to outlive just about any organization for which we work. It's hard to imagine a lifelong job at an organization whose lifetime will be shorter—often much shorter—than your own.

The end of America's economic adolescence; cheap, housable means of production; prosperity; the shrinking half-life of organizations: When these four ingredients combined—when each one flavored and solidified the other, and when they cooked together for a decade—the result was 33 million independent workers. Now that they've emerged, what do we know about how these people approach their work and lives? What's going on inside those free agent heads? The answers may surprise you.

THE BOX

CHAPTER 3

THE CRUX: How did free agency happen? Four ingredients were essential: 1) the social contract of work—in which employees traded loyalty for security—crumbled; 2) individuals needed a large company less, because the means of production—that is, the tools necessary to create wealth—went from expensive, huge, and difficult for one person to operate to cheap, houseable, and easy for one person to operate; 3) widespread, long-term prosperity allowed people to think of work as a way not only to make money, but also to make meaning; 4) the half-life of organizations began shrinking, assuring that most individuals will outlive any organization for which they work.

THE FACTOID: Eighty-five percent of Americans today were not alive during the Great Depression, which means most of the country lacks any conscious recollection of widespread economic privation.

THE QUOTE: "Netscape was formed in 1994. It went public in 1995. And by 1999, it was gone, purchased by America Online and subsumed into AOL's operation. Life span: four years. Half-life: two years. Was Netscape a company—or was it really a project? Does the distinction even matter?"

THE WORD: *Digital Marxism*. With the proliferation of inexpensive computers, wireless handheld devices, and ubiquitous low-cost connections to the Internet, workers can now own the means of production.

PART TWO

The Free Agent Way

The New Work Ethic

*"Our work ethic? Work where and when it makes the most
sense, doing the things you do better than anyone else. It's like
a gym class for the mind—a little stretching, a lot of aerobics,
and a very small cool-down, versus the traditional work ethic,
which feels like one endless push-up."*
> **—Nancy Halpern (New York, New York)**

This chapter is about two movie characters, a famous psychologist, two seventeenth-century theologians, a hip-hop impresario, and a folk rocker. Connect the dots, and you've sketched an outline of the American work ethic, newly redefined by free agents.

The first movie character is Tom Rath. He's a man in a gray flannel suit. Actually, he's *the* man in *the* gray flannel suit, the protagonist of Darryl Zanuck's 1956 film (based on Sloan Wilson's 1955 novel of the same name). Tom, played by a dashing Gregory Peck, is an army veteran living in the martini-soaked calm of postwar suburban Connecticut. He has a job at a foundation and a wife who covets a larger house. (He also has a secret—a child he fathered with an Italian woman while serving overseas.) Prodded by his wife, tantalized by an $8,000 annual salary, and hooked up by his seatmate on the morning commuter train, Tom secures an interview for a new job—in the public relations department of the giant United Broadcasting Corporation.

The scene in which Tom applies for this new position is a classic in the cinema of work. He arrives at UBC's wood-paneled corporate suite shortly before noon, and meets with Gordon Walker, head of the network's PR department, who describes the exercise that will determine Tom's occupational fortunes.

Go into a nearby room, Walker tells Tom, and write your autobiography. At the end, finish this sentence: "The most significant thing about me is . . ." Be done by 1:00 P.M.

Tom walks into the room. He lights a cigarette, scrolls a sheet of paper into the typewriter. Then he sits. And stares. And stares some more. The clock ticks. He rises. He paces. The words won't come. He looks out the window. He paces again. By 12:40, he's written barely a paragraph, and hasn't even begun crafting the self-defining concluding sentence. Grudgingly, Tom folds himself into his chair, and ever so slowly begins pecking on the Smith-Corona. When he's finished, he exits the room and hands his flimsy one-pager to Walker.

"Is this all?" Walker asks, surprised.

"That's all."

"But you've still got twelve minutes."

"I've written all that I think is necessary," Tom replies.

Walker reads Tom's essay, looks up at the job applicant, then continues reading silently until he can't help himself and begins reading aloud:

> "The most significant thing about me so far as the United
> Broadcasting Corporation is concerned is that I am applying
> for a job in its public relations department, and after a
> reasonable period of learning, I believe I could do a good job.
> I will be glad to answer any other questions relevant to this
> application for employment. But after giving it serious
> thought, I am unable to convince myself that any further
> speculation on my importance could be of any legitimate
> interest or value to the United Broadcasting Corporation."

Tom Rath is a man of few words. And before long, Tom Rath is a man with a job at UBC. He calculates, correctly it turns out, that in the realm of work, introspection and self-expression are bunk. As he later tells his wife, "I never wanted to get into this rat race, but now that I'm in it, I think I'd be an idiot not to play it the way everybody else plays it."

Cut. Fade out. Enter your local cineplex forty years later, and you'll encounter our second movie character—and a very different attitude toward work. In 1996, Tom Cruise starred in *Jerry Maguire*, a film about a slick sports agent who decides to play the game by a new set of rules. A few minutes into the movie, in a scene oddly similar to Tom Rath's essay-writing exercise, Jerry attends a corporate conference in Miami. On his final evening there, he confronts a dark night of the soul. Sweating and hallucinating, he begins pondering his life, hearing the voices of people he's betrayed.

"And then it happened," he says in a voice-over.

"It was the oddest, most unexpected thing. I began writing what they call a Mission Statement. Not a memo, a Mission Statement. You know, a suggestion for the future of our company."

No Rathian writer's block for Jerry Maguire:

"What started out as one page became twenty-five. Suddenly I was my father's son again. I was remembering the simple pleasures of the job, how I ended up here after law school, the way a stadium *sounds* when one of my players performs well on the field. The way we are meant to protect them in health and injury. With so many clients, we had forgotten what was important."

Lit by the screen of his laptop, clad in his underwear, Jerry writes and writes and writes. And soon his despondency becomes epiphany:

"Suddenly it was all pretty clear. The answer was fewer clients, less money. More attention. Caring for them, caring for ourselves. Starting our lives, really."

"I'll admit it," Jerry says. "What I was writing was somewhat touchy-feely." But he says he doesn't care. "I had lost the ability to bullshit. It was the me I'd always wanted to be." He finishes his manifesto, and in the middle of the rainy night runs it to an ersatz Kinko's. He titles his opus "The Things We Think and Do Not Say: The Future of Our Business," and compares its cover to the cover of *The Catcher in the Rye*.

"That's how you become great, man," the copy clerk tells a sleep-starved Jerry when he retrieves his copies. "You hang your *balls* out there."

"I was thirty-five," Jerry says in his final voice-over. "I had started my life."

For Tom Rath, in a movie that arrived in theaters the same year that *The Organization Man* arrived in bookstores, work meant submerging his identity and suppressing his genuine character to pursue another goal. For Jerry Maguire, in a movie released at the dawn of the free agent revolution, work held almost the opposite meaning. The very goal was to express genuine conviction, to act on deeply held values, and to be true to thine ownself. Rent these two videos, watch them back-to-back—and you'll learn far more about the changing nature of work than you ever would analyzing this month's government release on nonfarm payrolls or reading the latest million-dollar Booz-Allen-Hamilton study. The journey from Tom Rath to Jerry Maguire—from gray-flanneled reticence to Jockey-briefed garrulousness—speaks volumes about how the values of the free agent have broadened the Protestant work ethic and reshaped our attitudes about labor. But to understand exactly how and why, we'll need to bring in a professional—a psychologist by the name of Abraham Maslow.

Maslow's America

Anybody who's taken an introductory psychology course or sat through a corporate training seminar has at least a faint recollection of Abraham Maslow. An American born in 1908, Maslow became one of psychology's great names by challenging the theories of two of its most legendary figures, Sigmund Freud and B. F. Skinner. In thirty-nine years of field studies, lectures, and books, Maslow argued that human beings were more than a Freudian stewpot of subconscious urges—and that their behavior was more complex than the Skinnerian, laboratory-rat-like quest to seek reward and avoid punishment.

Instead, Maslow maintained that human motivation had deeper causes and a loftier purpose. Our highest need—indeed, what makes us human—was what he called self-actualization, the yearning to engage our talents and realize our potential. To establish his unconventional theory, Maslow defied some of the conventions of his discipline. Rather than study unhealthy people—how they got that way and how the rest of us can repair them—he studied healthy people, the better to discover how they got that way and how the rest of us can follow their happy path. Through this work, Maslow conceived what he termed "the hierarchy of needs." Individual human beings developed, he said, by climbing a pyramid. At the bottom level of the pyramid were basic physiological needs—food, sex, and oxygen, for example. One layer higher were safety needs—such as protection from illness, calamity, and danger. And still higher came love needs, esteem needs, cognitive needs, and aesthetic needs, proceeding all the way to the apex of personal growth—self-actualization. Before advancing to a higher level, humans had to satisfy the lower needs. (Someone who's homeless or hungry doesn't quite have the luxury of divining and fulfilling his aesthetic desires.) But when we are able to make this climb—even for a brief, ecstatic moment—we have had one of the transcendent "peak experiences" that deepen our humanity. Jerry Maguire was having a peak experience and seeking to self-actualize; Tom Rath was not.

Self-actualization, hierarchy of needs, peak experiences. That's Maslow on a postcard.[1] And it's a key to understanding the free agent workforce. Deep into the middle class, Americans are enjoying a standard of living unmatched in world history and unthinkable to our ancestors just a hundred years ago. As a result (and as I discussed in the previous chapter), for tens of millions of people the default assumption of American life has profoundly changed: The expectation of comfort has replaced the fear of privation. In other words, tens of millions of Americans have satisfied the physiological, safety, and even social needs on the lower levels of Maslow's pyramid—liberating them to pursue self-actualization. Thirty or forty million people attempting to self-actualize is staggering, if not a bit scary. And it has broad economic consequences, because for reasons that Maslow himself discovered as far back as 1962, one of the best—perhaps *the* best—mechanism for achieving self-actualization is work. "All human beings prefer meaningful work to meaningless work," Maslow wrote in his journal forty years ago, when he spent the summer observing a factory in Southern California. "If work is meaningless, then life comes close to being meaningless."[2]

The trouble is, many traditional workplaces—whether they are colorless Organization Man monoliths, cynical Dilbertian cubicle farms, or even sleek high-tech corporate campuses with volleyball courts and cappuccino machines—often don't allow this pursuit of a person's highest potential. So for many, the only way to ascend Maslow's hierarchy is to abandon the corporate hierarchy. In our new age of comfort, work has taken on a larger purpose—one that many large organizations seem incapable of accommodating. Though paychecks and stock options still matter, work is not just about making money. It's also about making meaning.

Making Meaning: The Four Pieces

The question, then, is how this new workforce makes meaning. The answer is by assembling four pieces—freedom, authenticity, accountability, and self-defined success—that together comprise a new free agent work ethic.

Freedom

Freedom isn't just another word for nothing left to lose. It's the first building block of the free agent work ethic. A bit of etymology helps explain why. The earliest recorded use of the phrase "free agent" came in 1662 when a British theologian named Edward Stillingfleet penned a religious tract called *Origines Sacrae*. Stillingfleet used "free agent" as a synonym for "free will," at the time a radical and controversial concept. A prevailing belief in the West, articulated by John Calvin, another seventeenth-century theologian, held that God chose certain people for salvation, and consigned the rest to eternal damnation. Free will? According to Calvinism and its doctrine of predestination, it didn't exist. Our fates were sealed like a manila envelope, and there wasn't much we could do about it. But since nobody knew whether he was on a stairway to heaven or a highway to hell, most Calvinists aspired to lead a pious life. Piety was a sign, though never a means, that you were among God's elect.

Calvinism had a lasting influence on Western culture—particularly in the United States, where Puritans adopted the doctrine. It became the foundation for the Protestant work ethic, which discouraged fun and frivolity and prized frugality and self-sacrifice. Some scholars, most prominently Max Weber, credited this ascetic ethic with creating the conditions that allowed industrial capitalism to flourish.[3] And this philosophy certainly prevailed in the Tayloresque factories and Organization Man bureaucracies of the twentieth century, where keeping one's head down and nose clean was considered both pragmatic and virtuous.

But, as Weber wrote, these Calvinist values and the work ethic they established could become "an iron cage."[4] That may be tolerable when opportunities are scarce. But when opportunities abound, it becomes truly imprisoning. After all, it's hard to climb Maslow's pyramid when you're stuck behind Weber's bars.

For example, most of the free agents I met in my travels—no matter what they did or where they did it—complained about the office politics of the organizations they'd left. The frequency with which the topic came up and the depth of the emotions were astonishing. Public relations free agent Deborah Mersino in suburban Chicago was one of these New Economy political prisoners. She said that at the downtown public relations firm she recently departed, "office politics was the foundation of the organization—somehow, all of that negative energy is what they thought held it together."

In the Organization Man's day, people like Mersino would likely have accommodated themselves to the stubborn reality of corporate politics. In an iron cage, you may not be happy—but you're usually safe. Today, however, increasing numbers of people have the opportunity to break loose. Among workers under thirty, for instance, 62 percent want to be their own boss, according to a *U.S. News & World Report* poll.[5] And more than one third of Fortune 500 executives say they would own their own company if they could relive their life.[6] Roll over, John Calvin. Send Tom Rath the news: In the hearts and minds of the new American workforce, free will has trumped predestination.

Freedom—the ability to exercise one's will—has become essential for making meaning in work. This is increasingly true throughout the workforce, but may find its most robust expression among free agents. Autonomy means different things to different people. For Virginia Klamon, a consultant in Seattle, it's freedom of speech—the ability to say what she thinks and be taken seriously. For Chicago management consultant Dan Feely, it's the freedom to take off the afternoon and go to Wrigley Field without asking anyone's permission—as well as the larger freedom to select the projects on which he works. "There is always a cost to not working or turning down a client, but at least *you* make the call," he says. For most free agents, freedom means mobility, variety, and control. Mihaly Csikszentmihalyi, the legendary University of Chicago psychologist and author of *Flow*, has written that "work requiring great skills that is done freely refines the complexity of the self"—but that few things in life are more deadening than "unskilled work done under compulsion." Indeed, sometimes freedom can literally be a matter of life and death. A Johns Hopkins study found that workers with little autonomy are 70 percent more likely to die from heart disease than workers with significant control of their work.[7]

For other free agents the highest liberty is freedom of conscience. In my conversations across America, a surprisingly large number of these new independent workers cited ethics as one reason for leaving a large organization. Mersino is one example. At that Chicago firm energized by internal politics, she had some serious concerns. "You would send out invoices, but I didn't feel like clients were getting their money's worth." At her own one-person operation, she sets the ethical standards. "I cannot bill a client for one quarter of an hour I have not worked. I cannot do it; it is not within me." Mersino's concerns turn out to be widespread. A 1999 Hudson Institute study found that 30 percent of employees have seen or suspect unethical behavior on the job.[8] According to *USA Today*, one out of four workers says they've been asked to do something unethical.[9] Mersino's solution likewise may reflect a broadening gap in on-the-job values. Case Western Reserve's Robert D. Hisrich studied entrepreneurs and business managers, and found that entrepreneurs place a far greater emphasis on ethics than do their counterparts in conventional jobs, perhaps because they have the freedom to do so.[10]

"To me, being a free agent is all about being free to follow my path and my purpose," New York outplacement consultant Leslie Evans told me. "I don't think corporate America has caught on and created an environment where people can exercise enough freedom to be able to do that."

One approach some companies, particularly those in the tech sector, have taken to respond to these concerns is to smother employees in affection. These corporations have established on-site gyms, on-site restaurants, on-site showers, on-site child care, and on-site concierge services—so nobody ever has to go "off-site" (a place also known as "home"). In Silicon Valley, companies vie to hire the best chefs to prepare employee meals—and they keep refrigerators bulging with soda and snacks—all so that employees don't wander away. A few corporations, perhaps the same ones whose employees guzzle those free sugared soft drinks, hire what one might call "toothmobiles," dentists in large vans who pull into the company parking lot so that employees can get checkups without leaving campus. Some Internet start-ups, such as now-defunct TheMan.com, have taken brand loyalty to new extremes, and urged employees to get tattooed with the company logo.[11] Business school professor David Arnott claims that some companies have gone so far they've become what he calls "corporate cults."[12] They display, he says, the three characteristics of cults: devotion, charismatic leadership, and separation from family. William Whyte himself feared just this turn of events—that "the people on the other side of the table wouldn't be Big Brother's bad henchmen; they would be a mild-looking group of therapists who, like the Grand Inquisitor, would be doing what they did to help you."[13]

Other companies have tried purchasing individual freedom with potentially lucrative stock options, keeping employees tethered to the New Economy plantation like gilded indentured servants. While these arrangements are freely bargained, and hardly a cause for weeping about the fate of this cyberproletariat, for many workers such arrangements amount to a bribe that proves effective only so long as the currency remains valuable. In many parts of the economy, corporate paternalism is alive and well. It's just that Mom and Dad now have a bit more money. But whenever the stock market goes south, as it did for many technology companies in 2000, even the finest father can quickly become a deadbeat dad.

Still other companies, in their push for productivity, have been less outwardly benevolent. Many now routinely deploy sophisticated software to monitor their employees' e-mail and Web use. In one survey, 54 percent of employers said they had "caught" employees surfing to sites that were not related to work.[14] In 2001, International Data Corporation estimates that 80 percent of large companies will use employee-monitoring software such as WEBsweeper, Disk Tracy, and Telemate.Net.[15] And several organizations—among them Xerox and the New York Times—have fired employees for "unauthorized" or "unofficial" surfing, the twenty-first-century equivalent of canning somebody for making a "personal" phone call.[16] In their defense, companies say they must track this activity to ensure that workers are doing their jobs rather than clogging bandwidth with MP3 tunes, or downloading cyberporn. But the impact on individual integrity and freedom is severe: Ma Bell may be gone, but Big Brother is baby-sitting.

Little wonder then that free agents often refer to traditional work as "going captive." And little wonder that many people are finding the only way to have the freedom they seek is to go out on their own. Dan Feely sums up the appeal of free agency like this: "Working when, where, how much, under what conditions and for whom you want." As both Edward Stillingfleet and Abraham Maslow would have understood, free will—not free cola—quenches the thirst for meaning.

MASLOW AND MAGUIRE ON FREEDOM

"The people who have been living in a world which always told them what to do—which made life easy for them and told them what the next step was, and put them on an escalator so to speak—this world never let them discover their weaknesses and failures, not to mention their strengths."
—*Abraham Maslow*

"I'm starting a new company, and the fish will come with me."
—*Jerry Maguire (eyeing the office aquarium after being fired from his job)*

Authenticity

Perhaps the ultimate freedom is the freedom to be one's self. But in the traditional workplace, authenticity is often neither condoned nor rewarded. As free agents around the country told me their stories, they repeatedly used the language of disguise and concealment to describe their previous jobs. They spoke of putting on "masks" or "game faces" at work. They talked about donning "armor" and erecting "smoke screens," because exposing themselves in a large organization could be perilous. Only when they returned home after work could they shed the costumes and protective gear and return to being who they truly were.

This personality split—Mr. Hyde at work, Dr. Jekyll everywhere else—can take its toll. Public relations guru Mersino recalled a conversation with her fiancé that convinced her to go solo. After she'd returned from another bruising day on the job, he told her, "You are not *you* anymore." Walt Fitzgerald, the GE veteran we met in Chapter 1, told me that compromising his identity was his greatest workplace fear: "I think the biggest ongoing risk I faced was being myself in a corporate environment." Both the Calvinist ethic—and the Organization Man workplace it infused—tended to flatten identity and homogenize individuality. The Gregory Peck movie wasn't called *Tom Rath.* It was called *The Man in the Gray Flannel Suit* because to the giant corporation where he worked, the costume was more important than the soul that inhabited it.

Karl Marx, hardly a film critic, would have understood this decision. Central to his critique of capitalism was the notion of "alienation." He believed one of the most corrosive features of the industrial economy was that it split workers in two. By dividing "being" from "doing," this form of capitalism inhumanely separated who workers *were* from the jobs that they *did.* Marx essentially warned the laboring class, "You are not you anymore, comrade."

Joan Tyre, hardly a Marxist, would have understood this analysis. She spent twenty years working for large organizations like Sheraton and Miller-Freeman, where she planned meetings and organized conferences. But in her late forties—in an act that "was the single most scary thing I had ever done in my life"—she became a free agent. She now works for herself from her home in Brooklyn.

"When I was working in a corporate environment, I would put on my little corporate suit—a Stepford Worker—and I went in there and did what was expected," she told me. "The minute I walked out of the building, I was Joan Tyre again. But this way [as a free agent], I'm me all the time." She says the thought of returning to traditional work "terrifies me. It would be like muzzling myself, gagging myself."

Peter Krembs, a solo industrial psychologist in Minneapolis, echoes Tyre's feelings. "Optimizing" the organization, he says, almost necessarily means "suboptimizing the individual." That's something he's seen in his consulting practice—and experienced firsthand. Krembs began work in 1974 at Honeywell, worked there for three years, then did time at a consulting firm before going out on his own. "A lot of people who have chosen to [become free agents] in some ways perceive themselves to be marginalized in their organizations. I happen to be a gay man. In 1974, Honeywell was a very homophobic company. I have to tell you, a very strong reason for my leaving was saying, 'I'm not going to run this risk of them discovering that I'm gay and have them throw me out on my ear. I'm going to create my own world.' "

Free agents, however, don't sit around waiting for authenticity to rain down on them like a summer shower. They express that authenticity by being passionate about their work. Indeed, where the Calvinist work ethic called for self-denial, the free agent work ethic permits—and at times, demands—self-expression. The advertising campaign of Kinko's—a crown jewel of the free agent infrastructure that I'll examine in Chapter 9—reflects this attitude. Kinko's began targeting free agents with the slogan "Your Branch Office." But once the free agent population reached a critical mass, and Kinko's importance to this population became widely known, the company switched its message from value to values. One print ad brilliantly captures this emerging free agent mind-set. It features a nicely bound document, prepared at Kinko's of course, sitting on a plush leather executive chair. The document's title? *Hell: Visitor's Guide for My Boss.* Sprinkled on the cover are promises of "Suggested Routes," "What to Wear," and "How to Beat the Heat." And beneath is the new Kinko's slogan: "Express Yourself."

In free agency, work becomes more fully integrated with who you are. That can be rewarding. But because work is more deeply woven into your self, it can be harder to cast off—which means work can occasionally consume and even smother identity.

Yet this urge for authenticity and self-expression is pervasive. "These are all byline occupations," Charles Handy says of independent workers, "meaning that the individual is encouraged to put his or her name on the work."[17] Joan Tyre's one-person microbusiness is Meetings by JT. Allison Cutler calls her Nashville, Tennessee, political consultancy the Cutler Group—a "group" that she says consists of "me, myself, and I." Nothing new about this approach to naming. Think of the millions of Americans whose surnames describe some ancestor's occupation: Baker, Miller, Farmer, Skinner, or Taylor. Even the ultimate free agent movie, unlike its buttoned-up predecessor, bears the name of its protagonist. And it's probably no accident that Jerry Maguire compared his manifesto to *The Catcher in the Rye.* What did Holden Caulfield detest more than anything else? Phonies.

As *Fast Company* declared in its inaugural issue, and as free agents affirm each day, "Work is personal." So forget the Pledge of Allegiance. In Free Agent Nation, people take a Pledge of Authenticity.

> ## Maslow and Maguire on Authenticity
>
> *"We can learn from self-actualizing people what the ideal attitude toward work might be under the most favorable circumstances. These highly evolved individuals assimilate their work into the identity of the self, i.e., work actually becomes part of the self, part of the individual's definition of himself."*
> —*Abraham Maslow*
>
> *"I had lost the ability to bullshit. It was the me I'd always wanted to be."*
> —*Jerry Maguire*

Accountability

Yeah, freedom and authenticity are groovy. But if they're your only goals, it can be hard to get anything done. That's why the third piece of the puzzle is accountability—putting one's livelihood and reputation directly on the line. Most people *want* to be held accountable for their work, provided they reap both the rewards for success and the penalties for failure. And most people instinctively seek variety, challenge, and passion in their endeavors. However, many free agents told me that in traditional jobs accountability is often diffused through layers of management. They said they got a little blame and even less credit—and rarely had a clear sense of how they were doing.

But free agency is different. "In working on your own as a free agent, you have freedom, tremendous freedom. That's one of its great lures," consultant Michele Foyer told me over salads near South Park in San Francisco. "But you have immense responsibility. You're determining everything." For some people, such pressure can be withering. So they're willing to push some of the accountability to the organization—and thereby sacrifice freedom and authenticity. This is one reason perhaps that several free agents I met referred to traditional jobs as a kind of "corporate welfare." The people in them, they said, felt entitled to the job but not inspired to do it well. They were wards of the state, not independent, accountable citizens.

For many free agents, though, accountability means liberation. They put their names on their businesses and their livelihoods on the line. "You don't have administrators who don't understand what you do telling you when and how to do what they don't understand," Claudia Slate, a "virtual assistant" who lives on the Rosebud Sioux Reservation in south-central South Dakota, explained to me. "You succeed or fail on your own merits." Says Brian Clark of Austin, Texas, "It's scary sometimes waking up in the morning and thinking I might not be able to pay my bills. If you're the type of person who likes a challenge, that gets you out of bed and working right away." Tom Anderson of Los Angeles takes this can-do American attitude even further: He calls himself not a consultant, but a "resultant." And Penn State University professor Peg Thoms has confirmed that these individual voices amount to a chorus of consensus about work. Her research has shown a tight "relationship between accountability and job satisfaction."

Jim Ziegler, who runs the Professional Association for Contract Employees from an office in Pleasant Hill, California, is especially blunt on the topic: "Free agents are accountable. Period. Employees are responsible but seldom held accountable for anything. Free agents and other independent professionals are accountable for the success of their own careers. They are accountable for acquiring the specific marketable skills and experience that bring value to their clients. They are accountable for the quality of their work. They are accountable for identifying business opportunities and for marketing their services. They are accountable for developing and maintaining satisfying and productive relationships with their clients."

In the traditional economy, the organization buffers the individual from the market. That means the slackers and do-nothings get paid more than they're worth—and the workhorses and creative minds subsidize them by earning less than their own true value. But free agents neither enjoy nor suffer from this organizational buffer. They're accountable directly to the market.

They occupy the same fast-feedback world that allows us to learn the price of a stock with a few taps on a keypad. By contrast, most companies still evaluate employees with six-month performance reviews. Six months? Imagine if you owned some stock, but could learn its price only twice a year. You'd be miffed. Even worse, you'd be lost. Free agents know where they stand. A client asks for a project. The free agent bids $10,000. The client says the job is worth only $7,000. That's feedback. A customer buys Lindsay Frucci's latest brownie mix. Or the customer doesn't. Either way, Frucci and her microbusiness know and are responsible. That's feedback. That's accountability. That's putting yourself on the line.

MASLOW AND MAGUIRE ON ACCOUNTABILITY

"Everyone, but especially the more developed person, prefer[s]
responsibility to dependency and passivity most of the time."
—*Abraham Maslow*

"I was thirty-five, I had started my life."
—*Jerry Maguire*

Self-Defined Success

Sean "Puffy" Combs opines, "It's all about the Benjamins." And for many people, that remains the purpose of work—accumulating cash and trying to get wealthy. But for most free agents, money is neither the primary motivator nor the greatest source of satisfaction. Nor do other traditional workplace goals—getting promoted and growing an enterprise larger—matter much to them. It's yet another way free agents are influencing American attitudes toward work: They are redefining our notions of what constitutes "success."

Money and Success

Begin with the almighty dollar. Combs is not the first to equate money with success. It's a grand American tradition—stretching from Ben Franklin to Andrew Carnegie to Suze Orman. But as prosperity widens, and as the expectation of comfort becomes the default assumption for ever more Americans, money matters less in determining individual satisfaction and personal notions of success. Indeed, a welter of psychological studies has concluded that "satisfaction simply is not for sale. Not only does having more things prove to be unfulfilling, but people for whom affluence is a priority in life tend to experience an unusual degree of anxiety and depression as well as a lower overall level of well-being," according to the *New York Times*.[18]

Take Liz Tobiason, a thirty-something marketing consultant in San Francisco. California-born, and the youngest of seven children, she began her career selling advertising, and then doing market research for Bay Area newspapers. In the mid-1990s, she landed a job at Wells Fargo Bank, where by all measures she was a high achiever. But after five years, she decided to leave and go solo.

"The light bulb really went on in February, during bonus and salary increase time," she told me. "I got by far the biggest bonus I'd ever gotten—triple the year before—and I was totally disappointed."

"Disappointed it was less than you expected?" I asked her.

"No. I was disappointed that I didn't care. I realized it's not the money that would make me happy, because I didn't like the job."

Two weeks later, her bank account flush but her soul depleted, Tobiason became a free agent.

Let's be clear, though. It's not that free agents don't care about money. They do. And it's not that they don't make money. They do. In fact, when Thomas Stanley and William Danko studied one thousand millionaires for their best-seller, *The Millionaire Next Door*, they discovered that two thirds of their sample worked for themselves. Self-employed people were four times more likely to be millionaires than those who worked for others.[19]

However, what prompts people to declare free agency and

pursue independent work is rarely financial. For example, a 1999 Lou Harris survey of one thousand self-employed Americans and small entrepreneurs found that money was not their top motivator. Nine out of ten respondents said that "setting their own priorities and independence influenced their decision most" to strike out on their own.[20]

This has huge implications for traditional employers. According to a 1999 Vault.com survey, a key reason people leave jobs is boredom.[21] A survey of executives by Robert Half, the staffing firm, found that autonomy, challenge, and learning were the things that really made people like their jobs. And an American Management Association study concluded that the best way to keep employees from leaving was not to fatten their salary or sweeten their benefits, but to offer flexible schedules, sabbaticals, and opportunities to learn.[22] In other words, the best strategy for managing employees isn't to bribe them, but to treat them like free agents.

PROMOTIONS AND SUCCESS

Free agents are also trampling on another traditional motivator of people and measure of success: promotions. In the Organization Man economy, the higher you climbed, the more successful you were. Each spot above you on the org chart was like a mechanical bunny at a greyhound track, prodding you to race faster to attain it. But a funny thing happened when people actually caught the bunny. They discovered it wasn't a natural creation of God, but an artificial product of man—and not nearly as delectable as they'd imagined.

Denise Apcar began working for pharmaceutical and medical devices companies in 1980. In 1995, a larger company acquired the company where she was working, and "I was promoted into a meaningless, thankless job where I was on a plane to New York almost every other Monday." A few months in that position were enough to inspire her to head for the exit. "It was middle manager hell," she told me on a rainy November night at a cramped Starbucks in Foster City, California. "The mentality was politics first, quality second." For Apcar, moving up was the impetus for moving out. "I lost everything I enjoyed doing, the higher up I got," she says. "I wanted to do what my staff people were doing. It was one of those things in the corporate world you're not supposed to admit."

Liz Tobiason tells a similar tale. At Wells Fargo, her "big boss"—a woman Tobiason likes and admires—helped Tobiason land a promotion to vice president. She also tried to further Tobiason's career by tapping her to do a presentation before the company's president. "I begged her not to make me do that," Tobiason told me. "I knew it would be two weeks of making this PowerPoint presentation, where no value would come out of it except that I was going to try and make the president think I was smart and remember my name." The more time she spent in the high reaches of her company, the more she yearned for the freedom of the flatlands. "I realized I had no desire to have more people working for me. More responsibility was fine. But I was having to manage people who were doing the actual work I wanted to do. I had to give away the fun part of my job."

I call this the Peter-Out Principle. Remember the Peter Principle? It held that people would rise through the ranks of an organization until they reached a position where they were incompetent. Its successor, the Peter-Out Principle, holds that people will rise until they stop having fun. When the fun peters out, talented people walk out—usually to become free agents. In Maslow's America, one of the surest ways to crush somebody's job satisfaction, particularly creative and technical types, is to promote them.

GROWTH AND SUCCESS

If money and promotions are no longer the sole measures of success, what is? One sensible answer would be growth. In the mythology of business, the goal of a small enterprise is to become a larger enterprise—the garage becomes an office tower, the corner drugstore becomes a national chain. But on this dimension, too, free agents are questioning what truly constitutes success.

Two men I encountered in different parts of the country offer examples of what I mean. Dennis Benson runs a Columbus,

Ohio, business called Appropriate Solutions, which conducts public opinion surveys, education research, and other quantitative analyses mostly for state governments. When he started the company in 1978, he and his four partners worked out of their homes. Then the company grew and found "real" space. "When we signed our office lease, it was sort of a symbol that we'd made it," Benson told me one afternoon on his backyard deck. By 1993, the firm employed thirty people. But an expanding company got to be an expanding hassle. So the following year, Benson began paring back his operation. While he could have made more money, it wasn't worth the aggravation. So he downsized his own firm, canceled his office lease, and moved the company into his suburban home. By 1998, Appropriate Solutions was down to a two-person microbusiness, just Benson and his wife, Sandy. Instead of growing, traditionally a sign of success, he shrank, traditionally a sign of failure. But Benson sees it differently. Like the promoted managers, he was spending less and less time on what he enjoyed doing and did best. And that proved inconsistent with Appropriate Solutions's philosophy: "It has to be good. It has to be fun. It has to be profitable. When it stops being fun, do something else."

Tom Crosley also downsized himself. An Iowa native and son of a small-businessman, he began his career in the early 1970s as an engineer in GTE's Chicago offices. Over the next few years, he did great work during the day and earned a master's degree in computer science at night. By age twenty-seven, he had reached the highest level a GTE engineer could attain, which left him with two options: jump to the management track or take a hike. Management wasn't for him. "I love to code," Crosley says. "I'm born to code." So he took another job in California, until his new employer told Crosley that any software he wrote at home during the evening belonged to the company. Crosley left that company, too, and never returned to traditional work. "I haven't had a W-2 since 1978," he bragged when we chatted in a coffee shop across from a Universal Studios lot outside Los Angeles.

But he performed so well as an independent software writer that he soon began issuing W-2s himself. So much business flooded in that he had to hire others. By 1985 he had four employees and revenues of a quarter-million dollars—a California success story in the making. Except for this: "I hated it," Crosley says. "I found myself in my dad's situation, head of a company with a bunch of employees. Except that he likes management and I don't." Cutting back, though, wasn't an easy decision. "Mid-to late 1980s I was making more money than ever before, but I was unhappy because I didn't like what I was doing." So he did something they don't teach you in business school: He decided to shrink his operation—to become, in the eyes of some, less successful. "By 1990 I was down to just myself," he says. "And I was happy."

For Benson and Crosley, and most free agents, bigger isn't necessarily better. Better is better. Gone is the One Size Fits All approach to success—measured in promotions and denominated in dollars. In is the My Size Fits Me approach to success—measured by personal metrics and denominated in anything from time to freedom to authenticity to prestige to challenge.

There's ample evidence that this tailor-made approach has made free agents the most satisfied people in the world of work.

- A 1999 study by economists David Blanchflower of Dartmouth College and Andrew Oswald of the University of Warwick found that the self-employed have greater job satisfaction than any other group of U.S. workers.[23]

- An eight-year study of workers in the U.K. found that "The happiest group of workers, in spite of their often long hours in pursuit of success, are the self-employed," according to the *Financial Times*. Workers in big companies were consistently less satisfied than those in small firms. Although workers in general were surprisingly satisfied, the smaller the operation, particularly when the operation was very small, the happier the worker.[24]

- Another Blanchflower and Oswald study—a mammoth effort that tracked the attitudes of more than a half-million Americans and Europeans—found that the highest satisfaction levels were reported by people who work for themselves.[25]

So maybe it's not all about the Benjamins . . . or the promotions . . . or the growth. Maybe Bob Dylan, and not Puff Daddy, holds the answer. "A man is a success," Dylan sang, "if he gets up in the morning and does what he wants to do."

MASLOW AND MAGUIRE ON SUCCESS

"To do some idiotic job very well is certainly not a real achievement. I like my phrasing, 'what is not worth doing is not worth doing well.'"
—*Abraham Maslow*

"Suddenly it was all pretty clear. The answer was fewer clients, less money. More attention. Caring for them, caring for ourselves. Starting our lives, really."
—*Jerry Maguire*

THE FREE AGENT WORK ETHIC

If I told you that you had a good work ethic, you'd probably take it as a compliment. Most Americans would. Most of us believe a "good work ethic" is something we should display in our lives and inspire in our children. Yet fewer of us have given much thought to what "work ethic" really means.

The Calvinist work ethic that reigned in America practically since the nation's inception went roughly as follows: Work hard and long, because in the end you'll be rewarded. You may not enjoy it. At times, you'll detest it. But buck up and don't complain. If you trudge to work every day and do your job, the rewards will eventually come. You'll earn enough money to house your family, feed your kids, and retire when your working days are done. Work is a bearable burden that's sometimes enjoyable but at its heart represents the antithesis of pleasure. Besides, tramping to work every day—even though you hate it—is a sign of good character. That's what we ought to teach our kids.

In the last decade, though, the four values I've described in this chapter—having freedom, being authentic, putting yourself on the line, and defining success on your own terms—have combined to expand our notions of the work ethic. They have formed a broad new attitude toward work—a free agent credo that's expressed most starkly in the independent workforce but that is shaping the rest of the workforce as well.

This credo abandons many of the tenets of the Protestant work ethic—particularly its intense seriousness and disdain for joy. It is as much about play as it is about work. Indeed, the essence of free agency may be that it's hard to distinguish between work and play. The result is not pure frivolity—but something more akin to "hard fun," "serious play," or "deep play," as some other authors have described it.[26] Besides, in an information-drenched, creativity-fueled economy, all work ethic and no play ethic can make Jack a less valuable free agent. Geoff McFetridge, a Los Angeles graphic designer, says he knows he's doing great work for a client when he wants to tell them, "I'm rocking on your dime."[27]

Equally important, the free agent ethic generally does not succumb to what *Wall Street Journal* columnist Sue Shellenbarger calls the "tomorrow trap"—which she says captures people "who essentially live for the future, taking refuge in visions of a relaxed, rewarding personal and family life somewhere down the road,"[28] instead of gaining pleasure and satisfaction in the moment. For free agents, work is often like virtue—it becomes its own reward.

Listen to some free agents try to define this new philosophy:

- "Work hard when you must work—and if at all possible, have fun at it." (Sara Jalali; Dallas, Texas)

- "I get to define my own work, and do what challenges and excites me the most—with the occasional Okay-I'll-do-that-because-it-pays-well stuff thrown in." (Dianne Jacob; Oakland, California)

- "It's freedom to pursue a line of work that is satisfying—not that every day is an absolutely joyous experience, but when I reflect (and that's a freedom, too) on my body of work at the end of the week, month, or year I can smile and say, 'It was good.'" (Lloyd Lemons; Austin, Texas)

In short, the emerging free agent credo goes something like this:

Working hard for a far-off reward is often a valuable exercise, but the act of work itself should produce its own intrinsic rewards. And since no position is permanent—but other positions are usually available and destitution is not around the bend—you might as well enjoy what you do. Produce quality work that's a genuine reflection of who you are. Use your freedom to accept responsibility for your work. Decide for yourself what constitutes success. And if you're not having fun—at least some of the time—you're doing something wrong.

THE BOX

CHAPTER 4

THE CRUX: As work becomes about both making money and finding meaning, free agents are expanding the American work ethic—and sometimes turning it inside out. For independent workers, freedom matters more than stability, and self-expression has replaced self-denial. Instead of hiding behind an organization, free agents make themselves directly accountable. And rather than accept a prefabricated notion of success, they are defining success on their own terms. (For instance, in Free Agent Nation, bigger isn't better; better is better.) The result is that free agents have refashioned the Protestant work ethic into a free agent work credo composed of four key elements: having freedom, being authentic, putting yourself on the line, and defining success on your own terms.

THE FACTOID: A 1999 Lou Harris survey of one thousand self-employed Americans and small entrepreneurs found that money was not their top motivator. Nine out of ten respondents said that "setting their own priorities and independence influenced their decision most" to go out on their own.

THE QUOTE: "Maybe it's not 'all about the Benjamins . . . or the promotions . . . or the growth.' Maybe Bob Dylan, and not Puff Daddy, holds the answer. 'A man is a success,' Dylan sang, 'if he gets up in the morning and does what he wants to do.' "

THE WORD: *The Peter-Out Principle.* Successor to the famous Peter Principle, which held that people would rise through the ranks of an organization until they reached their level of incompetence. The Peter-Out Principle holds that people will move up the ranks of an organization until they stop having fun. When the fun peters out, the talented people walk out—usually to become free agents.

The New Employment Contract

"Whenever someone tells you that a company really cares about its employees, repeat this simple mantra: 'Bullshit! Bullshit! Bullshit!'—and you'll dispel all dangerous illusions."
—Rick Cohen (Agoura Hills, California)

As squadrons of Organization Men marched through American companies, William Whyte pondered where their footprints would leave the deepest imprint. It wouldn't be on the carpet of the corporate boardroom, he decided, or even on the broader landscape of business. Instead, the Organization Men would make their enduring mark on the national psyche as their values "set the American temper."

The same is true for free agents. In the twenty-first century, free agent values are setting the American temper. And nowhere is this more pronounced than in how free agents are recasting the two core values of the Organization Man's social contract of work: security and loyalty.

SECURITY

What's the brightest star in America's constellation of values? Consider the name of the country's most popular, most successful, and most politically untouchable government initiative. It's not called "Social Opportunity" or "Social Possibility" or "Social Pretty Safe Bet." It's called "Social *Security*." "Security" is an American watchword, something we treasure when we have it and seek when we don't. And for much of the last century, "security" formed one half of the American workplace compact. Individuals received it from an organization in exchange for their loyalty. But in the new era of work, soloists, temps, and micropreneurs have been forced to redefine this American ideal.

The backdrop for this change is one of the most significant economic developments of the late twentieth century. Look at the street map of American life these days, and you'll find an intersection that was barely under construction ten years ago: Main Street now intersects Wall Street. In the space of barely a decade, a large portion of the middle class has joined the investor class. The numbers are staggering:

- In 1952, 96 percent of Americans did not own a single share of stock. In 1983, only one in five households owned stock. Today more than half of American households own stock.[1]

- As recently as 1987, the average household had only 13 percent of its total assets in the stock market, less than it had in checking and savings accounts.[2] Today, American households now have 28 percent of their assets in stock, more than they have in their homes.[3]

- More than 65 million Americans now own shares in a mutual fund—and 70 percent of these fund owners have annual household incomes of less than $75,000.[4]

Or consider this fact and its implications for American life: In 2000, for the first time in U.S. history, more citizens owned stock than cast a ballot for President of the United States. High finance has been democratized. And the result is that Americans have become increasingly sophisticated about financial matters.

Suppose we pulled a middle-class couple off the streets of Topeka or Tallahassee and sought their financial advice. "I've just inherited $6,000 from my Aunt Helga, and I'd like to invest it," you tell them. "IBM stock looks really strong these days. I think I'll plunk down the whole thing and buy $6,000 worth of IBM shares. What do you guys think?"

Chances are, this couple would tell you that you were nuts. "Don't invest the whole wad on one stock," they'd likely say. "If you want growth over the long haul, you've got to diversify." More and more, Americans understand this simple principle. And more and more, they are importing this financial reasoning to the world of work.

Churn, Baby, Churn

In a chapter called "A Generation of Bureaucrats," Whyte described college seniors interviewing for jobs with big companies. He wrote that "once the tie has been established with the big company, they believe, they will not switch to a small one, or for that matter, to another big one. The relationship is to be for keeps."[5] These college seniors entered a workforce warmed by the sun of the benevolent corporation—a quasi–welfare state that offered all the security they could need in return for all the submissiveness they could offer. And the job interview was often the place where the kabuki theater of this arrangement first unfolded. The classic interview question was "Where do you see yourself in five or ten years?" And the classic answer—the *right* answer—was that you saw yourself at the same company in an incrementally higher position than you were now seeking, climbing upward to still another incrementally better internal job.

Oh, how the American temper has changed. Imagine that job interview with a college senior today. Suppose the interviewer asked her "Where do you see yourself in five years?" And say she responded, "Five years? Jeez, how about twenty-five years? I'll be right here, working for this company. I intend to be here the rest of my working life." That's a perfect way *not* to get the job. After all, the interviewer himself is probably awash in office politics, worried about being let go, and contemplating striking out on his own. If he's not going to be there in five years, why should you? And who's to say the company itself will even be around five years hence? Product cycle times are shortening, corporate half-lives are shrinking, and time-to-market is now measured in months and sometimes weeks.

Many of the forces that have produced a faster computer chip every year have infiltrated the world of work, and accelerated work's every aspect. Throughout the new labor market, the churn is especially intense. For example:

- In 1982, in the trough of a recession, 12 percent of workers feared they'd lose their jobs. In 1999, with a 4.3 percent unemployment rate, 37 percent feared they'd lose their jobs. Says the redoubtable Alan Greenspan: "The rapidity of change has clearly raised the level of anxiety and insecurity in the workforce."[6]

- Even in the booming economy of the late 1990s, one in five California workers had lost a job in the previous three years. One in ten had lost a job in the previous twelve months.[7]

- In 1998 and 1999, with the unemployment rate at its lowest level in thirty years, American companies laid off 1.3 million people—nearly six times the rate of ten years earlier.[8] The once hot Internet sector canned more than 45,000 people in 2000 alone.

In a climate of churn and heightened risk, attachment is a poor strategy and cradle-to-grave security a false promise. Free agents therefore are employing the same strategy investors use in volatile markets: Because they are shouldering more risk than ever, they are hedging against it as much as they can.

Hedge, Baby, Hedge

For years, most Americans did not diversify their work lives—largely because they didn't need to. Signing up with one company—investing your entire account of human capital in one stock, as it were—was usually a prudent move. But for most people today, investing all your human capital in a single company makes as little sense as investing all your financial capital in shares of IBM. (Curiously, economists and investors didn't fully understand the power of diversifying investments over a broad stock portfolio until 1952, when a twenty-five-year-old University of Chicago graduate student named Harry Markowitz wrote a short article in an esoteric finance journal making this point. The stunning simplicity of his argument won Markowitz a Nobel Prize thirty-eight years later.) Just as in the newly democratized world of finance, in the newly liberated world of work, it's diversify or die.

Deborah Risi embodies this new approach. A forty-three-year-old marketing guru, Deb Risi is nothing if not self-sufficient. If disaster ever struck her airy ranch house in Menlo Park, California, she and her two young children could eat extremely well for months—without ever leaving the property. In her front yard is a massive vegetable garden with enough variety to stock a Safeway produce section. In the back are trees that grow olives, plums, and figs. Her living room shelves groan under the weight of several dozen cookbooks.

For many years, Risi worked at companies like Apple Computer and Pacific Bell, making her way smoothly, landing ever better positions at ever higher salaries. But eventually she tired of working for bad bosses. So she chose free agency, and charted a new route to a secure future.

Today she operates out of a room in her house, chock-a-block with computer equipment and file cabinets. She designs marketing plans for high-tech companies like Sun Microsystems, Oracle, and Cisco Systems, juggling four to six clients at a time. Her income is higher and so is her sense of security.

Indeed, she actually feels *more* secure than she did in a job. She approaches her work guided by the same principles that guide her investments—plenty of research, solid fundamentals, and most of all, diversification. Just as that middle-class couple from Topeka or Tallahassee said you'd be a fool to invest your entire stock of financial capital in one stock, free agents have figured out that you're equally foolish investing all your *human* capital in a single *employer.*

Not everyone Risi encounters grasps this new way of thinking. A few years ago, she was applying for a mortgage. The bank demanded every scrap of paper about her life and her finances. "How could we lend money to you?" the bankers sniffed. "You don't even have a . . . job."

"I showed them my résumé and said, 'You're kidding me. I've been at Apple, Pacific Bell, Culinet Software, all these high-tech companies. And you're telling me that I would be a safer bet at one of those versus having six active clients at once? If one of those goes away, I'm going to make my payments. But if I'm employed by Apple and they let me go, I'm out on the street.'"

She got her loan.

"Job diversity" is essential because "job security" has evaporated. Indeed, by the time Risi's young son and daughter enter the workforce about the only place they'll find the phrase "job security" will be in America's linguistic ash can, next to words like "icebox" and "motorcar."

The Game of Risk

The ascendance of diversity over security results largely from that indomitable force of casinos, insurance policies, and market economies: risk. In the security-for-loyalty bargain, the organization bore most of the risk of the enterprise. Organizations were willing to assume the risk, because in an economy insulated from foreign competition, dominated by extremely large enterprises, and made stable by predictable technologies, that risk was often minimal. Meanwhile, individuals, prizing stability above all, were willing to accept less of risk's upside—in exchange for protecting themselves against more of its downside. But when competition intensified and new technologies proliferated, the total volume of risk increased, sometimes substantially. Companies grew weary of carrying the full load, so they started shifting risk onto their employees.

Consider how Americans now save for retirement. For decades, most retired workers received what are called "defined benefit" pensions—that is, their former employer sent them a check every month from the moment they left the company until the moment they left the world. Sixty-five percent of workers over age sixty-five have defined benefit pension plans—but only 25 percent of younger workers.[10] Why? Since the mid-1990s, a greater number of workers have had what are called "defined *contribution*" pensions. These plans—the most prominent of which are 401(k)s—allow employees to set aside money on their own (sometimes matched by the company), invest it as they choose, and carry the pension with them from job to job. Defined contribution pensions are cheaper for employers—and both riskier and potentially more lucrative for employees.

Or take another example: the explosion in variable pay schemes such as stock options, commissions, and performance bonuses. A survey of 1,069 employers by Hewitt Associates found that 72 percent offered variable pay arrangements, compared with 61 percent only two years earlier.[11] While Organization Man pay scales were based largely on seniority, and therefore were easy to predict and didn't vary much from person to person, these new pay arrangements are quite different. They reward individual performance, sacrificing predictability and equality along the way. As in many other realms, the risk, responsibility, and reward have shifted from the organization to the individual.

Another example is education and training. In the old economy, the organization trained its workers. Whyte describes how companies would devote an entire year to training new employees. But with the churn so great, employers don't want to make

those investments—so they've pushed onto individuals the burden of acquiring new skills and the risk of letting current skills
grow rusty. Thus the increase in distance learning and the soaring adult enrollment in community colleges.

Some people have recoiled at taking on more risk. More risk
might mean more pain. Others have embraced it. More risk
might mean more payoff. Most are somewhere in between—wary
of the challenge, but accepting its inevitability. One of these men
in the middle is Bob Milbourn. Milbourn earned his MBA in
1974, and spent the next two decades working as a loan officer
for banks in the San Francisco Bay Area. As his career pro-
gressed, and his industry consolidated, he sensed that each day
he stayed his risk expanded—and that total risk in his work life
was ballooning. "For the longest time, I was so terrified of being
laid off," he told me. "Then I got to the point where I *hoped* they
would lay me off. Then I *asked* to be laid off."

He walked into his boss's office one day in 1995, told her that
he was miserable in his job, and offered himself as a sacrifice to
the cost-cutting gods. His boss said no, that the bank needed
him. "The next step for me," Milbourn says, "was to take the bull
by the horns." He needed time to muster the courage, but two
years later he walked into the same office of the same boss and
quit to go solo. "I figured it was a bigger risk to stay," he explained.

"I felt more and more confined. My networking circle had
shrunk. I only knew people within the four walls that I worked. I
knew that was dangerous," he told me one afternoon in San
Francisco. In other words, Milbourn was not diversified. Like
Milbourn, more individuals, accustomed to managing risk in
their financial lives, have slowly begun warming to it in their
work lives. Of course, different workers—like different investors—have different appetites for risk. And many of us don't
always approach risk—whether financial or vocational—as
purely rational calculators of our economic self-interest. But
many free agents have discovered that the risk they are now
forced to bear may not be as weighty as they imagined. The
downsizings of a decade ago delivered pain to millions of fami-

lies, and deepened distrust of large institutions, but it was hardly the enduring calamity many predicted. Says Paul Starobin, a canny American public policy journalist, "Yesterday's paternalistic society has evolved into today's take-a-chance one; the idea that society should shelter the individual from risk has been supplanted by the notion that society should enable the individual to profit from risk."[12] What profiting from risk requires, though, is that individuals begin acting like high-priced financial managers sitting atop billions of dollars, and start deploying an array of hedging strategies to manage the intensified risk in their work lives.

Diversification—that is, an independent worker spreading her risk across a portfolio of projects, clients, skills, and customers—is the best hedging strategy. But there are other hedging techniques afoot in the new world of work. Take the resurgence of moonlighting. In the Organization Man era, moonlighting was a big no-no. The very name implied that you were doing something illicit—concealing your behavior under the cover of darkness. No more. Today, anybody who holds a job and *isn't* looking for a side gig—or crafting a business plan, writing a screenplay, or setting up shop on eBay—is out of touch. Moonlighting is a way to diversify your human capital investments—and hedge against the risk of your company collapsing or your job disappearing. It represents an economic side bet not much different from derivatives or soybean futures. Indeed, as most companies resist training workers in new specialties, and as they claim to prefer people with entrepreneurial pluck, moonlighting, once a way to get fired, now may have become a way to get hired. Workers of the world, paste on your reflective strips. You have nothing to lose but your day job. In some sense, we're all moonlighters, because in every sense, we're all risk managers.

Some Silicon Valleyites are hedging by working for one year each at several companies to accumulate stock options at a diversified set of companies. Another hedge against risk is size itself: Enterprises with fewer than ten people are less likely to fail than fuller blown start-up companies.[13] Downshifting and simplifying can also be a hedging strategy. If you can't reduce the risks of free agency itself, you can at least cushion the impact that volatility has on your family's life.

Free agency itself may more broadly reduce risk in the total economy. In an economy dominated by a few giant companies, if one of those companies failed, it often brought down many others as well. When General Motors sneezed, America caught pneumonia. But the free agent economy operates differently. When Pink, Inc. sneezes, America remains 99.99 percent germ-free. If one microbusiness collapses, the tremors reach only a tiny portion of the business terrain. The result is something of a microeconomic paradox. Free agents are more exposed to risk—particularly in a broad economic downturn. But that sort of downturn is less likely to occur, because the collapse of any single enterprise is unlikely to tear down the whole economy. In this sense, free agency may minimize its own risk.

One result is that many free agents actually appear more secure than typical workers, a view confirmed by economists who have studied the matter. Government labor economist Sharon Cohany has concluded that most "data make clear that intermediated, irregularly scheduled, or consulting jobs are not necessarily perceived as unstable by the workers who hold them."[14] And in their study of 3,600 workers over a four-year period, Northwestern University economist Charles F. Manski and University of Wisconsin economist John D. Straub found that "Self-employed workers see themselves as facing *less* job insecurity than do those who work for others."[15]

As free agents like Deb Risi and Bob Milbourn reckon wisely with risk, they are teaching the rest of the workforce a crucial lesson about work in the twenty-first century: Freedom and security are not necessarily trade-offs. Not only is it more interesting to maintain a portfolio of clients and projects than it is to answer to a single boss, it may be safer. The more clients you can assemble, the more projects you can land, the more nodes you can add to your personal network, the more secure you will be.

Freedom, once a detour from security, is now a pathway toward security.

LOYALTY

When security collapsed, and then was reconfigured by free agents, its counterpart—loyalty—met the same fate. In the Organization Man's world, loyalty ran up and down. It flowed from a subordinate to an authority figure, who graciously conferred some benefit in return. Call this brand of loyalty *vertical loyalty*. And consider it dead—at least in the workplace.

According to one study, about 40 percent of workers say they would leave their current employers if they were offered only slightly higher pay.[16] No surprise there. If there's no security offered in return, loyalty becomes at best an act of charity, at worst an act of folly. And while organizations may decry the disappearance of this form of allegiance, there's little question who waved the magic wand. In 1987, IBM chairman John Akers said, "Full employment is the cornerstone of the loyalty of our employees to the company."[17] Five years later, as we learned in Chapter 3, the company began shedding more than 100,000 employees. "Companies killed loyalty," Stanford professor Jeffrey Pfeffer told *Fast Company* founding editor Alan Webber, "by becoming toxic places to work!"[18]

What's more, vertical loyalty—where individuals offer fealty upward to some benevolent institution—is crumbling more broadly across American culture. In politics, party loyalty is down. (The fastest growing political affiliation in America today is Independent.) In retail, consumer loyalty is down. (AT&T says 1.7 million customers are "spinners," who change long distance companies three or more times a year, always searching for the best deal.) Like workers, voters and buyers are free agents, too.

To some, vertical loyalty's disappearance is yet another slippage in the rock slide of American morals. Harvard professor Henry Louis Gates, Jr., who himself has hopscotched from university to university in search of better positions, has even lamented "The End of Loyalty," citing free agency as one of the more pernicious expressions of this dangerous trend. But the truth is, vertical loyalty, while perhaps superficially comforting, can be dangerous. For instance, unstinting loyalty to a single organization can become a liability for individuals. Too many years with one employer can dull skills and limit exposure to a fast-changing world, degrading loyalty into dependence. And what holds for individuals may hold equally for organizations. Researchers at New York University and Northwestern found that employees grow less loyal after only two years on the job.[19] Besides, writes author and former *Reason* editor Virginia Postrel, "The world we've lost wasn't all today's stability zealots make it seem. 'Loyalty' sounds good in the abstract, but it exacts a terrible cost in economic stagnation and personal repression."[20] William Whyte made much the same point in his chapter on the organization's role in suffocating freewheeling scientific discovery, exploration, and genius. The idle curiosity that often sparks innovation had no place in organization life, he wrote. "Company loyalty . . . is not only more important than idle curiosity; it helps prevent idle curiosity."[21]

Alas, no one need plan loyalty's wake just yet. In Free Agent Nation, loyalty isn't dead. It's different.

"I'm loyal to individuals, but I can't think of any institutions," says Bob Milbourn. Loyalty is alive and well in Free Agent Nation—if you look for it in the right places. What you'll find is not vertical loyalty—but *horizontal loyalty*, loyalty that flows laterally.

Loyalty to Teams, Colleagues, and Ex-Colleagues

"My loyalty isn't really to the corporation," says Charlie Bofferding, who heads the labor union that represents engineers at Boeing, the company that metamorphosed one weekend from a family to a team. "That's an abstract thing. What I do understand are my colleagues and the technical community at Boeing." While loyalty upward has weakened, loyalty sideways has intensified. Free agents harbor deep loyalty to their peers, who return that loyalty with equal intensity. Such loyalty often blooms from genuine human connection. But enlightened self-interest also helps nourish it. As a free agent, your network is your safety net. The vaster it is and the tighter its connections, the more likely you'll be able to survive. Every connection you make and maintain connects you to another person's network—and it likewise connects her to yours. Tom Peters puts it beautifully: "Logo loyalty" is dead; "Rolodex loyalty" is essential.[22] This form of horizontal loyalty also breeds fierce loyalty to teams. It's one reason that some free agents move from project to project in teams—just as some directors make movies only if they can work with the same cinematographer and sound crew. One interesting version of this variety is loyalty to *former* colleagues. As I'll explore in Chapter 7, former employees of many companies are forming "alumni networks" to sustain the horizontal loyalty that developed when they worked together. The horizontal relations between teams, colleagues, and former colleagues have become more important and more plentiful.

Loyalty to Professions and Industries

Silicon Valley, the saying goes, is the only place where you can switch jobs without switching carpools. Independent contractors abound. Nearly everyone, it seems, skitters from job to job to job. To some observers, this serial employment leaves the air along the Valley's Highway 101 thick with disloyalty. But those with a refined sense of smell detect something more subtle—the aroma of a new kind of allegiance. "Some say they wake up thinking they work for Silicon Valley. Their loyalty is more to advancing technology or to the region than it is to any individual firm," writes AnnaLee Saxenian in *Regional Advantage*, her influential examination of Valley culture.[23] One survey of information technology professionals found that when asked what they did for a living, three fourths answered with their skills or profession. Only 23 percent responded by citing the company they worked for.[24] For free agents, another strain of horizontal loyalty is loyalty to communities of practice: If you're not well connected to your profession, it's harder to sharpen your skills, keep up to date on trends, and find new gigs. This helps explain why membership in professional associations (generally based on occupation) is rising as sharply as membership in labor unions (often based on employer) is falling. Patrice Molinarolo, a Seattle computer consultant, says that her loyalty is to a particular project—and to the larger industry. In particular, she expresses much of her loyalty through the Association of Women in Computing. "I formulate great friendships I never would have had prior," she explained to me. "We, as women in the high-tech industry, have to support each other."

Loyalty to Clients and Customers

Since free agents focus more on the task than on the organization, they understandably express great loyalty to projects and products. This, too, is a form of enlightened self-interest. If you're only as good as your last project, that project better be excellent. But it also reflects the pride of a craftsperson, which is how many soloists and microbusinesses see themselves. And because the relationship between free agent and client is inherently and explicitly short-term (in contrast to the traditional employment relationship, which is inherently short-term but explicitly not), free agents seeking respect must earn it with every contract or customer. Talk to free agents for any length of time, and you'll hear comments like those I heard from San Francisco–based copywriter Carla Detchon. "I have tons of loyalty to my clients," she told me. "Because we have more of a friendship, we've created a bond. They respect me. They applaud me." Says Tom Crosley, the Los Angeles–based infotech free agent we met in the previous chapter, "I'm very loyal to my clients. There is a misconception that consultants and contractors are get-up-and-go and you never can count on them for the long term. But in Silicon Valley, where you have employees staying in the company for less than two years, I am the one that is the continuity."

Loyalty to Family and Friends

"I don't think an organization can be loyal to me," free agent Sally Duros told me at a Starbucks in Chicago's Loop. Instead, loyalty can flow only from person to person—and it's the people closest who deserve it the most. Where the Organization Man might have sacrificed his duty to his family in favor of his allegiance to the company—say, by always missing dinner or by relocating anytime the company issued the word—free agents often do the reverse. Those who've left traditional jobs to spend more time with their families, those who work at home to be near their kids, and those who work what the industrial economy called "part-time" in order to fulfill family obligations are examples of this form of horizontal loyalty.

One final difference between up-and-down loyalty and side-to-side loyalty is also crucial to understanding the newly reset American temper. Vertical and horizontal loyalty differ not just in quality, but in quantity. Where vertical loyalty depended on *one* strong connection, horizontal loyalty depends on *multiple* connections—all of varying strength and endurance. Vertical loyalty resembled a thick and sturdy rope. Horizontal loyalty, as I'll explain more fully in Chapter 8, creates a complex and intricate web.

STRIKING A NEW BARGAIN

In the end, security and loyalty have acquired new meanings. Security, once achieved through attachment to a large institution, is now achieved by hedging risk and diversifying across several clients, customers, and projects. Loyalty, which once ran vertically, has been turned on its side. It now runs horizontally— to colleagues, teams, professions, and families. The result: For good or ill, the loyalty-for-security bargain that nearly defined the American workforce for several generations is gone. The question: What new bargain has taken its place?

Free agents themselves offer some possibilities:

- "What has taken the place of the old social contract is me being responsible for my livelihood versus someone else (a company) being responsible for me. This is both freeing and scary as hell. But scary only because we're not used to it. The fear will subside as the paradigm shifts. Our grandchildren probably won't believe that most of us actually went to work for someone else." (Pete Siler; Herndon, Virginia)

- "I try to look at whatever I do as getting paid to learn what I need to know." (Tom Durkin; Colfax, California)

- "The superior-subordinate, boss-employee paradigm is replaced by the peer-to-peer, business-to-business one. As a free agent, you don't go into a job as a subordinate. You go in as an equal. This may be subtle at times, but it fundamentally changes the nature of the relationship between the two parties in a transaction." (Mark Haas; Kensington, California)

These three answers and the perspectives I heard from other free agents distill to the following new social compact of work, the implicit employment contract of Free Agent Nation:

The free agent gives talent in exchange for opportunity.

Talent can be solving a problem—a computer contractor figuring out how to set up a company's LAN or a plumber unstopping a clogged kitchen sink. Talent can be offering a set of niche skills that allow a large team to solve a sprawling problem. Or it can be completing a project—like a housepainter putting a new coat of paint on the living room walls. The buyer doesn't purchase the person; the buyer rents that person's abilities. Or in the case of a microbusiness like a taco stand, or a soloist like a freelance speechwriter, the buyer purchases not the person, but the artifact of the person's abilities. Talent—performance, skill, and results—is what organizations and other buyers seek and what free agents must offer.

Opportunity, what free agents receive in exchange for their talent, comes in many forms. It can be the opportunity to work on a cool project, to learn new skills, to meet new people and broaden your network, to have fun, and, of course, to earn money. Opportunity—money, learning, connections—is what free agents seek and what organizations and other buyers must offer.

The new talent-for-opportunity employment contract answers the imperatives of the market—and therefore has all of the market's elegant efficiency and icy logic. Unlike the old bargain, it is neither static nor universal. It will vary over time. It often will not be equitable. Power and relative advantage will shift based on the conditions of the employment market. When talent is scarce—that is, when the employment market is tight—those who offer it will hold the better cards. When opportunities are scarce—that is, when the employment market is slack—those who dispense them will have the upper hand. This bargain will also vary from person to person—as buyers seek specific talent for finite purposes and free agents seek opportunities based on their My Size Fits Me ethic.

However, each time a free agent strikes a talent-for-opportunity bargain, he adds another investment to his work portfolio—and may increase his security. And each time he strikes this bargain, he can broaden his web of loyalty—to the client, the project, the team, his profession, and his own family. Ultimately, the new employment contract of talent-for-opportunity not only replaces loyalty-for-security, but it enhances both loyalty *and* security.

THE BOX

CHAPTER 5

THE CRUX: In the old social contract of work, the organization offered the individual security—and in return, the individual gave the organization loyalty. That bargain, we all know, has crumbled. As the churn of jobs, technologies, and companies has intensified, free agents have responded to this heightened risk by hedging. Today, just as they do in their financial lives, individuals are achieving security through diversification. Security means investing their human capital in several clients or projects rather than tying it up in a single company. Likewise, loyalty has changed. Vertical loyalty—giving loyalty *up* to an authority figure or institution—has been replaced by horizontal loyalty. The result is a new and more challenging social contract of work: The free agent provides talent (products, services, advice) in exchange for opportunity (money, learning, and connections).

THE FACTOID: More than half of American households now own stocks, up from only one in five households in 1983. In 2000, shareholders outnumbered voters: More citizens owned stock than cast a ballot for President of the United States.

THE QUOTE: "Freedom, once a detour *from* security, is now a pathway *toward* security."

THE WORD: *Horizontal loyalty.* The successor of vertical loyalty, which flowed upward—from an individual to an institution or authority figure. By contrast, this new loyalty flows laterally. It is a fierce, and usually reciprocal, allegiance to: teams, colleagues, and ex-colleagues; to clients and customers; to industries and professions; and to family and friends. (See also: *Free Agent Org Chart*, Chapter 8.)

The New Time Clock

"The worst part about going out on your own is that you have to work twenty-four hours a day. The best part is that you get to pick which twenty-four."

—**Micah Jackson (Chicago, Illinois)**

It's amazing what people will tell you if you just ask them. One week during my year-long effort to strap an EKG to the beating heart of Free Agent Nation, I asked a few dozen free agents to keep time diaries—to record how they spent every half-hour of every day for an entire week. They complied—often sharing intimate and surprising details about their personal and professional lives over the course of those seven days. (For a peek into one independent worker's life, see the sidebar in this chapter, "A Monday in the Life of a Free Agent.") Their reports also confirmed something else I'd suspected about the impact free agents are having on work and life: They are reconfiguring our relationship with time.

Time is tough to fathom. Even Albert Einstein had trouble figuring out what it was and how it worked. Physicists think of time as a separate dimension. Philosophers and cognitive scientists consider time less a natural feature of the universe than a creation of the human mind. But most Americans view the subject more concretely. Time, the saying goes, is money. It's something we "spend," "save," and sometimes "waste." But time is unlike money in at least one crucial respect: It is resolutely democratic. We all get the same amount—168 precious hours every week.

Yet despite time's democratic distribution—or perhaps because of it—there's one aspect of time on which we all seem to agree: Nobody has enough of it. In an economy awash in capital and information, time is scarce. And scarcity, as any Econ 101 graduate can tell you, generally makes something more valuable. For many people today, time is more valuable than money, because throughout the workforce, Americans seem to be suffering from time bankruptcy.

Juliet Schor, whose influential 1992 book, *The Overworked American*, described the time vise gripping American families, has calculated that since 1969 the average worker now spends an additional month on the job every year.[1] Cornell University research found that on average Americans work 350 hours more per year than Europeans—and seventy hours more per year than even the Japanese, whose language contains a word, *karoshi*, that means "death from overwork."[2] On the other hand, there are also some who say the time bind is a myth—that people chronically overreport how much time they work and underreport how much time they devote to less worthy pastimes such as watching television. Using different data sets than Schor, John Robinson, a University of Maryland professor and a leading time researcher, has found that the average time an American works has *declined* by roughly seven hours per week since 1965.[3] In the rarefied realm of university sociology and economics departments, time is a roaring controversy.

But on the front lines of the New Economy, time anxiety is more than simply the hours a person logs, whatever those hours may be; it's also the sense of control that person has over her time. When I worked at the White House, what eventually crushed me was not the long hours—although regular fourteen-hour days certainly didn't help—but the utter lack of control I had over my schedule. I was never truly free. One glance at my belt could tell you that. Hanging off of it, at all times, was a government-issue pager, which kept me tethered to my job psychologically no matter where I was physically. For some of my colleagues, that little vibrating box was a status symbol. And for a time, that may have been true for me. ("Excuse me," you'd say, dutifully pushing yourself away from the restaurant table, sponging up the awe of your meal mates, and then lowering your voice an octave. "The White House is calling.") The pager was proof that you had arrived. But it quickly became equal proof that you could never leave. Some people called the device an electronic leash—but to me, it was more like an electric fence. When dogs are surrounded by an electric fence, they need be zapped only a few times before they learn their boundaries. Even though the fence is invisible, the dog is never free to roam—and after a while doesn't even bother to try. That was me—a dog in a high-prestige job.

And it turns out that I wasn't the only put-upon pooch in the American workforce. In the last decade, time anxiety has become rampant.

- According to a Families and Work Institute study, 63 percent of Americans say they want to work less, up from only 17 percent in 1994.[4]

- In another study, an NYU economist and her University of Pennsylvania colleague found that "45 percent to 50 percent of workers (and 80 percent of those working more than fifty hours a week) said they would prefer to work fewer hours, and more than 25 percent said they would take a pay cut to make it happen."[5]

- Even college students and recent graduates place "flexible hours" at the top of the list of the job benefits they most desire—above health insurance, vacations, and stock options.[6]

What's going on, I suspect, is that time had one meaning in an industrial age—and a different meaning today. Yet we haven't rebuilt the structures or shed the expectations that the old meaning created.

In the industrial economy, time was a unit both fundamental and fungible. And workers, in this sense, were mostly just bushels of hours that the employer could purchase and deploy to serve his needs. The employer's goal was to get those hours cheaply and wring as much out of them as possible—just as the goal of an applesauce maker is to purchase Granny Smiths at a good price and squeeze out of each apple the maximum amount of juice and pulp. The worker's goal was also simple: to fetch the highest price he could get for the fruit that was his labors.

This approach to time fundamentally shaped American business. Indeed, the most important feature of the industrial age may not have been the manager, the production worker, or the assembly line. Each of them bowed down to the almighty clock. What put Frederick Winslow Taylor's Scientific Management on the business map were his time-motion studies, which became a minor obsession in early-twentieth-century factories. (In fact, when Taylor died in his sleep one afternoon in 1915, his nurse found him with a watch in his hand.) The bushels notion of time and work gave us the hourly wage. It generated astounding productivity gains and made America a mass production titan. But it required the workplace to devote considerable technology and brainspace to measuring and monitoring time—factory whistles, time cards, and stopwatch-toting foremen. And for all its efficiency, there was something deadening and demeaning about the individual's place in such a system. Think of Charlie Chaplin throwing a wrench into the machine in *Modern Times* or Lucille Ball gobbling chocolates as they raced down a Taylorist conveyor belt.

In the new workplace, however, most workers—whether free agents or employees—are not merely bushels of hours. Many are selling more than just units of their time. They're selling insight, talent, expertise, ideas, creativity, and solutions—all of which are hard to measure, and harder still using Taylorist time tools. Yet it's extraordinary how much the industrial notion of time still prevails. Even idea-based endeavors like law and public relations typically bill by the hour—which means that if you're the client, a bad idea that takes a long time to hatch will cost more than a good idea the firm comes up with instantly. That's why many free agents charge by the project or the task—rather than by the hour. People know in their bones that there's something awry with the old economy notion that the more time you log, the more valuable you are.

The Rutgers University Work Trends survey showed that across the workforce, a variety of pressures, particularly time pressures, were undercutting job satisfaction. Ninety-five percent of respondents said they were concerned about spending more time with their families. Eighty-seven percent said they were concerned about getting enough sleep. But this clenched face of stress and tension masked a psychological split. As the survey reported, "The experiences of full-time and part-time workers differ sharply from the self-employed. Only 32 percent of the self-employed are very concerned about spending enough time with their immediate family as compared to 42 percent of full-time and 43 percent of part-time workers. Only 29 percent of the self-employed report being very concerned about flexible work arrangements as opposed to 38 percent of full-time and 42 percent of part-time."[7]

In my interviews around the country, free agents said that what matters is what you accomplish, not how many or which hours you're at your desk. "Face time," they said, was false time, which is why many left time-stupid organizations to fashion their own schedules—to align them more closely with their own values and with the new realities of the modern economy. "People respect your time so much more when you're a free agent," public relations consultant Pookie Melberg told me. "They know they can't control you. They can't exert some kind of force on you to get you to do what they want you to do." Instead, independent workers have more control. And at every unit of time—the day, the week, the year, and even the lifetime—they are applying the My Size Fits Me ethic.

THE DAY

Prior to the Industrial Revolution, many people did not rely on clocks to assess time. Instead, as historian E. P. Thompson wrote, they built their time vocabulary on how long it took to do something. Eight hours was "a sleeping time," a minute "a pissing time." But factories couldn't operate according to such idiosyncratic measures, so after some nasty struggles, capital and labor struck a bargain. Time would be chopped into standardized chunks, the most famous chunk of which was the nine-to-five day.

Working nine to five became the standard for most (though, of course, not all) workers in the industrial age. Anything longer was considered "overtime," anything shorter "part-time." The phrase, which crept into movies, songs, and the wider culture, became shorthand for the workday. Nine to five. This regime had many virtues. For workers, it was predictable and fair. No employer could force on people the fourteen-hour sweatshop days many workers endured early in the twentieth century. For employers, the regime was easy to measure, monitor, and enforce. And for both sides, it offered clarity. Some time belonged to the employer; other time belonged to the worker. During certain hours you were "off"; during others you were "on." Some of the day was work; other parts were leisure. It was all very simple.

But now it has become very archaic. As consumers, we expect 24/7 service, which means that someone has to staff those 5:00 P.M. to 9:00 A.M. shifts. As workers, we understand that technology makes us accessible 24/7—as I discovered with my White House–issued electronic fence. The boundaries are far less clear than they were in a world where wailing whistles signaled a day's beginning and end. For instance, if you can answer client e-mail at 10:00 P.M. from your den, where does work end and home begin? What exactly is the "workday"? What exactly is, to borrow a labor movement rallying cry, "a fair day's pay for a fair day's work"? Whose time is it anyway? This daily smokiness, and not the hours themselves, may be stoking America's time anxiety.

And it may be why free agents have less time anxiety than the typical worker. At the unit of the day, free agents are refashioning the nine to five regime to suit their own needs. Some soloists and temps do indeed work nine to five. But most others have customized their schedules to suit their own needs. For free agents, an eight-hour day can mean working 7:00 A.M. to 8:00 A.M., 10:00 A.M. to 11:00 A.M., 1:30 P.M. to 4:00 P.M., 5:00 P.M. to 6:00 P.M., and 8:30 P.M. to 11:00 P.M. Or it can mean, as it does for many parents, working whatever eight hours of the day the kids are not around. In my own modest time diary study, the more than two dozen free agents who opened a window onto their lives worked an average of seven hours and thirty-seven minutes each weekday, a total remarkably consistent with the eight-hour industrial standard. But nobody in the study configured those total hours exactly the same way. Instead of marching to a single, universal beat drummed out by a boss, free agents are finding their own rhythm.

This has advantages, of course. But it also brings annoyances. There are no paid sick days in Free Agent Nation. Even more important, if you work for yourself, it's hard ever to be "off" work (except perhaps during some existential crisis). That can turn many a free agent into what I call a "New Economy 7-Eleven." Like an all-night convenience store, their work life occasionally may be empty, but it's never closed. This feeling of being ever "on"—which I bridled against in my role as a wage slave in a "real" job and which I accept as my moral responsibility in my role as a parent—takes some getting used to as a free agent.

"I think being on your own is really hard because you don't have all of the typical ritual social structures—like company picnics, beer day, casual day on Friday, coffee breaks, going to lunch with somebody," says David Garfinkel, a free agent copywriter in San Francisco. Commuting, saying hello to colleagues, deciding where to get lunch are all important markers and transition points for traditional work. They help establish boundaries. As a result, free agents have had to establish their own time rituals— but as with so many other things, they tailor the rituals themselves instead of buying them off the rack.

For example, Theresa Fitzgerald says: "Every morning I get up and walk the dog. I'm out in the park. I see the same people, my park people. I eat breakfast out every day. So I start my day out, then I come home and work." Cyndi Froggatt, a free agent facilities designer in Manhattan, usually begins each day by taking a long shower and then working naked at her computer for a few hours. (Try *that* one in your ninth-floor cubicle.) Closing rituals matter, too, especially if you work at home. Since my own commute is the roughly ten-second journey between our home's second and third floors, I have tried, with varying degrees of success, to end my work day the same way each evening: filing the day's stray papers and clippings, backing up my computer files, and making a list of things to do the following day. Without these rituals, many independent workers can get lost in a time warp. But with them, they are once again unambiguously in charge of their time priorities. "That's not flexibility," says free agent Dennis Benson, whom we met in Chapter 4. "That's power."

So what do these free agents actually do all day—in between the opening and closing rituals, when they're not walking their dogs, filing their papers, and answering e-mail in the buff?

Their workdays, of course, vary considerably. In my study, they averaged more than two hours per day working in their offices directly for a client. They spend nearly an hour a day answering e-mail—and much of their other work is done online. This is consistent with other workforce studies that have found that the typical worker spends one third of the day on a computer—and 23 percent on the Internet.[8] The free agent time diarists averaged thirty-six minutes a day on the phone—and forty-three minutes a day marketing themselves. Perhaps surprisingly for a group of people who are trying to escape two of the drearier aspects of traditional work, they averaged thirty-eight minutes a day in meetings with clients or customers and thirty-six minutes per day in the car.

But in other respects, particularly those involving health and well-being, their days diverge considerably from the norm. For instance, the free agent time diarists with children spent nearly four hours a day with their kids, far higher than the national norm and far less reliant on orchestrated perfect moments. "With children, the whole idea of quality time is fiction," says free agent Mimi Denman. The majority exercised regularly, averaging slightly more than a half-hour a day hitting the pavement or sweatin' to the oldies. And while several reports have chronicled a national sleep deficit—and some have estimated that more than 100 million Americans are sleep-deprived[9]—free agents seem to be snoozing somewhat more comfortably, slightly more than seven and a half hours per night.

But quantity itself is not the most important element in understanding free agents and time. It's the sense of control over those quantities. Theresa Fitzgerald may work the occasional ten-hour day, but it's *her* ten hours—apportioned, as much as possible, as she decides. Such time-tailoring is powerfully attractive, something companies are discovering, often to their chagrin. Allowing an employee to reconfigure her day can often lead to free agency. First, she takes work home and leaves early on certain afternoons. Then she arranges to telecommute three days per week. Then, while she's telecommuting, she begins moonlighting—or "sunlighting," if she's working on side gigs during the day. Finally, she becomes the genuine article, a free agent. Those few sweet drops of time liberty become intoxicating.

The old way was nine to five. The free agent way is now-to-then—and that probably will change tomorrow.

THE WEEK

If the discussion about work and time were a movie, "the week" would play the starring role. While days are variable and years are long, weeks tend to be the unit around which much of the discussion occurs.

In the middle of the nineteenth century, the typical industrial worker toiled some sixty-four hours each week, with farmworkers racking up seventy-two hours. By the turn of the century, a sixty-hour week—often in horrendous conditions—was typical. But by the 1920s, organized labor beat back that exploitation—

and established a forty-eight-hour workweek. In 1926, at his plant in Dearborn, Michigan, Henry Ford—practically a deacon in the church of Taylorism—did labor one better and put in place a five-day, eight-hour workweek. And by World War II, forty hours a week became the norm—both as custom and as legislation. (Even today, federal law requires that most employees who earn an hourly wage receive time-and-half for the forty-first, and every subsequent, hour they work in a given week.)

Ever since, Americans have heard a steady stream of predictions that the forty-hour week would eventually shrink even further. At a 1967 Senate subcommittee hearing, experts predicted that within twenty years Americans would enjoy a twenty-eight-hour workweek. The very same year, nuclear theorist Herman Kahn speculated that by the year 2000, productivity gains could reduce the typical workweek to only twenty hours.[10]

Alas, it hasn't quite happened. Morgan Stanley Dean Witter chief economist Stephen S. Roach says that the government's official statistics put the average workweek in the service sector—where the vast majority of both free agents and salaried employees work—at 32.9 hours, which is the same as 1987 and actually five hours less than 1969. But, says Roach, "The dirty little secret of the information age is that an increasingly large slice of work goes on outside the official work hours the government recognizes."[11] And several studies have shown an increase in the length of the working week—the explanations for which vary from wages that have stagnated to individuals who are addicted to consumption. The International Labor Organization says that 80 percent of American men and 62 percent of American women work more than forty hours per week.[12] Other reports indicate that two thirds of American workers now log more than forty hours per week.[13]

But for free agents, the mathematics of work time is not as simple as eight times five. "There are some weeks where I may only put in two days. There are some weeks when I will put in nine days!" Neil Brown, a free agent marketing consultant, told me at a strip-mall coffee shop in central Ohio.

The people in my ministudy logged an average of forty-two

hours of work per week. Nearly four of those hours, on average, were over the weekend. But several people worked long days on weekends, only to vacate work on weekdays. As we saw in how they spent their days, at the unit of a week, these free agents arrive at traditional numbers via untraditional routes. Says Brown, "I wouldn't call my schedule the Protestant work ethic because the kind of thing I'm doing would be abhorrent to Puritans." Independent workers may log about forty hours every week, but how they configure those forty hours is highly fluid. Unlike employees, free agents mostly control the faucet.

In most of the non-free-agent workforce, the boundaries are rather clear. Monday through Friday is work. Saturday and Sunday, if not exactly leisure, are not work. The downside of that arrangement: inflexibility. The upside: predictability. You know where the boundaries are. Even at the White House, although I worked just about every weekend, when I went into the office on those days I wasn't "required" to wear a tie—which, if not spiritually reassuring, is sociologically revealing. Weekends weren't made for speechwriting—even if you spent Saturday and Sunday writing speeches. But free agents seem to be on their way to blurring the boundary between the workweek and the weekend. "I can take off Thursday if I need it," self-employed lawyer Brian Clark, whom we met briefly in Chapter 4, told me one morning in Austin, Texas, over plates of migas, a South Texas specialty that's a glorious amalgam of scrambled eggs, sausage, onions, cheese, peppers, and crushed tortilla chips. "But I work most Saturdays and Sundays because that's what I'm interested in doing." And others are mirroring Clark's habits. For instance, even though most people use the Web at "work" rather than at "home," it turns out that the most active day on the Web is Saturday, suggesting the carefully crafted distinction between "the workweek" and "the weekend" may be melting.[14]

The old way was Monday through Friday—five days of work and two days of weekend. The free agent way is Monday through Sunday—seven days of everything.

THE YEAR

Europeans outdo Americans on one—and perhaps only one—dimension: vacations. Many Europeans receive paid vacations of four to six weeks every year. In Australia and Belgium, those vacations are the law. But in the U.S., vacations are more a matter of custom—or at least negotiation. The standard is two to three weeks, and there's some evidence that may be declining. Today, the average worker at a midsized or large company gets 9.6 paid vacation days per year.[15] Juliet Schor maintains that the typical U.S. worker receives three and a half fewer days of paid vacations, holidays, and sick days each year than he did at the beginning of the 1980s.[16]

But at the unit of the year, too, things can get murky. And once again, free agents are often the ones mucking things up. The traditional arrangement at most workplaces usually calls for fifty weeks of work and two weeks of vacation. But for free agents, that plain vanilla option is hard to swallow in a thirty-one-flavors economy. At her previous job, free agent copywriter Carla Detchon got two weeks of vacation and "a decent amount of holidays." But that didn't do it for her—and even worse, revealed who held the power. "Two weeks is not where I'm at," she told me at a Starbucks in San Francisco. "I always took more, took it unpaid, but I always had to ask. I always had to wheedle, make it happen, do my work before and after. But it was like going to my parents constantly. I never felt like I owned my life or job."

Control of their lives over the course of the year was fundamental for most of the free agents I interviewed. Some took long vacations if they had the funds to finance them. Others, who didn't have the money or who just wanted to work, took fewer and shorter vacations. Austin lawyer Clark argued that in the conventional workforce, "a vacation is parole from a job," but since free agents have more liberty, they need this kind of release less urgently. And many free agents I talked to blurred the distinction between toil and leisure, taking their families with them on business trips or getting some business done while on holiday.

The old way was fifty weeks of work and two weeks of vacation. The free agent way is as much vacation as you can afford and as much work as you need.

THE LIFETIME

Time also operates across the span of someone's existence. This stretch of years, after all, is called a "lifetime." And here, too, free agents are beginning to make some changes. As at the unit of the day, the week, and the year, the old way was fairly uniform. The typical lifetime also generally followed a set course: a dose of education, followed by several decades of work, followed by a short period of retirement. The free agent way rejects that standard approach—and most dramatically is changing how and when people participate in those first and last stages, education and retirement. I'll wait to explore those fascinating topics in Chapters 14 and 15, because for this section and this chapter, I'm out of time.

THE BOX

CHAPTER 6

THE CRUX: Free agents are reconfiguring the relationship between work and time. The nine to five day has become the now-to-then day. The forty-hour week may still contain forty hours of work, but free agents apportion those hours as they see fit—often blurring the boundary between the "workweek" and the "weekend." During a year, free agents are rejecting the fifty-weeks-of-work, two-weeks-of-vacation regime for whatever tailored arrangements they want or can afford. The advantage of working in the free agent time zone is the ability to control your schedule instead of ceding that control to a boss. The disadvantages are murky time boundaries and unpredictability.

THE FACTOID: Americans work 350 hours more per year than Europeans—and seventy hours more per year than even the Japanese, whose language contains a word, *karoshi,* that means "death from overwork."

THE QUOTE: "The boundaries are far less clear than they were in a world where wailing whistles signaled a day's beginning and end. For instance, if you can answer client e-mail at 10:00 P.M. from your den, where does work end and home begin? What exactly is the 'workday'? What exactly is, to borrow a labor movement rallying cry, 'a fair day's pay for a fair day's work'? Whose time is it anyway? This daily smokiness, and not the hours themselves, may be stoking America's time anxiety."

THE WORD: *New Economy 7-Eleven.* What many free agents become, because they are never fully "off" work. Like an all-night convenience store, their work life occasionally may be empty, but it's never closed.

A MONDAY IN THE LIFE OF A FREE AGENT

NAME:	Michelle Gouldsberry*
AGE:	35
WHERE SHE LIVES:	San Jose, California
WHAT SHE DOES:	Marketing and Communications Consultant

* What follows is Gouldsberry's half-hour by half-hour account, in her own words, of how she spent her time one Monday in November.

Overnight

Midnight to 4:00 A.M.:
> sleep

4:00 to 4:30 A.M.:
> sleep, wake up to let cat in, back to sleep

4:30 to 5:00 A.M.:
> sleep

5:00 to 5:30 A.M.:
> woken up by husband's snoring, back to sleep

5:30 to 6:00 A.M.:
> sleep

6:00 to 6:30 A.M.:
> shower, dress

6:30 to 7:00 A.M.:
> sleep

Morning

7:00 to 7:30 A.M.:
> baby wakes, play with her until nanny arrives

7:30 to 8:00 A.M.:
> play with daughter

8:00 to 8:30 A.M.:
> hand over daughter to nanny, dry dishes, pick up around house

8:30 to 9:00A.M.:
> pick up around house, eat breakfast

9:00 to 9:30 A.M.:
> continue eating breakfast, call friend to set lunch date

9:30 to 10:00 A.M.:

    check/respond to client e-mail and personal e-mail

10:00 to 10:30 A.M.:

    follow up on newsletter story information for client, firmly respond
    to officious and condescending e-mail from client (one of the many
    reasons I stopped being an employee was to avoid this behavior
    as much as possible, so why should I tolerate it in my business)

10:30 to 11:00 A.M.:

    attempt to put out client "fires" needlessly created by above
    mentioned client; consider the pleasure I'd get from fanning the
    flames, but decide against it

11:00 to 11:30 A.M.:

    conduct interview, review tape of interview

11:30 A.M. to Noon:

    continue putting out needless client fire

Noon to 12:30 P.M.:

    continue putting out needless client fire, assist ant exterminator in
    identifying problem areas inside house (that would be just about
    everywhere), remove all contents from bathroom cabinets (scary!)

12:30 to 1:00 P.M.:

    continue putting out needless client fire

Afternoon

1:00 to 1:30 P.M.:

    continue putting out needless client fire, meet friend for lunch, half-
    hour late

1:30 to 2:00 P.M.:

    lunch with friend

2:00 to 2:30 P.M.:

    lunch with friend

2:30 to 3:00 P.M.:

    lunch with friend, drive back home to work

3:00 to 3:30 P.M.:

    send several follow-up e-mails to troublesome client contact to
    make sure she can have no misunderstanding of what I've done
    for her and what information remains outstanding

3:30 to 4:00 P.M.:

    check personal e-mail

4:00 to 4:30 P.M.:

nanny hands daughter back

4:30 to 5:00 P.M.:

play with daughter

5:00 to 5:30 P.M.:

play with daughter, start making family dinner

5:30 to 6:00 P.M.:

making dinner

6:00 to 6:30 P.M.:

eat dinner

6:30 to 7:00 P.M.:

clean dishes

Evening

7:00 to 7:30 P.M.:

leave for rehearsal for church Christmas play

7:30 to 8:00 P.M.:

rehearse as a Hebrew dancer and angel with seven adolescents and one woman in her forties; feel better about having someone closer to me in age on stage

8:00 to 8:30 P.M.:

rehearsal; wondering if I'm cut out for these dance numbers

8:30 to 9:00 P.M.:

rehearsal, return home

9:00 to 9:30 P.M.:

clean remaining dinner dishes, work on various newsletter stories for clients

9:30 to 10:00 P.M.:

work on various newsletter stories for clients

10:00 to 10:30 P.M.:

work on various newsletter stories for clients

10:30 to 11:00 P.M.:

work on various newsletter stories for clients

11:00 to 11:30 P.M.:

respond/send client e-mails

11:30 P.M. to Midnight:

respond/send client e-mails—go to sleep

PART THREE

How (and Why)
Free Agency Works

7

Small Groups, Big Impact: Reinventing Togetherness in Free Agent Nation

"Every day, entrepreneurs, free agents, and individual business owners face challenges that they cannot discuss with their clients, their employees, or their families. So where do they turn? To their peers. With peers, they can establish a level of trust that allows them to talk openly and intimately about what's going on. Developing a support system, which includes peer-to-peer groups, is critical to the sanity of sole entrepreneurs."

—Larry Kesslin (New York, New York)

Vic's Restaurant sits on a sliver of a street in what passes for downtown in San Carlos, California, a cozy city twenty-five miles north of San Jose. Vic's isn't fancy. Its cuisine isn't memorable. (The most exotic dish on the burger-and pasta-packed menu: "crispy onion petals with ranch dressing.") But on the third Thursday of every month, the back room of this restaurant off Silicon Valley's El Camino Real becomes a staging ground for one of the most fascinating and revolutionary developments in Free Agent Nation.

Work even a few months as a free agent—and whether you're a home-based brownie entrepreneur or a freelance C++ programmer, your friends and family likely will pepper you with the same questions. Don't you get lonely? Don't you miss the water cooler? Don't you feel isolated? The first part of the answer, of course, is yes. Free agents sometimes do feel lonely and isolated; they do occasionally long for a conversation around the corroded coffeepot in the employee break room. But the second part of their answer is often a surprise. They don't *stay* isolated. Instead of laboring in loneliness, free agents across America are inventing an array of new groups to replace the workplace communities many have left behind.

That's what's happening at Vic's. About two dozen women have gathered on this April evening to talk business and trade stories. The women are all free agents—one runs a training microbusiness with her husband, another is an education consultant, a third is a marketing strategist who says she's "between start-ups." They've come to Vic's tonight for the same reasons they show up every month—to network, to find new clients, and simply to get out of the house. Born in 1998 as the Self-Employed Women's Network—and rechristened the following year as Women Independent Consultants (WIC)—this group is what I call a Free Agent Nation Club, or F.A.N. Club. It helps members find new gigs and new customers, but it also offers them a forum to discuss issues close to their hearts with people who understand what work is like when you're a pilot instead of a passenger.

WIC members sit at long tables arranged in a large square. The conversation is easy, the conversationalists relaxed. The women take turns. They offer advice. They listen. The session has the flavor of a graduate seminar, a chamber of commerce meeting, and an encounter group—all blended into an utterly new form. Becoming a WIC member costs $100 a year, not a bad deal since it buys ten dinners at Vic's and is tax deductible. WIC has eighty paid members—and another two hundred on its free e-mail list. At each monthly gathering, the group brings in a speaker—an expert who discusses how to negotiate contracts, how to deliver a knockout presentation, or how to price their services. But whatever is on the agenda, the broader purpose remains the same: to offer and receive business advice—and to break the isolation that often accompanies life beyond the water cooler.

"My monthly meeting is something I look forward to," WIC member Elaine Starling told me. "I count down the days! It's fun to see my monthly friends again, meet new attendees, and learn something. WIC is an opportunity to mingle with people who understand what I do. We face the same challenges and are often competitors, yet we all benefit from sharing ideas, concerns, challenges, solutions, opportunities—even goals and aspirations. I get so pumped after a WIC meeting that my husband wishes we'd have one every week!"

Small, self-organized, decentralized groups like WIC are flourishing in every realm of American life. Princeton University sociologist Robert Wuthnow estimates that "four out of every ten Americans belong to a small group that meets regularly and provides caring and support for its members."[1] Alcoholics Anonymous, a self-described "informal society" begun in 1935, now has more than fifty thousand groups with nearly 1.2 million members.[2] Book clubs have become a national phenomenon: In 1990, for example, only one Barnes & Noble store had its own book group; today, nearly all of Barnes & Noble's more than nine hundred stores have at least one in-store book club.[3] And independent religious small groups, in which people meet to pray and discuss faith outside the auspices of institutional denominations, are surging. The U.S. has some 300,000 religious congregations, but as many as four *million* religious small groups.[4]

But the world of work is where small groups might produce their deepest influence. F.A.N. Clubs and other clusters of independent workers are mushrooming throughout Free Agent Nation. Their bond is the horizontal loyalty I described in Chapter 5. Their purpose is both hardheaded and softhearted. Because they're decentralized, ad hoc, and self-organized, they have eluded much notice. But their impact is enormous. These groups challenge the popular notion that America is fragmenting, that community is collapsing—and that the rise of the independent worker only makes matters worse.

F.A.N. Clubs

On a blazingly sunny August afternoon, amid the soaring crimson rocks of northern New Mexico, the Ghost Ranch Alliance has convened. At the entrance to an adobe building, a hand-lettered sign on butcher block paper reads, HELLO AND WELCOME TO GLOBAL SHARING RETREAT II. Inside, twenty-four cross-cultural trainers and consultants—most of them independent workers, all of them independent spirits—sit in a circle for the first session of this three-day event. About fifty people, representing fifteen nationalities and toting six kids, have come here at the behest of Jeremy Solomons, a forty-year-old Englishman and Oxford graduate transplanted to the American Southwest.

Solomons assembles this group once a year at the Ghost Ranch, a rustic Abiquiu, New Mexico, retreat where Georgia O'Keeffe once spent her summers. The people sitting on card table chairs and wearing their summer camp best—T-shirts, shorts, and sandals—tell what's happened since they last met: business they've landed, clients they've lost, and what's changed in their family life. Later they'll break into smaller groups to talk about marketing, pricing, and referrals—or attend small seminars on stress management or "The New Europe." While some schmooze, others cook dinner for four dozen in huge vats and gigantic serving trays. Tonight, they're having baked ziti—tomorrow, a Pakistani feast. Later they'll play a rousing game of "Intercultural Bingo."

Welcome to a commune for capitalists, one of the many varieties of F.A.N. Clubs that free agents are assembling.

Solomons told me that the idea for the Ghost Ranch Alliance and its annual Global Sharing Retreat was born of isolation. He'd worked for large institutions like J.P. Morgan and the World Bank before declaring free agency. But after a few years on his own—he advises international business executives on global leadership and runs training programs for their companies—Solomons grew weary. "I figured if I'm isolated and want to spend more time with others without going to a ten-thousand-person conference where you feel even more isolated, let's see if other people would have the same idea as me." So he e-mailed several dozen friends, colleagues, friends of colleagues, and colleagues of friends to "see if they wanted to spend three days together, to relax, share ideas, and just 'be' for a while instead of doing."

The first year, 1998, fifty-five people attended. They pow-wowed, cooked meals together, swapped ideas and business cards, and then returned to their own free agent lives. But they stayed connected through regular e-mail and phone calls. Now the Ghost Ranch Alliance meets every August.

The agenda is fluid. The rules are nonexistent. Yearly turnover is about 50 percent. And what happens afterward is almost as important as what happens in the shadow of these red rocks. When someone needs a partner on a large project, he calls a fellow "GRAmmy." When someone has a client she can't take on, she often refers that client to someone else in the group. Members get commissions for these referrals, but how much is up to the person who receives the business. They're obligated to pay only what they think the referral is worth. No set percentages, no prescribed formula, no explicit requirement to hand over even a dime. "The minute you start building a fixed relationship," Solomons says, "you're breaking the trust."

On the final day of the meeting I attended, the members voted on whether to formalize their arrangement, and create a more official organization. The vote was nearly unanimous: thumbs-down. Nearly everyone preferred remaining what they call "a loose alliance."

"We decided to work with each other on an ad hoc basis," Solomons told me on a dusty road leading from the Ghost Ranch conference center. "We don't want to create another corporate structure.

"We're focused on results, but even more we're focused on relationships. The only way for all of us to succeed is if we're out there marketing for each other. That's what this helps us do." But even more important, he says, "This is just a great way of keeping in touch."

F.A.N. Clubs are one part board of directors, another part group therapy. They combine the search for clients with the quest for meaning, the urge for authenticity with the need for sociability. They emerge from self-interest, but endure through trust. Their forms vary. Some, like Ghost Ranch, meet once a year. Some, like WIC, meet once a month. Others meet by telephone. Yet all confirm what author and consultant Terri Lonier told me once and what remains essential for understanding how free agency flourishes. "Working solo," she said, "is not working alone."

The only thing harder than counting free agents is tabulating the ad hoc groups of them that have sprouted in every industry and region. There's no National Association of F.A.N. Clubs in downtown Washington, D.C., recording their numbers or crafting their bylaws. There's no central office where every club must register. Like so many of the operational elements of Free Agent Nation, F.A.N. Clubs are self-organized. Nobody is in charge, because everybody is in charge. Yet for all their modern blossoms, F.A.N. Clubs have roots that stretch to colonial America.

In the fall of 1727, well before the birth of both Free Agent Nation and the American nation, twenty-one-year-old Benjamin Franklin convened the first meeting of a dozen friends and associates who would meet every week for the next thirty years. As Franklin described it in his autobiography, "I had form'd most of my ingenious acquaintance into a club of mutual improvement, which we called the JUNTO."[5] Franklin's Junto, which he also called the Club of the Leather Aprons, met each Friday night in a room above a Philadelphia alehouse (the thirteen colonies' answer to Vic's). Joining Franklin were several fellow printers, a shoemaker, a cabinetmaker, a self-taught mathematician, a surveyor, a silversmith, a cobbler, and a scrivener—free agents all—who gathered to talk current events, offer political opinions and business advice, and find ways to educate and assist each other. At most meetings, Franklin would assign one member to write an essay about some hot topic—which the writer would read at the next meeting and which the group would debate "in the sincere spirit of inquiry after truth, without fondness for dispute or desire for victory."[6] While Franklin kept his group small, exclusive, and mostly secret—the Junto never had more than twelve members—he encouraged his colleagues to form spin-off groups. They tried, with varying success, giving rise to similar clubs with names like the Vine, the Union, and the Band.

In the days before formal education, learning came not from teachers or textbooks but from one's social network. Franklin—a soapboiler's son who attended school only from age eight to age ten, and entered the workforce when he turned thirteen—called the Junto "the best school of philosophy, morality, and politics that then existed in the province."[7] Since there were almost no bookshops south of Boston then and colonists had to order most books from London, Junto members pooled all their own books and traded them among themselves. This book-pooling cooperative gave Franklin the idea of a "subscription library," which he launched in 1730 and which eventually became the first public library in America.[8]

"It was part mutual aid society, part social fraternity, part academy," Franklin biographer Esmond Wright said of the Junto. Its "motivation was self-improvement, the 'wish to do good' that would also bring them advantages, or even profit."[9] In both spirit and execution, Franklin's Junto was the forerunner of groups like WIC and Ghost Ranch Alliance.

Juntos are not F.A.N. Clubs' only precursor. Another emerged in the 1960s, spilling from the pen of one of the country's first success gurus, Napoleon Hill. In his odd but long-lived book *Think and Grow Rich*, Hill advocated what he called the Master Mind—a collection of people an aspiring businessman would put together to help him and his mates think and grow rich. "Perhaps you may need much more specialized knowledge than you have the ability or the inclination to acquire," Hill told his readers, "and if this should be true, you may bridge your weakness through the aid of your 'Master Mind' group."[10]

As Hill further explained, "Economic advantages may be created by any person who surrounds himself with the advice, counsel, and personal cooperation of a group of men who are willing to lend him wholehearted aid, in a spirit of perfect harmony.

This form of cooperative alliance has been the basis of nearly every great fortune. Your understanding of this great truth may definitely determine your financial status."[11] Master Mind groups still flourish (though not, as Hill assumed, limited to business*men*). Lonier has been part of one for more than five years. Every two weeks, she and three colleagues hold a conference call to discuss their microbusinesses, exchange tips, and counsel one another.

F.A.N. Clubs, whether Master Mind groups or some other form, are not easy to sustain. Interest wanes. Personalities clash. For several years, a Washington, D.C., group of home-based workers met each month at an Uno's Pizza in northwest Washington. For a time, the group—called Home Alone—had about a hundred members. But after a few years, people stopped coming, the leaders stopped leading, and the organization drifted into oblivion. Marilyn Zelinsky of Fairfield, Connecticut, started a F.A.N. Club in her suburban town—but summer break made it hard for the mothers who were members to participate, and the group withered. Later, Zelinsky grew so isolated working alone that she returned to a traditional job after five years as a free agent.

Yet for all their difficulties, F.A.N. Clubs serve a crucial purpose. Even though Lonier's group sees each other in person just a few times a year, they all understand the value of these sessions. "I have a lot of great friends," says David Garfinkel, the free agent copywriter we met in Chapter 6 and who is part of Lonier's Master Mind. "But they haven't chosen this path. No matter how kindhearted they are, they just can't cheer you on. They're on a different emotional frequency."

Erika Tauber, 67, is twenty years older than Garfinkel, lives three thousand miles away, but operates on the same emotional frequency. Tauber is a member of Women Entrepreneurs Home-based, a F.A.N. club in Belmont, Massachusetts, outside Boston. On the first Monday of every month ("except when it's a snow day or a major holiday," marketing consultant Tauber explains), twenty-five or so women meet in the Belmont Public Library, a local synagogue, or the town's Armenian Church. All the women run their own home-based businesses—and the format of their meeting is similar to that of the others I've described. Women Entrepreneurs Homebased is an amazingly eclectic group: The youngest member is in her twenties, the oldest in her seventies. And the micropreneurs run the gamut—including a lawyer, a computer animator, an architect, and a chef. But its goals are the same as most F.A.N. Clubs: The women offer one another advice, connections, and sometimes simply a set of ears.

Some members also form four-or five-woman Accountability Groups that meet between the official sessions. These subclusters, says Tauber, serve as a "focus group or sounding board." And as the name suggests, they reinforce that important element of the free agent work ethic—putting yourself on the line. The women make promises out loud to the other members—for example, to finish a brochure, to confront a client about an unpaid bill, or to make ten cold calls—because public exposure often activates peer pressure's benevolent gases. "It's easier to break a promise to yourself than to others who are sitting there with you," Tauber says. "When you have told three or four other people you'll do something, you will do it." (This is also the principle behind the microfinancing initiatives I'll discuss in Chapter 18.)

Tauber, who's been a micropreneur since 1979, says her group formed in response to the old boy network—which didn't have room for free agents, particularly the female variety.

"But we create a nonthreatening, supportive environment," she says. "Women aren't ashamed to say 'It's been a rough year for me.' Men are more loath to open themselves up in that way."

Women-only or women-predominantly are among the most common types of F.A.N. Clubs. There's Second Shift, a group of working mothers in Chappaqua, New York; MOMents, a working mother support group in suburban Chicago; the Wednesday Morning Group, which meets in Chevy Chase, Maryland; Lawyers at Home, a group of attorney moms who meet each month in Washington, D.C.; and the Homebased Businesswomen's Network in Danvers, Massachusetts.

But whatever the gender of the members, the industries in which they work, or the communities where they live, F.A.N.

Clubs tend to follow a similar structure and philosophy. They're tailored to individual needs. They depend on horizontal loyalty and reciprocity. They aim to deepen both human connection and professional connections. And in contrast to labor unions, PTAs, or other giant, older groups whose ranks are thinning, F.A.N. Clubs succeed precisely because they have no central authority. That's one reason why those who use the decline of large established groups to support their claim that community is disappearing have it wrong. Community hasn't disappeared. You just have to look for it in the right places. Indeed, this free agent style of forging community is quintessentially American, something Alexis de Tocqueville discovered and remarked upon during his visit to America 170 years ago: "The art of association . . . [is] . . . the mother of action, studied and applied by all."

Confederations, Entreprenetworks, and Alumni Associations

F.A.N. Clubs are the most prevalent ad hoc work group, but they're not the only new communities of independent workers the free agent economy has spawned. Confederations are akin to the partnerships formed by lawyers and accountants, but they're more laid-back and usually fixed by informal agreements rather than written contracts. Entreprenetworks operate like a Rotary Club crossbred with Alcoholics Anonymous. And alumni associations are groups of people who've all graduated not from the same college, but from the same company.

Confederations

Whitney Vosburgh has a business card. So does Ellen Mann. In fact, they've got the same business card. On one side of the card is Vosburgh's name—along with his address and phone number in Berkeley, California. On the other side is Mann's name—along with her address and phone number in Oakland. And at the top of both sides is a logo for WE Communications.

WE Communications doesn't have its own address or Web site. In the eyes of the law, it doesn't even exist. It's an informal collaboration between free agents that I call a confederation. In their marketing confederation, Vosburgh handles the images, Mann takes care of the text. His side of the business card labels him "Creative Director—Art." She's "Creative Director—Words." Sometimes they work together, sometimes they don't. Their affiliation rests on the general principles of an informal pact rather than the specific provisions of a twenty-page partnership agreement.

Like F.A.N. Clubs, confederations are abound in Free Agent Nation. And they're growing in the same ad hoc, self-organized fashion. There are no world headquarters, monthly newsletters, or annual conferences keeping it all together. Yet free agents are forming confederations in droves—often with similar structures and underlying ideals.

The hub of one such confederation is a mod apartment in Half Moon Bay, California, home of Brian Gruber, directing principal of Principals.com. For fifteen years, the Brooklyn-born Gruber was a hard-charging cable TV marketing executive. He worked in the United States at such organizations as TCI and C-SPAN—and in Australia for Rupert Murdoch's News Corporation. But at age forty, Gruber felt something was amiss. "I basically had this realization that I had been unhappy in my work life ever since I got out of college," he told me one afternoon in November as a storm pelted his apartment windows.

"At a certain point, I thought to myself, 'What's happening here?' I'm using an alarm clock to wake myself, shock myself up in the morning. I'm rushing through the morning, driving in rush-hour traffic, wearing a noose around my neck in the form of a tie and suit. I'm going into a poorly ventilated building with fluorescent lighting and breathing other people's toxins. I'm doing things I don't necessarily want to do, sometimes working for psychos under intense stress. I would look around me and see ten, twenty, or thirty years more of it—and say, 'What's the fruit of this?'"

Even worse, his marriage had crumbled and he'd been diagnosed with an underactive thyroid, a condition that left him flat-out exhausted. So he left Australia, moved back to the United States, and spent a year climbing back onto his feet. He knew that when he worked again, he'd want to do it his way.

And the best way, he figured, was by starting a confederation—though he didn't call it that. Instead, he called it a "connected marketing team" and named it Principals.com. Principals.com is a virtual community of fifteen people who work in eleven disciplines ranging from brand strategy, to public relations, design, and market research. Each person has his or her own microbusiness, and they come together only when necessary. But when Gruber brings these people together, Principals.com can deliver what he calls "custom-built marketing teams." Some clients, for example, might need only two people from Principals.com—say, a strategic planner like Dana Christensen and a brand strategist like Richard Carter. Other clients may need as many as ten people. "So the promise to the client," says Gruber, "is that we'll deliver exactly the right talent in exactly the right quantity, at exactly the right time."

Gruber says this approach allows him to do better work for a lower price than traditional ad agencies or marketing firms. "No mahogany conference rooms, no perky personal assistants, no fees for layers of bureaucracy," boasts the Principals.com Web site. In ad agencies or large law firms, the name partners often pitch the business, but low-level copywriters, junior associates, and other faceless minions do the actual work. In Gruber's confederation, everybody is, well, a principal. "We all come together based on the mission and the opportunity, not based on the fact that we all work in an agency and need more billable hours.

"Everyone is part of this connected marketing team, but they have their own identities and are principals of their own companies. They know how to collaborate, and can work in a different kind of structure where there is no hierarchy," Gruber says. "Everyone on the team is a peer." The peers each kick in a small amount for stationery and Principals.com business cards. And when somebody brings in business for the others, he or she gets 7 percent of the fee.

But what's perhaps most intriguing is that this agreement has no formal contract. "There's no legal structure," Gruber says. "At first, we wondered how we would protect ourselves. A corporation was out. A partnership was out. We looked at it and ultimately decided there should be no legal relationship between the principals. The idea is simply that everyone has a moral commitment that when the call comes, you make it a priority because you want this to succeed." The bonds of Principals.com are informal, flexible, and impermanent rather than tight, rigid, and legally prescribed.

The right mix between individual freedom and group power is the secret to confederations. "We're like the Justice League of America," Gruber jokes. "We've got these different superheroes and different superpowers, and we come together when the world is threatened. Then after we achieve the mission, we disperse to do our own stuff."

Entreprenetworks

Like most business leaders, Norm Stoehr has an inner circle. What makes Stoehr's inner circle different is that he's franchised it in six cities. During the 1970s, Stoehr, fifty-nine, made a tidy sum running a construction business, owning restaurants, and developing real estate in Peoria, Illinois. In 1978, then in his late thirties, he moved to Minneapolis. "It took me two years to go broke in the restaurant business," he says. Hoping both to rebuild his finances and to help others avoid some of entrepreneurship's pitfalls, Stoehr began organizing seminars for fledgling businesspeople to teach them the basics of running a small operation. As he brought these mircopreneurs together, he made a surprising discovery: They initially came to the seminars to listen to him, but they continued coming to subsequent seminars to talk to *each other*. And the more meetings they attended, the more their questions and concerns began moving away from the nuts and bolts of hiring and financing, and toward murkier issues like how to balance the demands of being both an entrepreneur and a parent or what to do if your business partner decides he doesn't want to be in business anymore.

"I discovered that the single biggest problem inherent in business ownership, entrepreneurship, and free agency is isolation," Stoehr told me one Sunday afternoon in Minneapolis's Calhoun Square. So he began a company called Inner Circle, which brings together individual entrepreneurs from different industries to talk business strategy. One morning a month, a dozen of them meet at a hotel for breakfast and a skull session. Unlike in most F.A.N. Clubs, Inner Circle members pay to join: $5,600 per year. "How does that grab you for breakfast once a month?" Stoehr chuckles. Stoehr facilitates each session, which usually centers around a particular member discussing her business and seeking advice from the others. While they're required to "be positive," Stoehr says, they also aim to make the presenter uncomfortable—to ask tough questions, to challenge her assumptions, and to make her clarify what her business is, where it's going, and how she'll get there. Stoehr, who's now franchised Inner Circles in Baltimore, San Diego, Fargo, and Seattle, says 90 percent of Inner Circle members renew—despite the hefty price tag. "It's an expensive breakfast, but very inexpensive strategic thinking."

Inner Circles and its cousins are what I call entreprenetworks. They're more formal than F.A.N. Clubs and usually more expensive. In some ways, they've become the chambers of commerce of Free Agent Nation. Entreprenetworks are often less explicitly social than their counterparts, but they operate and succeed by nearly identical values. "Sometimes you even get business," Stoehr says. "That's a bad reason to join, but an outcome of the process." He bristles at calling what his members do "networking," since he believes that term has a "tarnished image." So he's redefined networking in the free agent economy: "It's being other-centered—letting go of your own agenda long enough to hook into somebody else's dream."

Stoehr's venture is just one variety of entreprenetwork that has emerged to serve free agents. Some entreprenetworks are more overtly about generating new business and finding sales leads. Yet what powers even these groups is less unbridled greed than a unique strain of free agent altruism. Consider Le Tip, one of the largest such "business leads" groups, with 450 chapters and nine thousand members. Its monthly meetings begin exactly at 7:16 A.M. and end by 8:31 A.M., and each attendee's task is simple: provide two sales leads to other members. The tips are recorded by a "tipmaster," and members who fail to help others are expelled. In entreprenetworks, it is better to give than to receive—in part because giving to others encourages them to give to you. Reciprocity oils the gears of horizontal loyalty. As one Le Tipper gushes in the firm's promotional video, "Where else in the world can I get over thirty people to represent my company and speak to people in the community about what I do without having to pay them? All they want in return is for me to do the same for them." Business Network International (BNI), another lead referral organization for self-employed business owners, with more than 24,000 members nationwide, is similar. BNI's motto is perhaps the most succinct expression of the ethic that animates these groups: "Givers gain."

An entreprenetwork with a slightly broader mandate is the New York–based Let's Talk Business Network. (One of LTBN's founders, Larry Kesslin—himself a refugee from General Electric and Westinghouse—is quoted at the beginning of this chapter.) LTBN began as a radio talk show and grew into an entrepreneurial support group with affiliates in Vancouver, Philadelphia, New Jersey, and Washington, D.C. LTBN's $1,495 membership fee entitles participants to monthly breakfasts, a library of videos and books, seminars, and a community of like-minded people. "It would be easy enough for me to stay in my own little virtual world, doing my own little thing with my business and not meeting other people face-to-face," says Arzeena Hamir, who runs her own Vancouver-based online organic gardening products company. "LTBN lets me meet other business owners and get the support that's so often missing for online entrepreneurs."

Entreprenetworks provide micropreneurs with a sales force, a team of strategic advisers, and a few dozen sympathetic ears.

And they succeed by abiding by Stoehr's notion of being other-centered.

"Let me tell you where the real value comes in," Stoehr told me, leaning forward in his chair. "Not when somebody's giving you advice. The real 'Ah-ha!' comes about when you're sitting there as part of a group assessing the other person's issue. It has no resemblance to yours. And all of a sudden, you get a break-through thought. Because you've emptied your mind of your own garbage to get into somebody else's, ideas can come out. I see that over and over again. The real value comes not when you're working on your own deal, but when you're working on somebody else's." In Free Agent Nation, givers gain.

Alumni Associations

Free agent Virginia Klamon, whom we met briefly in Chapter 4, talks about Arthur Andersen the way some people describe law school. Here's what Klamon tells college seniors considering a job at the Big Five consulting firm: Go for a couple or three years, as long as you can take it, and then you'll be set. The professional education you'll get there will be superb. Klamon worked at Andersen after graduating from St. Louis University, and says she learned more from her two and a half years as a systems implementation and development specialist than from her entire undergraduate education. Most of her fellow free agents share such sentiments. If I had a dollar for every time an independent worker told me something like, "I learned more from that first job than I did in all my years in school," I could have financed my entire trip through Free Agent Nation.

Call it the universitification of the corporation. While companies design "corporate campuses" and establish homegrown education institutions such as Motorola University, Dell University, and SunU, individual workers are treating companies like college. They think of them as places to gain knowledge, snag a credential, and make connections. And not surprisingly, this new approach has hatched a new entity: the corporate alumni group. When Klamon and her husband (whom she met while both were

Andersen employees) relocated to the Pacific Northwest, she landed a job at a Seattle hospital thanks to another ex–Andersen employee who knew about the opening and recommended her for the job. When Klamon declared free agency after a stint at the hospital, she got some of her first gigs by tapping other former Andersenians. For her, the only thing more valuable than being an Andersen employee was being an Andersen alum.

Traditional college alumni groups are remarkable things when you stop and consider them. Each year, alumni feel such fierce devotion to their alma maters that they donate billions of dollars to them—even though they left these institutions years ago and originally paid to attend. Corporate alumni networks tap related sentiments. They exist not because of ex-employees' allegiance to the corporate mother ship, but because of their allegiance to others who did time at the same place. Once again, horizontal loyalty is the bond. The connections they forge while working in traditional jobs help free agents find new clients and customers—as well as keep up with industry gossip and information—when they venture on their own.

Some alumni clusters, like Andersen's, are informal—but others have more formal arrangements. The Microsoft Alumni Network, for instance, has 2,500 members who pay a $100 annual fee. "Thanks to the network, teams that worked together at Microsoft have formed virtual teams to work on new projects," Katharine Mieszkowski reported in *Fast Company*.[12] Most alumni groups compile directories of former employees, which help those who have become free agents land new projects or locate partners for existing projects. Some groups publish job listings— an attempt to formalize the networking arrangements that led to Klamon's hospital job. Many also have e-mail discussion lists and social get-togethers—which have the added benefit of helping free agents overcome isolation.

McKinsey & Co., another giant consulting company, has an alumni program that it describes as "one of the world's most dynamic professional networks." Its Web site has a separate Alumni Center for the 8,500 people who once clocked in at McKinsey, and the company publishes a regular newsletter of alumni news.

The Web site of Morgan Alumni—the seven-hundred-member association of onetime employees of J.P. Morgan—includes links to alumni's solo enterprises and start-up companies along with recipes for Senegalese soup, Norwegian cake, and other favorites from the company cafeteria. Another potent cluster of ex-employees is the group 85 Broads, an alumni association of women who once worked for Goldman Sachs, whose headquarters is located at the New York City address 85 Broad Street. And, natch, there's an Internet company—Corporatealumni.com—to help you find an alumni group or start your own.

Alumni networks seem most prevalent in the high-tech world, where employee turnover is intense and free agency is the reigning ethic. I've come across AXLE (the Association of eX-Lotus Employees), ExPaq (former Compaq Computer employees), and alumni networks for Oracle, Prodigy, and Netscape. Even though the individuals no longer work in nearby cubicles, and often live in far-flung places, they remain united—a high-tech diaspora.

One free agent who left Symantec, a California computer and Internet security company, to go solo, and who asked that I not use his name, put it best: "The nice part of working at Symantec was that everybody left. Now we've got this great network of people we know at all these other companies."

The emergence of F.A.N. Clubs, confederations, entre-prenetworks, and alumni associations is one of the most important developments underway in America's independent workforce. These self-fashioned groups call into question the claim that free agency frays social ties or fractures community, and instead suggest that free agency is merely redefining those things—that Tocqueville's "art of association" is no less robust in the twenty-first century than it was in the nineteenth. Free agents may be bowling alone, but they're not going it alone. In Chapter 5, we saw that loyalty hasn't disappeared; it has simply changed from vertical to horizontal. The same is true for community. In Free Agent Nation, community isn't dead. It's different.

THE BOX

THE CRUX: Instead of laboring in loneliness, independent workers are inventing an array of small groups. Free Agent Nation (F.A.N.) Clubs are clusters of free agents who meet regularly to exchange business advice and offer personal support. Confederations are informal work collaborations of free agents. Entreprenetworks are groups of small entrepreneurs who pay a fee to participate in facilitated brainstorming and strategy sessions. Alumni associations are groups of people whose common bond is that they graduated not from the same college, but from the same company. Because most of these groups are self-organized and arise from the grass roots, they've eluded much notice. And they challenge the critics who claim that community is collapsing and that independent workers are speeding its demise. Community isn't dead in Free Agent Nation. It's different.

THE FACTOID: One of the earliest self-organized clusters of free agents—Benjamin Franklin's Junto, formed in 1727—created a "subscription library" for its members, which in turn became the first public library in America.

THE QUOTE: "F.A.N. Clubs are one part board of directors, another part group therapy. They combine the search for clients with the quest for meaning, the urge for authenticity with the need for sociability. They emerge from self-interest, but endure through trust."

THE WORD: *Confederation.* A regular collaboration between free agents akin to a law or accounting partnership—but in which the relationships are fluid and the structure is set by an informal agreement rather than a legal contract.

Getting Horizontal:
The Free Agent Org Chart
and Operating System

*"If you and I are on the playground and like to go on the
teeter-totter, and I'm a jerk who likes to jump off and leave you
to fall on the ground—how many times will you get on the
teeter-totter with me?"*

—Notty Bumbo (San Francisco, California)

In the previous chapter, I described ad hoc clusters of independent workers and their powerful role in the free agent economy. In this chapter, I'll show how the guiding values of these free agent small groups—trust, reciprocity, and horizontal loyalty—are essential nutrients of free agency itself. The story isn't simple. But its conclusions are straightforward, if a bit surprising: The emergence of an independent workforce will both reconfigure how work gets done and remind us that business is a fundamentally human endeavor. The place to begin telling this story is back inside the corporation.

A TALE OF TWO ORG CHARTS

Most companies have an organization chart—the firm's official map of who does what and who reports to whom. In Figure

8.1, I've drawn (based on the actual org chart of a multinational energy company) a stripped-down org chart of a fictitious corporation I'll call Gaki Enterprises.

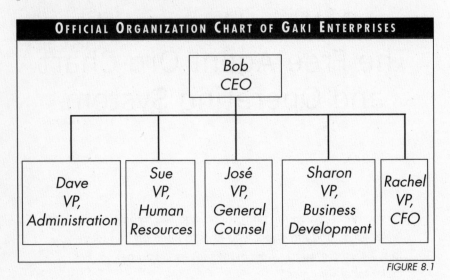

OFFICIAL ORGANIZATION CHART OF GAKI ENTERPRISES

Bob
CEO

Dave
VP,
Administration

Sue
VP,
Human
Resources

José
VP,
General
Counsel

Sharon
VP,
Business
Development

Rachel
VP,
CFO

FIGURE 8.1

As usual, the CEO is at the top. Beneath him is a phalanx of vice presidents, who have different functions but who occupy identical hierarchical positions. And beneath each of them (though not drawn here) is another collection of employees in each particular division, spiraling downward in ever larger rows of the corporate pyramid. The defining relationships are *vertical*. Bob is above José. José is above the people in his division, and so on.

Organization charts apparently serve some useful purpose. But most have a rather serious flaw: Anybody who's ever worked in an organization knows that these charts bear only a passing resemblance to how things really get done. For instance, suppose Sue the HR honcho is a dope. In that case, the only way to hire a new account executive is to go around her. Maybe Dave in Administration is looking for a new job. If so, you better go to someone else for a new department copy machine. And the deeper you burrow into the organization—that is, the closer you get to where work actually gets done—the more the org chart loses its explanatory power. Even though employees receive a copy of the company organization chart in their first-day orientation packets, they don't use this official map any more than someone in suburban Atlanta relies on the state highway patrol's map of Georgia to make their way around their own neighborhood. In the workplace, as in the neighborhood, people get where they need to go using shortcuts and alleyways more often than the officially sanctioned routes.

Again, this shouldn't surprise anybody who's worked in an organization. And, in truth, it's not a surprise to savvy CEOs. They know their companies have an unofficial org chart. So many of them have begun looking to an emerging academic discipline called "social network analysis," which has been used to study how diseases spread, how innovations diffuse, and how groups solve problems.

Here's how social network analysis works in a business setting. Anthropologists and computer technicians descend on a company to watch and record what happens. The researchers ask employees who they talk to most frequently, which colleagues they trust, where they get information or gossip, who they go to for advice, who helps them on tough projects, and even with whom they eat lunch. The analysts also examine telephone and e-mail logs to compile more data about who's communicating with whom. Researchers then run the numbers and patterns through a computer and draw a new chart that represents more accurately the relationships and connections that exist beneath the skin of the official chart. This organizational X ray shows who's getting work done, who's trusted by her colleagues, who's controlling information, and who are the organization's real leaders.

Social network theory is less novel than it seems. As one management journal explains, "Going back to the turn of the century, cultural anthropologists were using the same investigative methodology to map kinship and trade relations among tribes and cultures on civilization's fringes."[1] And inside every organization where I've worked, there's always been some top person who was absolutely clueless—and someone else with significantly less titular authority who seemed to be the linchpin of the operation. This latter person was a source of gossip and rumors, the sage who knew how to accomplish any task, and the only employee who seemed on a first-name basis with everyone else in the organization. What was most interesting, though, about these super-connected, extremely effective people is that they were never—*never*—the person on the top of the chart.

To understand social network theory better and to begin to unlock one of the secrets of the free agent economy, let's look at a simplified version of what social network analysis might reveal about one department of Gaki Enterprises. In Figure 8.2, I've drawn a simplified version of the org chart of the company's Human Resources department.

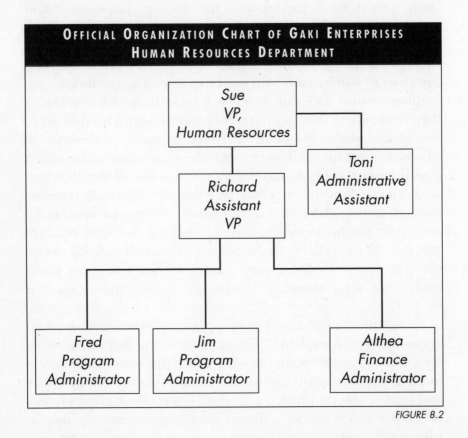

OFFICIAL ORGANIZATION CHART OF GAKI ENTERPRISES HUMAN RESOURCES DEPARTMENT

Sue
VP,
Human Resources

Toni
Administrative
Assistant

Richard
Assistant
VP

Fred
Program
Administrator

Jim
Program
Administrator

Althea
Finance
Administrator

FIGURE 8.2

In the official rendering, Sue, Vice President for Human Resources, holds the most important position. Toni, an administrative assistant, supports her. Richard, the assistant vice president and Sue's immediate subordinate, is the department's number two person. Helping the HR department run are two lower-ranked program administrators, Fred and Jim. Althea works in the Finance Department, but has to deal with HR on personnel and benefits matters. The lines connecting the six people are simple and vertical.

But if social network analysts watched what really took place in this department—that is, they went in and asked who talked to whom, who trusted whom, who relied on whom—they'd reveal a very different architecture of work. Suppose that Richard coveted Sue's job, never helped her, and tried to enlist Fred and Jim as his allies. Social network analysts would erase the line between Richard and Sue. If Richard regularly talked to Fred, social network analysts would draw a line from Richard to Fred. And if Fred regularly talked to Richard, and confided in him, they'd draw a line running the other direction as well. Now, suppose that Jim had a two-way relationship with Sue. And since he knew that administrative assistants have plenty of the information needed to get work done, Jim had a two-way relationship with Toni. Suppose Fred and Jim got on well, but that Fred was too intimidated to deal with Sue and too elitist to talk to her assistant. And suppose that Althea, from another department, went to Jim for everything instead of going above him in the official hierarchy. Map these connections, and we get the shadow organization chart shown in Figure 8.3.

On this new organization chart, the most important person in the Gaki Enterprises HR department is Jim—even though Jim occupies a very different slot on the official chart. He has relationships with everyone—and two-way, reciprocal relationships with everybody except Richard. Sue, nominally the top person in the department, has only a one-way relationship with Toni. (She tells Toni what to do.) And perhaps unintentionally and unknowingly, she relies heavily on Jim for most of her information on what's happening in the department because he's connected

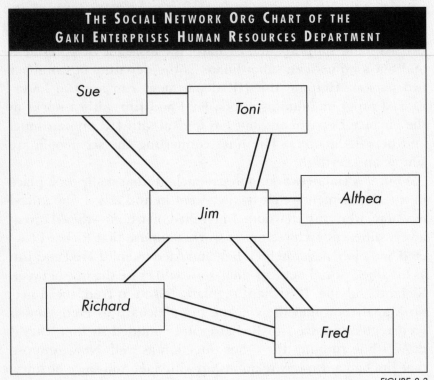

THE SOCIAL NETWORK ORG CHART OF THE
GAKI ENTERPRISES HUMAN RESOURCES DEPARTMENT

FIGURE 8.3

to people she isn't. Jim is also the only person with a relationship with someone in a different department, Althea. On this chart you can see Jim's influence by looking at how many lines connect to his box compared with the boxes of the others. On this unofficial, but more accurate, org chart, power is based on relationships, not a preordained pecking order. And the direction of these relationships isn't vertical, but *horizontal*. Every organization has a Jim. If you work in an organization, you probably know the person I'm talking about.

What does this have to do with free agency? Everything. *The implicit org chart of social network analysis is the explicit org chart of free agency. This is how free agency works.*

Let's look at the same chart through a free agent lens. Suppose that Sue, Toni, Richard, Jim, Fred, and Althea are all free agents. And suppose that they have the following professions:

Jim, Fred, and Richard are graphic designers; Sue and Toni are copywriters; and Althea is an accountant. Now, imagine that Jim has two-way relationships with Althea, Toni, Sue, and his fellow graphic designer Fred—that is, he talks with them fairly often, sees them at professional events, maybe even works on projects with them. Imagine, too, that the other relationships mirror those of Figure 8.3 when the individuals were employees. The free agent org chart would look like Figure 8.4.

When Sue and Toni look for a designer, whom will they seek? Jim. If Jim can't take on the project, he might pass it on to Richard or Fred—that is, become the bridge between two people who don't know each other and thereby strengthen his relationship with each party. What if fellow designer Fred were looking for a new accountant? He might ask Richard and Jim. But since Jim is the only person connected to an accountant, Jim is the one who could lend a hand. He'd help Fred solve a problem, and in

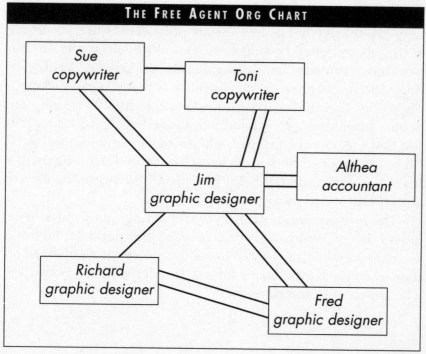

FIGURE 8.4

the process earn a chit with Althea that he can deposit in the favor bank and withdraw when he needs it. Jim likely has other relationships, too. Maybe he's organized a F.A.N.Club. Maybe he's part of a corporate alumni association. He's built a thick network based on authentic human contact. In Free Agent Nation, unlike inside most organizations, the Jims of the world become the most successful. They get the most work, earn the most money, and have the most fun. The secret to their success is relationships—horizontal, reciprocal relationships. Sara Jalali, the Dallas free agent quoted in Chapter 4, says that the way to suceed as an independent worker is to "build a strong network based on mutual respect and trust and then keep building and strengthening that network throughout your career and your life. The strength of your continuing relationships with current and former customers, colleagues, partners, mentors, employers, employees, friends, and family is what will provide you any security you can find."

In a corporate environment, a person's pool of contacts is inherited—that is, your co-workers are preselected when you arrive at the job and often beyond your control while you remain. But free agent contacts are deliberate and purposeful. "The nice thing about this versus a regular office is that you can pick people you really can connect with, whereas in an office, there are people I don't respect," Columbus, Ohio, free agent Diana Wilson told me. David Garfinkel, who belongs to one of the F.A.N. Clubs I mentioned in the previous chapter, says that what makes his group work and what helps free agency thrive are "deliberate affinity and stated purpose."

The new organization chart of free agency marks what sociologist Barry Wellman calls a broader transition "from little boxes to social networks."[2] What allows people to flourish when they leave their little boxes for the frontier of social networks? The answer is counterintuitive.

STRENGTH IN NUMBERS, STRENGTH IN WEAKNESS

When it comes to relationships, most people believe that strong is better than weak and that quality matters more than quantity. A close marriage is generally more satisfying than an endless string of quick entanglements. Having hundreds of acquaintances seems less personally fulfilling than enjoying the love and support of a few close friends. But free agency, in many ways, operates by a reverse logic. Loose connections are frequently more valuable than tight ones, the quantity of an independent worker's connections more valuable than the quality.

That's the lesson of one of the most legendary research projects of twentieth-century sociology. In 1974, a young academic named Mark Granovetter interviewed and surveyed 282 professional, technical, and managerial male workers in Newton, Massachusetts, about how they'd found their jobs. Granovetter discovered that nearly 19 percent of them found their jobs by using newspaper classifieds or an employment agency—and that another almost 19 percent simply had applied directly. But the clear majority—56 percent—found their jobs through personal contacts.[3] No great surprise in this discovery: Most of us know that the best way to get in the door is to have someone else turn the knob. And as Granovetter reported, "The more satisfied individuals are in their jobs, the more likely they are to have found them through contacts."[4] Again, this shouldn't startle. When we hear of a job through contacts, we usually get a more accurate picture of what it's like to work there than if we apply blind.

But what surprised Granovetter—and what gave his study its lasting impact—was *who* these personal contacts were. The contacts who led to new jobs weren't the job seekers' best buddies. Far from it. Of the applicants who landed their jobs through personal contacts, 55.6 percent reported they saw their contacts only "occasionally" and another 28 percent saw their contacts only "rarely." Fewer than 17 percent of the applicants said the people who connected them to jobs were people they saw often.[5] In other words, *about five out of the six applicants who found jobs through personal contacts found them from people to whom they were not particularly close.* Granovetter called this seeming paradox "the strength of weak ties."

The strength of weak ties is crucial to understanding the Free Agent Org Chart. Weak ties link free agents to acquaintances who move in different circles. Precisely because free agents don't know them intimately, these loose connections expose the free agent to ideas, information, and opportunities she might not have discovered on her own. Go back to the relationships charted in Figure 8.4. If Toni the copywriter relied only on her roommate and close friends for new work opportunities, she might not last very long as a free agent. Chances are that the people she's closest to know each other and share similar, overlapping contacts. If we mapped these connections of close pals, the result would look less like the outward-extending fingers of the Free Agent Org chart and more like an inwardly directed tangle of yarn. As Granovetter discovered, "close friends might indeed have been more *disposed* than acquaintances to use influence, but were simply less often in a position to do so."[6] In the free agent economy, structure trumps motivation. When looking for work is a permanent feature of life rather than an occasional nuisance, weak ties are essential.

Take the alumni networks I described in the previous chapter. Imagine two colleagues—Ed and Jenny. If they worked alongside each other for five years, seeing one another every day, talking all the time, they probably forged a strong tie. But if Ed is contemplating going independent, Jenny is not a particularly valuable contact. However, if Jenny leaves the company first, her value to Ed increases. Once she's on the outside rather than the inside, she'll likely know people, places, and opportunities that Ed doesn't. And if Ed eventually does leave, their mutual connection might become even more useful in spite of the fact that they don't see each other every day—indeed *because* of that fact. Their tie weakens; its value increases. Strong ties—to family and friends, for instance—still matter to our professional and emotional well-being. We can't live without strong ties. But as the surge of alumni networks shows, more of us—free agent and not—are depending ever more on weak ties.

The Free Agent Org Chart is fluid. And because it's fluid, it's less hierarchical. Your peer on one project could be your boss on another. Today's subcontractor could be tomorrow's customer. In this sense, the Free Agent Org Chart resembles a traditional organization chart less than it resembles the human brain. In our brains, existing neurons and new ones are continually forging and reforging connections, constantly laying fresh pathways to one another. That—literally—is how we think, learn, and remember. This is one reason that free agency might—just might—be more attuned to human nature than the typical twentieth-century employment structure. In fact, several prominent scientists have begun advancing versions of this argument. Alexandra Maryanski and Jonathan H. Turner of the University of California at Riverside, in their brilliant book *The Social Cage: Human Nature and the Evolution of Society*, show that evolutionary evidence suggests that humans prefer "open, fluid, and individualistic" systems. They argue that "the elaboration of social structures into more constraining patterns violates humans' genetic tendencies," and that "the lack of center, structure, and integration is highly compatible with human nature."[7] Maryanski and Turner dismiss those who believe that humans require "embeddedness in tightly woven social structures," and instead make the forceful case that humans intrinsically have "little trouble with weak tie relations, loose and fluid communities, mobility, and fluctuating social structures."[8] After all, there are striking similarities between free agent structures (small, shifting, temporary clusters) and the structures favored by hunter-gatherers, our evolutionary forebears (small, shifting, temporary clusters). Although Maryanski and Turner don't put it in precisely these terms, their ideas suggest that the Free Agent Org Chart—and not the rigid, vertical corporate form— is more compatible with human nature and our evolutionary heritage. If nothing else, the Free Agent Org Chart, a network, also resembles the Internet much more than the classic corporate org chart does—which suggests that free agency is better aligned with the information age than is the traditional corporate form.

DIFFERENCE IN RELATIONSHIPS BETWEEN FREE AGENCY AND TRADITIONAL WORK		
	Traditional Org Chart	**Free Agent Org Chart**
Direction of relationships	Vertical	Horizontal
Strength of relationships	Strong ties	Weak ties
How relationships are established	Inherited	Created
How relationships are organized	Centrally organized	Self-organized
Permanence of relationships	Fixed	Fluid

Figure 8.5

I've summarized in Figure 8.5 how the Free Agent Org Chart changes key aspects of the relationships between workers. But a question remains: In this brave new world of weak ties and social networks, what keeps everything and everyone together? Once again, the answer might surprise you.

THE FREE AGENT OPERATING SYSTEM

Every computer has an operating system, the underlying software that establishes the foundation for everything the computer does. An operating system—DOS, Windows, Mac OS 9, and Linux are examples—manages, regulates, and sets the standards that allow software applications such as word processing programs, spreadsheets, and computer games to run. These invisible lines of computer code schedule tasks, allocate storage, and allow your computer and printer to talk to each other. The operating system is the first program loaded when you turn on the computer, and its main part—called the "kernel"—resides in your computer's memory at all times. It sets the boundaries of what your computer can do and how it can do it, but most people are barely aware that the operating system exists. Here's a rough analogy: If this book is a software application, the English language is the operating system. This book wouldn't exist without the English language, but you (and I) probably never thought about that until just now.

The Free Agent Org Chart I've just detailed is akin to a software program. But beneath it runs what I call the Free Agent Operating System, the more fundamental piece of software that allows the programs on the surface to function smoothly.

The basic unit of this Free Agent Operating System—the 1s and 0s of the underlying code—is trust. Trust, as scholar Francis Fukuyama noted in a magnificent book of the same name, is essential not only to a just society—but also to a healthy economy: "One of the most important lessons we can learn from the examination of economic life is that a nation's well-being, as well as its ability to compete, is conditioned by a single, pervasive cultural characteristic: the level of trust inherent in the society."[9] If buyers can't trust that sellers will pay, and if sellers can't trust that buyers will deliver, commerce will collapse. Return to the Free Agent Org Chart in Figure 8.4. What connects the six individuals are what one anthropologist calls "invisible lines of trust."[10] Fred trusts Jim to recommend an accountant; Jim trusts Althea to provide good service to Fred. Break the trust, and you break the connection. And the consequences of doing that are dire: You disconnect not just from that person, but from the other people to whom that person is connected.

Respecting and maintaining trust is essential for free agency to flourish. Recall what F.A.N. Club leader Jeremy Solomons said in the previous chapter about his Ghost Ranch Alliance's decision not to formalize its arrangement: "The minute you start building a fixed relationship, you're breaking the trust." It's the same with the confederations I discussed in that chapter. The glue of those collaborations isn't a written contract, but the simple belief that each member will honor her obligations to the others. At first, this heavy reliance on trust may seem too loosey-goosey to succeed. But the system turns out to work remarkably well. One reason: Where there is no trust, there are plenty of lawyers, police officers, regulators, and other officials of the state. "Societies which rely heavily on the use of force," writes Oxford University sociologist and scholar of trust Diego Gambetta, "are likely to be less efficient, more costly, and more unpleasant than those where trust is maintained by other means."[11]

The trust I'm talking about here, however, is not the naive belief that everyone will unilaterally do what they say they'll do. That's gullibility. Genuine trust flows in two directions—which leads to the essential feature of the Free Agent Operating System: *reciprocity*. I'll help you because somewhere down the line, you'll help me.

Such reciprocity is imprinted in our DNA. "We are human because our ancestors learned to share their food and their skills in an honored network of obligation," says Richard Leakey.[12] Evolutionary biologists contend that most animals survive in part thanks to "reciprocal altruism," a process by which creatures from guppies to baboons appear to cooperate with one another, trade favors over time, and cut out those who cheat. Biologists explain what seems like selfless behavior—for example, a fish swimming away from its school in order to undertake the dangerous mission of looking for predators—as merely a way to generate goodwill and eventual payback from its fellow fish.[13] Little wonder then that the planet's most successful and advanced animal does this best and depends on it most. Sociologist Howard Becker says the formal name for human beings shouldn't be "Homo sapiens," man the knower—but "Homo reciprocus," man the reciprocator.[14] The principle of "givers gain" is not just a good idea. It's the (evolutionary) law.

Reciprocal altruism is the underlying process that allows the free agent economy to function. And it ruthlessly eliminates those who violate its terms. In the org chart in Figure 8.4, if Althea doesn't return Jim's good deeds, Althea is clipped from the network—and therefore severed from the connections to information, ideas, and opportunities she needs to survive. As San Francisco health care consultant Notty Bumbo told me, "The real power comes in the sharing, not in the withholding. Those people who are out there asking for information and not giving back get cut off. It's a peer process. If it becomes apparent that they're just sucking the lifeblood out of everybody else, they get cut out of the picture." Givers gain. Takers lose. What's more, in the above example, Althea's reputation suffers because Jim's account of her lack of cooperation can spread easily to his contacts—and then to their contacts. If you don't play fair with Notty Bumbo, plenty of people are going to learn that you're a lifeblood sucker. An employee can more easily hide behind the reputation of his employer. But a free agent is exposed to the outside world—and this exposure actually promotes more noble behavior.

The pragmatic reciprocity that is the platform of the free agent economy is a remarkably enduring concept. Let me haul out Alexis de Tocqueville one more time. When the Frenchman visited America in 1830, he remarked that American democracy was blooming not because its citizens were selfless—but because they were *not*. Instead, what allowed this remarkable new democracy to flourish was each person's pursuit of his "own interest, rightly understood."[15] Enlightened self-interest is as crucial for free agency as it was—and is—for democracy. Enlightened self-interest, indeed, is the oxygen of free agency. That may not be idealistic, but it just might be ideal.

But another expression of the reciprocal altruism principle is even more enduring and far more profound. Enlightened self-interest—that is, "do unto others as you would have them do unto you"—is the cornerstone of every major world religion. In Christianity, the principle comes from the book of Matthew. In Judaism, the Talmud teaches: "What is hateful to you, do not to your fellow men. That is the entire Law; all the rest is commentary." Islam holds, "No one of you is a believer until he desires for his brother that which he desires for himself." And this idea likewise is central to Buddhism, Taoism, Confucianism, and Hinduism. So we are left with what seems like the ultimate paradox: The underlying operating system of the freewheeling, individualistic, hypercapitalistic free agent economy is . . . the Golden Rule. The DOS, Windows, and Mac OS of the real new economy is one of the oldest principles of human civilization. In the world of free agency, the way to be better off is to be better.

THE BOX

THE CRUX: Free agency has its own organization chart—but this org chart doesn't look much like the traditional corporate version. The connections between individuals run horizontally, not vertically. Power depends on relationships instead of one's place in an established hierarchy. And the connections are loose, fluid, and purposeful rather than tight, permanent, and preordained. What keeps free agency running smoothly is the principle of enlightened self-interest. I'll help you, because in the future I know you'll help me. The great paradox of the freewheeling, seemingly treacherous, free agent economy is that it encourages people to behave extremely well. What keeps the free agent economy together is the Golden Rule.

THE FACTOID: In sociologist Mark Granovetter's classic study of how people find jobs, he discovered that most people found them jobs through contacts—and that in roughly five out of six instances, those contacts were people with whom the job seeker did not have a close relationship and did not even know particularly well.

THE QUOTE: "The Free Agent Org Chart is fluid. And because it's fluid, it's less hierarchical. Your peer on one project could be your boss on another. Today's subcontractor could be tomorrow's customer. In this sense, the Free Agent Org Chart resembles a traditional organization chart less than it resembles the human brain. In our brains, existing neurons and new ones are continually forging and reforging connections, constantly laying fresh pathways to one another. That—literally—is how we think. This is one reason that free agency might—just might—be more attuned to human nature than the typical twentieth-century employment structure."

THE WORD: *Free Agent Operating System.* The underlying instructions that allow free agency to function. Like Windows, DOS, or Linux on computers, the Free Agent Operating System establishes the platform on which the free agent economy operates. Its basic unit is trust, which is fashioned into reciprocal altruism. (See also: *The Golden Rule.*)

The Free Agent
Infrastructure

"I go out the back door, down the alley, and walk a block to Mail Boxes, Etc. I go in there and joke with everybody. It's my community."

—Janna King (Minneapolis, Minnesota)

Arranging a few hundred interviews with people I'd never met, often in cities I'd never visited, was a logistical challenge. So during my free agent tour, before I'd arrive in a town, I'd call or e-mail the interviewees to choose a place for our conversation. In about half the instances, the setting we decided on was Starbucks (or some other, similar high-end coffee joint). These coffee places, most of which didn't exist ten years ago, had several virtues. They were always in convenient locations. They permitted, even welcomed, patrons to sit and talk for several hours. And they had tables for spreading out my materials and electrical outlets for plugging in my equipment. In short, they provided a four-hour office rental for the price of a three-dollar latte.

Some days I'd station myself at a table at a single coffee place from early in the morning until nightfall, welcoming each appointment, as if I were a dentist. In Minneapolis, lower Manhattan, Foster City, California, and Glenview, Illinois, Starbucks barristas even took phone messages for me. (And since I tape-recorded my interviews, and since music invariably played in the background at every location, I now have the world's largest collection of bootleg Starbucks CDs.) Everybody knows that Starbucks serves a decent, if pricey, cup of coffee. But what far fewer people realize is that Starbucks is not in the retail beverage industry. It's really in the commercial real estate business. For me, and for many other independent workers, these coffeehouses have become free agent office centers.

Starbucks and its caffeinated cousins are part of what I call the free agent infrastructure. The components of this infrastructure, which I'll review in a moment, include copy shops, office supply superstores, bookstore cafés, overnight delivery services, executive suites, and the Internet. Like America's system of federal highways, the free agent infrastructure forms the physical foundation on which the economy operates. But unlike the federal highway system, which was planned and paid for by the government, this infrastructure emerged more or less spontaneously. Like so many other aspects of Free Agent Nation, it is self-organized. Nobody is in charge of it. That's why it works. It works so well, in fact, that few people realize that this collection of commercial establishments even constitutes an infrastructure. The free agent infrastructure has eight key elements.

COPY AND PRINTING SHOPS

A few years ago, I spent twenty-four hours working at a Kinko's in Houston. Here's what I discovered: Kinko's has become the *Cheers* bar of Free Agent Nation. It's the place that always knows your name and is always glad you came. Just as Starbucks is about more than coffee, Kinko's is about more than copies. Free agents often have a particular store they call "my Kinko's" and a particular clerk they favor. These clerks—or "coworkers," as they're known—talk about copy shop regulars the way Sam Malone talked about Cliff and Norm. Several free agents I interviewed have found partners for projects at Kinko's. One couple, who later married, even met at a Kinko's.

Kinko's founder, Paul Orfalea, who began his chain of copy shops in 1970 beside a taco stand near the University of California at Santa Barbara campus, was one of the first business leaders to understand the rise of free agency and the boom in home offices. He steered his company from its college roots to the new frontier of work. Kinko's is now the nation's largest copy chain, with 1,100 locations worldwide—many averaging seven thousand square feet and open twenty-four hours a day. "They're a great company," says Minneapolis free agent Eric Turnipseed. "I think they offer tremendous service. I have a lot of the hardware and software you can get at Kinko's, but what I don't have that Kinko's can give me is the high-speed copying and duplicating and color-printing capability. I can work at home and run down to Kinko's for an output for a lot less than going to a printer." More than 150 Kinko's locations have videoconferencing facilities—providing a service to many free agents that no single free agent could purchase on her own. The launch of kinkos.com in 2000 allowed micropreneurs to send documents and printing instructions over the Web—and now provides design tools and marketing advice for small entrepreneurs. And in another sign of how the infrastructure is knitting together, Kinko's has allied with Federal Express to deliver in person documents that users create over the computer. A partnership with America Online likewise strengthens this component of the infrastructure. Most free agents—or at least *this* free agent—couldn't imagine working independently without a nearby Kinko's.

COFFEE SHOPS

In 1971, in Seattle's bustling Pike Place Market, Starbucks opened its first store. In 1987, when current chairman and CEO Howard Schultz took over, Starbucks had seventeen shops, most of them in the Pacific Northwest. Today, Starbucks has some 4,000 locations. It sometimes seems like the entire American

population lives within five minutes of a double-tall machiatto—
a change on the American landscape that delights some and hor-
rifies others. One reason for Starbucks's explosive growth has
been the rise of the independent workforce.

In his book *The Great Good Place*, sociologist Ray Oldenburg
charts the decline of what he calls the "Third Place," a community gathering spot that isn't work or home but a place simply to
hang out. These establishments—beer gardens in Germany,
cafés in Italy, pubs in Great Britain, the corner bar in the U.S.—
invigorate communities and foster the sociability neighborhoods
need to thrive.[1] Starbucks's Schultz originally conceived his cafés
as sip-and-run establishments, but he soon latched on to Oldenburg's idea. As Schultz writes in his book, *Pour Your Heart into It*,
"Americans are so hungry for a community that some of our customers began gathering in our stores, making appointments
with friends, holding meetings, striking up conversations with
other regulars. Once we understood the powerful need for a
Third Place, we were able to respond by building larger stores,
with more seating."[2]

The design of Starbucks reflects this transition from beverage dispenser to free agent meeting ground. The first Starbucks
on the scene circled customers from the door, to the counter, and
back out the door again. The countertops were too narrow to
place many items, the high-back chairs too uncomfortable to sit
in for long stretches. But once the company realized that people
were visiting Starbucks for more than the expensive drinks,
Schultz and his team redid the furniture and the interior design.
In came comfortable, cushioned chairs—positioned near others
to encourage conversation. The thin, solitary countertops gave
way to tables for two and to larger conference-style tables capable of holding piles of free agent stuff. Now Starbucks is teaming
up with Microsoft to offer wireless Internet access at most of its
locations.

Of course, Starbucks is not the only coffee place that's woven
itself into the free agent infrastructure. Xando Café, Foster
Brothers, Peet's, and an array of local hot spots likewise serve as
Free Agent Nation's new commercial real estate. Free agent

Turnipseed says he prefers the local chain, Caribou Coffee. "I've met lots a clients and closed lots of deals in those places," he says. But not everybody delights in this development. One traditional employee complained to me in an e-mail not too long ago about "a free agent imposing her business on the general public" by setting up her laptop at a local coffee joint. "I went to that place to relax," this woman told me, "not to expose myself to the unfortunate soul that didn't have a proper office for her business meeting."

BOOKSTORES

Bookstores—both large chains and independent booksellers—are also entering the commercial real estate business. Their cafés provide a meeting ground for free agents, but have benefits the local Starbucks can't offer. "I use Barnes & Noble as my research library," said one free agent who understandably desired that I conceal his name. "The public library near me is awful. The material is either missing or out of date. But Barnes & Noble has everything. They've got the latest books, and everything is easy to find. I used to feel guilty about it, but not anymore—because it seems like half the people there are doing the same thing." In less urban settings, other free agents use public libraries as their public libraries.

EXECUTIVE SUITES

While the Xando Café and the local Borders are unofficially in the commercial real estate business, executive suites are officially in that industry. These operations rent micropreneurs and other free agents private offices with a shared reception area and receptionist. Many also provide meeting rooms, videoconferencing, mail and commercial package delivery, photocopying and secretarial services, and sometimes even child care and fitness centers. They offer free agents the trappings of corporate life without the hassles. Some of the big players in this market are Alliance Business Centers, HQ Global Workplaces, and Regus Business Centers. Regus alone owns more than five million square feet of real estate worldwide.[3] And the entire executive suite business is now about a $2 billion industry, with over four thousand business centers in the U.S. alone.[4] One company, Executive Office Clubs, rents workstations for $9 an hour and private offices for as little as $12 an hour. And its facilities offer customers—you guessed it—free Starbucks coffee. Think about that for a moment. At Starbucks, you buy coffee and get the office free. At Executive Office Clubs, you rent the office and get the coffee free.

THE INTERNET

This is hardly a news flash, but the Internet is huge. And free agents need it even more than they need caramel cappuccinos or colored copies. International Data Corporation projects that by 2002, home offices will spend more than $10.2 billion on Internet access and more than $71 billion on information technology in general.[5] Internet service providers such as Earthlink, Microsoft Network, and America Online are aggressively pursuing the free agent market—as are high-speed Internet providers such as Covad. Some researchers expect more than eight million American households to have their own home networks by 2002, while others claim that by 2003 "as many as 30 million new and existing homes may be networked."[6] And microbusinesses have been flocking to the Net. In 2000, 68 percent of the companies that registered Internet domain names had fewer than five people working for them; only 1 percent of the companies registering names had more than one hundred employees.[7] What's more, until the advent of the Internet, most computer software came on disks or CD-ROMs inside shrink-wrapped packages. But the Web has allowed free agents to access the latest versions of all sorts of software applications—from word processing programs to spreadsheets to e-mail. On the Net, free agents can find free fax services, free voicemail, free calendar programs, and through companies like BigStep.com, free electronic storefronts. I could probably live without a nearby cup of java—but without the Internet, I (and most free agents) would be hurting.

OFFICE SUPPLY SUPERSTORES

Office Depot, Staples, and OfficeMax are the supply closets of Free Agent Nation. These three national chains allow soloists and micropreneurs to get their office supplies almost as easily as when they just had to walk down the hall to pilfer Post-its. And free agents are fueling extraordinary growth in this industry. People who are self-employed and work at home are 41 percent more likely than the average person to shop at office supply stores.[8] And 80 percent of these superstores' sales are in the small office and home office market.[9] Office Depot, which opened its first store in 1986, today has more than 850 superstores in North America, and generates annual sales of more than $10 billion. Staples, the second largest office supply superstore, does about $9 billion of business each year—and has been opening an average of at least one new superstore every week. "The typical Staples superstore," says the company, "is about 24,000 square feet and targets small businesses, home office professionals, and consumers." Also in this category are OfficeMax, number three in the market, and online upstart AtYourOffice.com, which sells office supplies from its Web site instead of a traditional retail outlet. I knew I'd arrived as a free agent when I entered my local Staples and bought my first toner cartridge.

POSTAL SERVICE CENTERS

For free agents who work out of their homes, establishments like Mail Boxes, Etc. offer a post office box, assistance shipping packages, and a small selection of business services and office supplies. MBE currently provides post office boxes to more than 800,000 people in the United States. Founded in 1980, it is now the place where each day a quarter million people check their mail—and where some, like Janna King, quoted at the beginning of the chapter, hang out and shoot the breeze. Like other components of the free agent infrastructure, MBE is bubbling up quickly: With four thousand locations, it's growing faster than McDonald's did in its initial two decades.[10] MBE and its counterparts are the mailroom of Free Agent Nation.

Overnight Package Delivery

Overnight delivery services such as Federal Express have helped free agents attain the speed of a giant corporation. FedEx is a legendary business story, a critical part of how all business gets done—and a mainstay of the free agent work style. Some one million *individuals* now have their own FedEx accounts. And FedEx's latest advertising campaign is pursuing home-based workers with particular intensity. Its ads play up the camaraderie between a FedEx driver and the housebound free agent delighted to see another human being. "Signs by Donna. Delivered by Dave," says the caption—with copy below that reads, "FedEx couriers are more than just pickup and delivery people. They're familiar faces you can trust and count on." The ad rings true for me. On some days, Tony (my FedEx guy) is the only person outside my family I see face-to-face—which might say more about me than about the free agent infrastructure.

CHAPTER 9

THE CRUX: An economic infrastructure has emerged to provide a foundation for free agents' work. Composed of copy and printing shops, coffee shops, bookstores, executive suites, the Internet, office supply superstores, postal service centers, and overnight delivery services, this new infrastructure has two defining attributes. First, it is self-organized rather than centrally planned. Second, the infrastructure serves a fundamentally social role by creating a variety of "Third Places" where independent workers can come together.

THE FACTOID: By 2002, home offices will spend $10.2 billion on Internet access.

THE QUOTE: "Everybody knows that Starbucks serves a decent, if pricey, cup of coffee. But what far fewer people realize is that Starbucks is not in the retail beverage industry. It's really in the commercial real estate business. For me, and for many other independent workers, these coffeehouses have become free agent office centers."

THE WORD: *Free agent infrastructure.* The physical foundation on which the free agent economy operates. The infrastructure is self-organized and composed of private establishments.

10

Matchmakers, Agents, and Coaches

"We're doing in the digital age what the William Morris Agency began doing in the vaudeville days. We're representing talent."
—Paul Smith, President, Digital Talent Agency
(New York, New York)

So far in Part III, we've seen how small groups, the Golden Rule, and a self-organized physical infrastructure grease the gears of the free agent economy. In this chapter, I'll look at how some specialized new industries and professions have arisen to serve a similar function. Most of these new specialists didn't exist ten or fifteen years ago. But they have surfaced today because of two of free agency's most powerful underlying currents—one economic, the other emotional.

Begin with the economic tide. In a world dominated by large organizations, capital—especially financial capital—was arguably the economy's most important resource. You needed money, often lots of it, to finance tall buildings and giant machines. And not surprisingly, the rise of this organization-dominated economy created new ways to collect, distribute, and manage this key resource. Brokerages helped connect investors with cash to companies that needed it. Financiers invented new financial instruments so more firms could raise more funds. And money managers offered advice to wealthy people and pension funds about where to direct their loot for maximum return. Today, America has the most efficient capital markets in the world. But as power continues to devolve from organizations to individuals, financial capital may no longer remain the economy's most important resource. Instead, the scarcest and most valuable resource today is talent. "All that matters is talent," said a widely read 1998 McKinsey & Co. report. "Talent wins."[1] Raising lots of money is often easier than finding lots of capable people, because the market for talent operates far less efficiently than the market for financing. So, much as we saw last century with capital markets, in this century an array of new enterprises and professions has emerged to boost the efficiency of the free agent talent market.

The second underlying current giving rise to free agency's new specialists is emotional. In the Organization Man's day, managing your career was like riding an elevator. You pressed a few buttons, tried not to rock your surroundings, and waited almost effortlessly until you arrived at your destination. Today, though, careers for many people are more emotionally fraught. As I've argued, work has increasingly become a source of meaning. And that has made careers resemble mountain climbing— full of great heights and potential peril, a self-directed quest rather than a passive ride. That's why more American workers are turning to self-styled career sherpas to help them trek across work's new emotional terrain.

Economics and emotions—the rise of a market for talent coupled with the increasing emotional complexity of work—are *why* a new breed of specialists has emerged. But the best way to understand how they function is to see these specialists in action. To do that, we'll go to Walnut Creek, California, and meet a talent matchmaker, drop down near Hollywood and see a New Economy talent agent, and travel to Brookfield, Connecticut, and visit a personal coach.

MATCHMAKERS

The free agent economy, as I've said, is a market. On one side of the market are buyers—those seeking talent. On the other side are sellers—independent workers with products or services for sale. And in between are companies like M-Squared, a $10 million venture headquartered in San Francisco's financial district. In the new talent market, M-Squared is one of the many enterprises that link buyers and sellers, trying to hook up companies that need help with free agents who need work. The company bills itself as "the premier broker of independent consultants to companies in need of 'spot-market' expertise and just-in-time management staffing." Co-founder and president Marion McGovern has called the company "an arbitrageur of talent." That is, M-Squared profits from price discrepancies in different markets: It "purchases" talent at a price that sellers are willing to accept—and then "sells" the talent to buyers willing to pay a higher price, pocketing the 30 to 35 percent markup. But M-Squared's Claire McAuliffe has a slightly different take on the company's business, one perhaps more consistent with the kinder, gentler ethos of Free Agent Nation. "We are a hybrid," she told me. "We're not a search firm. We're not a consulting firm. We're not a temp agency. We're not a dating service. We're sort of a corporate yenta."

If you'd thought I'd exhausted the supply of metaphors for describing free agency, think again. Maybe the new economy is an old-fashioned Ukrainian village—a shtetl, like the one in *Fiddler on the Roof.* Recall that in *Fiddler*'s shtetl, one of the most prominent residents was Yente. She was the matchmaker. Today, many of Yente's descendants have left Eastern Europe and immigrated to Free Agent Nation. An array of free market yentas now helps connect free agents with potential suitors. These matchmakers assist large companies in locating the talent they need, and aid soloists and micropreneurs in landing lucrative, satisfying work. Sometimes these matchmakers improve independent workers' lives, introducing them to opportunities they could never have found on their own. Sometimes, as happened in *Fiddler*, parties spurn the matchmakers as overpriced meddlers. But whatever their virtues or vices, the specialized yentas of the free agent talent market are here to stay.

The U.S. labor market has always had middlemen—usually in the form of employment agencies or temporary staffing firms such as Manpower, Kelly Services, Olsten, and Robert Half. But in the era of free agency, matchmaking has become big business. Manpower alone has more than 3,200 offices in fifty countries, and generates sales in excess of $11 billion a year.[2] In 2001, the entire temporary staffing industry is expected to produce revenues of nearly $100 billion.[3]

These talent intermediaries run the gamut of size and scope. Take René Shimada Siegel. Fed up with life as an executive at Novell, she launched HiTech Connect from an office in her Silicon Valley home. Her small company connects free agent marketing and communications specialists (most of them, like Siegel, talented women who'd had it with the Valley's family-flattening corporate culture) with high-tech companies desperate for experienced talent. Siegel's partner, Nancy Collins, works from her home in New Jersey—and together they've fashioned a specialized nationwide talent network of six hundred home-based free agents. Meanwhile, another matchmaker, IMCOR—founded by John Thompson, a downsized accounting executive turned visionary entrepreneur—swims in a different talent pool. With offices in Stamford, Connecticut, Chicago, Dallas, Los Angeles, Atlanta, and New York, IMCOR draws on a network of some sixty thousand people who call themselves "portable executives."

Bob Weis—a mustachioed six-foot-ten former Portland State University basketball player, who looks enough like Phil Jackson to play the coach in a TV movie—was once such a portable executive, though he didn't work through IMCOR. After earning a master's degree in finance and working in banking and venture capital in Northern California, Weis says that helping companies get off the ground proved more satisfying than "doling out cash—and then owning the project at the end when they couldn't make the payments anymore." So when he reached his mid-thirties, he took a three-month trip to Australia, and spent much of his time writing about what he wanted to do with his life. He suspected it would be fun to move from company to company advising them on IPOs and financial structures. He wrote a business plan for how he could do that himself, and figured some friends might join his band of nomadic chief financial officers. Weis called his fledgling company Strategic Financial Services. "That," he says, "was a stupid name." But in a burst of whimsy, Weis had fitted his car with a vanity license plate that read, "CFOS2GO." That, he realized, was a great name.

Today, CFOs2GO is a thriving talent market matchmaker with a roster of more than five thousand senior financial and accounting executives that start-up companies can call on for interim positions, directorships, consulting gigs, or even full-time jobs. As in any market, supply and demand created the opportunity. On the supply side, Weis says, "It didn't take an Einstein to figure out that financial management careers were changing." Finance types once worked like crazy for seven or eight years to secure a partnership at an accounting firm. Then the firms began requiring as much as fifteen years for partnership—and extending offers to far fewer people. That left plenty of seasoned professionals looking for something to do. Meanwhile, on the demand side were the acres of technology companies that had mushroomed near San Francisco Bay. At the helm of these companies were usually a technology person and a marketing person, but rarely anyone who could read a balance sheet. Enter Weis with his Walnut Creek–based boutique. "In my business, finance and accounting people are usually not worth a crap until they're about forty," he told me one December morning. "It's a skill position. Nobody was born a good accountant or a good finance person." By connecting experienced free agent talent with inexperienced tycoon wannabes, Weis established a critical place in the Silicon Valley talent market.

And while he acknowledges that matchmakers like himself make the market more efficient, he disdains those who describe the process in the cold-blooded language of high finance. "There are some companies that think of themselves as an arbitrageur between what talent is willing to sell themselves for, and what purchasers are willing to pay for it. There's always that element in what I do—but it's not one I want to encourage." The only people he'll consider, he says, are those who "get fulfillment from their business or their craft."

As with most aspects of American economic life, free agent matchmaking is moving online. Forrester Research estimates that online recruiting will be a $1.7 billion business by 2003.[4] Monster.com—the Internet's largest and most influential career site—operates what it calls the "world's first online, auction-style marketplace for talent." Its name? "The Talent Market," of course. Free agents can place offers—"I'll write your marketing materials for $50 an hour"—and potential clients can respond with bids, sometimes driving up the price if more than one buyer is interested in the same seller. Dozens of other online matchmakers and marketplaces have sprouted in the last two years. Ventures like Guru.com, Elance.com, and eWork.com allow companies and others to post projects—and free agents to offer themselves up for the gigs. Some of these online agora have several hundred thousand registered free agents—and more than $500 million worth of work up for bid at a time. Other ventures—young, publicly held companies such as Opus 360 and Niku—take a somewhat different approach. While they also maintain marketplaces, they provide sophisticated software to large companies to allow them to track and deploy talent as efficiently as possible. (Full disclosure: I have a very small financial interest in two of the companies mentioned in this paragraph.) Some analysts predict that these digital matchmakers will morph into "career networks—that aggregate job postings across multiple sites, link Web services to the HR desktop, and offer a full array of training, assessment, and placement services."[5] The trajectory is similar to the one followed by Charles Schwab & Co. It began as an offline discount broker that connected buyers and sellers, evolved into an online discount broker, and then added an array of research and analysis to help investors make wise decisions. You've come a long way, Yente.

AGENTS

They call themselves The Muses. But as they sit in a café off South Park in San Francisco, Betsy Harkavy and Jodi Hadsell seem focused more on representation than inspiration. "We work with talent to figure out what their goals and aspirations are. We counsel them, and guide them in the direction we think is best for them," Harkavy says. Harkavy and Hadsell are two of the new Jerry Maguires of Free Agent Nation. They are agents—talent agents. They represent many of the free agent designers, producers, writers, programmers, and strategists who ply their trade in San Francisco's Multimedia Gulch. Harkavy and Hadsell, founders of The Muses, find these workers gigs, scout for new projects, and advise them on their careers.

Kristin Knight takes a similar approach. Ten years ago, this former Microsoft temp founded Creative Assets, which now represents more than one thousand free agent creatives in Seattle and six other cities. "My whole premise of starting this is that I wanted people to work in cool and interesting jobs," she told me in Seattle's Pioneer Square. "People really like the idea of having an agent; it's almost like having a status symbol." Aquent Partners—which began as MacTemps, a temporary staffing firm run out of founder John Chuang's Harvard dorm room—has become the world's largest specialized talent agency, representing more than twenty thousand independent professionals in twelve countries. Authors, actors, athletes, and artists are no longer the only people with agents. More independent workers are turning to places like Aquent, Creative Assets, and The Muses. According to one estimate, more than five percent of workers who earn more than $75,000 per year now have agents to negotiate their employment contracts.[6]

Talent agents straddle the economic and emotional realms. They help the talent market run more fairly—by boosting the bargaining power of independent workers. But they also serve a kinder, gentler function—helping these independents contend with career vicissitudes, and occasionally balming bruised free agent egos. Because they stand at the intersection of money and meaning, talent agents may be the most representative figures of the free agent age.

But in Southern California—where free agent work styles and talent reps are nothing new—I met a man named Jim Delulio who is pushing the concept even further. For seventeen years, Delulio worked for public relations firms—when, in the late 1990s, he began seeing dramatic changes in his industry. "A lot of the best people were getting hard to hold on to at the agency," he told me at a Los Angeles coffee shop. "They were leaving to go freelance. There was this burgeoning pool of freelancers that was developing out there. Some of the most experienced and seasoned people, the best PR talent, were out there freelancing."

Like Weis of CFOs2GO, Delulio saw a gap in the talent market. "A lot of freelancers were out there, but there was no conduit between them and the companies that were likely to buy their services." So borrowing a page from Hollywood, Delulio launched James Communications, a New Economy talent agency. Using his own contacts and word-of-mouth referrals, he built a pool of 350 free agent public relations people—from speechwriters to account executives to graphic designers—that he could tap for assignments. If the box office bigwigs of public relations were leaving large PR firms to go solo, then Delulio wanted to be the William Morris Agency of their lives.

Now companies call him in search of help. Delulio checks his computerized database of free agents, and tries to match talent to task. He says the buyers seeking talent took readily to this new way of doing business. "Companies are starting to realize that a lot of the creative talent, a lot of the best brains and smartest people, are going out on their own." And the talent, he says, appreciate having someone who looks out for their interests and is willing just to chat about life.

Even better, at least from Delulio's perspective, is that this arrangement confers on him several competitive advantages over traditional public relations firms. The most obvious edge is that James Communications is leaner and cheaper. His monthly overhead, including his own salary, is less than $15,000 per month, while at a typical forty-person agency, monthly overhead can run well over $250,000. High overhead can create urgencies that Delulio lacks. "In an agency, if I have three people sitting on their hands in the back, they've got to work on the next piece of business that comes in the door." In that sort of system, the project goes to the most available people, not necessarily the most qualified ones. But Delulio believes he can serve clients better. He finds precisely the right person in his pool, connects that person to the buyer—and like any good agent, takes his cut.

In this sense, James Communications may not even be a PR *talent* agency. Instead, it may be the larval form of the new PR agency. In Chapter 1, I described the Hollywood model of production. Today, a firm called Jefferson & Rogers Public Relations may consist of Jefferson, Rogers, a secretary, and a computer database full of talented free agents. The value that Mr. Jefferson and Ms. Rogers bring to clients is the ability to assemble the right team for a particular task—and then disband that team when the project is done. "When a client hires a PR firm," Delulio says, "they're buying brains. It doesn't really matter whether the brains are sitting in a chair at a particular address." If Delulio can get better brains—faster and cheaper—he'll beat the established firms every time. That's how the talent market works. And that's why—in Free Agent Nation as in Hollywood—talent agents are fast becoming power brokers.

COACHES

When work was governed by the loyalty-for-security bargain, and when Organization Men prized getting along with the boss over getting in touch with themselves, the workplace was startlingly free of emotions. People parked their feelings at the office door or factory gate—and once inside, did what they were supposed to do. Although it made work life humdrum much of the time, the arrangement was neat and predictable. But when the bargain crumbled and individuals faced both greater opportunity and heightened uncertainty, many workers felt loosed from their moorings—and they needed help sailing these choppier, more emotionally turbulent seas.

That's where people like John Seiffer have come in. He's a coach. But inside his cluttered Brookfield, Connecticut, office, you won't find any baseball gloves or badminton birdies. Instead of screaming from the sidelines at a soccer team or pitching batting practice to Little Leaguers, Seiffer coaches individual New Economy workers. The shingle outside his office in a small retail park identifies him as a "business and executive coach."

Matchmakers enable the new market for talent to operate efficiently. Talent agents negotiate on the talent's behalf. But coaches serve a squishier, though no less important, function. They help free agents reckon with the new emotional complexity of work. Independent workers can discuss with their coaches issues they can't talk about with anyone else. Should they leave their job? How should they handle a troublesome new project? Why do their days seem out of balance? Coaches, most of whom work by phone, are sounding boards and motivators who talk through problems with solo entrepreneurs, help them set deadlines, hold them accountable for their actions, and lead them down the path of self-discovery. Coaches are career counselor and priest rolled into a single voice on the other end of the telephone. And coaching has become a booming business—despite the fact that "executive coach" sounds like a bus that takes grandmothers to Atlantic City. The U.S. now has some ten thousand full-and part-time coaches. There's a two-thousand-member professional association, the International Coach Federation, that certifies coaches—and a network of institutions that train them, including one called Coach U.

Seiffer, who built a window-washing business in Dallas and has dabbled in other industries, says he'd never heard of coaching until 1994 when a financial planner he knew told him about an odd turn his professional conversations kept taking. The financial planner's clients began asking him questions that had little to do with money—things like when to have kids, or whether to divorce their spouse. Sensing an opportunity, the financial planner became a "life planner," and ended up calling what he did "coaching." Seiffer, a gregarious and helpful sort who was looking for a new challenge, decided that he, too, would give coaching a try. Clients seek him in a variety of circumstances—when they're confronting a microbusiness that's stalled, when their lives feel out of whack, or when they're undertaking a daunting project. He charges $400 a month, which gets clients three or four half-hour coaching calls. Some clients receive his coaching for a few months. Others maintain the relationship for several years.

It may sound peculiar to some. But Coach Seiffer has a ready response. "Pete Sampras has a coach," he explains. "Tiger Woods has a coach. Opera singers have coaches. Coaching pulls out of them abilities they already have." That's what he tries to do—although he focuses less on performance and more on questions such as "how do you want what you're doing to fit with your bigger life issues?" He says coaching reflects an accommodation of sorts between baby boomers' 1960s pursuit of personal knowledge and their 1990s pursuit of personal wealth. Bringing those urges into alignment is the secret. "If every part of your life is working in balance, you will be more successful," he says. Another executive coach I met, Wendy Wallbridge of San Francisco, coaches businesspeople to become what she calls "soul proprietors."

In a sense, coaches are shrinks without the couches, management consultants without the flow charts, and sympathetic bartenders without the row of shot glasses. It's easy—very easy—to make fun of them. "Isn't this just rent-a-friend?" Seiffer says some people ask him. But coaches serve a purpose for some free agents similar to the small groups I described in Chapter 7. In the idealized world of several decades ago, Americans had plenty of people to talk to—the neighbor over the back fence, the priest of the local parish, the neighborhood cop who strolled down the sidewalk each morning. But with more people living alone—and working alone—more people are seeking another form of connection and conversation. The added benefit, Seiffer says, is that "When you hire a coach, you can expect that their main goal is to do what's best for you. It's the coach's job to help people clarify, to see through stuff, and help them become who they really are."

Vince Lombardi, meet Abraham Maslow. Self-actualizing isn't everything. It's the only thing.

THE BOX

CHAPTER 10

THE CRUX: The free agent economy differs from the Organization Man economy in two fundamental ways. First, as power has shifted from organizations to individuals, talent has replaced capital as the economy's most important resource—and a new talent market has emerged to organize, price, and allocate it. Second, instead of being humdrum and personality-free, work has become more emotionally complex. These two forces have created a new breed of professional specialists who help Free Agent Nation work. Matchmakers, an outgrowth of the temporary staffing industry, connect buyers seeking free agent talent with free agent talent seeking projects—and thereby make the new talent market run more efficiently. Agents—like the talent agents that have long represented actors, authors, and athletes—straddle the economic and emotional realms. They represent independent workers, negotiate on their behalf, and advise them on personal and professional matters. And coaches serve a squishier role—part career counselor, part priest—helping free agents answer more fundamental questions about their work and lives.

THE FACTOID: More than 5 percent of workers who earn more than $75,000 per year now have agents to negotiate their employment contracts.

THE QUOTE: "In a sense, coaches are shrinks without the couches, management consultants without the flow charts, and sympathetic bartenders without the row of shot glasses."

THE WORD: *Corporate yenta.* An entity that matches independent workers with firms or projects that need their short-term help.

11

Free Agent Families

"If I could just get my three-year-old off 'her' computer, I might be able to get some work done."
— *Allison Cutler (Nashville, Tennessee)*

I want to see Bubbe's office," Sophie said, pausing between swigs of orange juice from her sippy cup. Sophie is our older daughter. Bubbe is my mother. And during the Midwest leg of my family's free agent jaunt, we'd squeezed in a quick visit to the Pink grandparents at their central Ohio home.

"Okay," I said to our firstborn, then nearly two and a half. "Let's get in the car, and we'll go." Bubbe works at a community center about a mile from the house where I grew up and where she and my father still live.

"Noooo," said Sophie, laughing. "I want to see her *office*."

"Yeah, no problem. Her office. Let's put on your shoes—and we'll drive there."

But Sophie didn't budge. She just looked at me, trying to discern which was malfunctioning—my ears or my brain. "Her *office*," Sophie said again.

Then I got it. Sophie's mom and I both work from offices in our home. Telling our toddler that we had to leave her grandmother's house to see her grandmother's office was like telling her that we'd have to jump in the station wagon to visit Bubbe's kitchen.

So I explained to our daughter something no one needed to explain to me when I was a kid: "You see, some people have offices other places. Bubbe's office isn't in her house like Mom's and Dad's offices are. Her office is somewhere else. We have to drive there."

"Oh," Sophie smiled. "*That's* funny."

BALANCERS AND BLENDERS

Sociologist Christena Nippert-Eng says two kinds of people inhabit the world of work: segmentors and integrators. Segmentors lay down clear, inviolable boundaries between what is "home" and what is "work." Integrators do the opposite: For them, the border—if it exists at all—is murky and often moves. Of course, few of us are total integrators or segmentors. At any given moment we find ourselves somewhere on what Nippert-Eng calls the "integration-segmentation continuum." But if you watch people long enough, you can learn which side of the continuum they occupy most of the time—and how that shapes their thinking and their lives. That's what Nippert-Eng did in her breakthrough 1996 book, *Home and Work*. She asked how people sculpted and maintained boundaries between home and work.[1] The answer, it turned out, was in their pockets and on their walls.

Using a 103-item questionnaire, Nippert-Eng got up close and personal with six dozen scientists, machinists, and administrators at an unnamed lab in the Northeast United States. She asked her subjects to open their wallets, show her the photos on their desks or toolboxes, explain their appointment books, take out their key rings, and reveal what they talked about in bed. Here's what she found: The best way to tell segmentors from integrators was by looking at their calendars or examining their keys. Segmentors kept one calendar at the workplace for job-related appointments (meetings, assignments, and professional obligations)—and another at home for personal matters (doctor visits, kids' events, and those sorts of things). Some segmentors even carried a third pocket calendar to transport information to and from the first two calendars. Segmentors usually had two separate key rings—one with keys that unlocked doors and desks at work, and another with keys that opened the front door or started the family car. Integrators carried one chain with all their keys for home and work—sometimes going to extremes to maintain the integration. ("On several occasions," writes Nippert-Eng, "Dave has duct-taped holes in his pants pockets rather than give up the forty-odd keys he carries with him."[2]) And not surprisingly, segmentors rarely talked about work at home or home at work. But integrators yapped about everything anywhere.

Nippert-Eng's book is fascinating—and not just because it inevitably makes you look at your own key chain, wallet, and pillow talk in a fresh light. What adds to the fascination is that work-home boundary sculpting is something we somehow taught ourselves to do. Like commuting, it wasn't necessary until the twentieth century. "We have moved away from the 'craftsman' model of work in which work, home, and leisure are merely different facets of a single crystalline existence," Nippert-Eng writes.[3] Instead, she says that home and work for most Americans became "two entirely different matrices of order and meaning."[4] Suburbs (*places* that aren't work) and weekends (*times* that aren't work) are products of this segmentist outlook.

As I explained in Chapter 3, only after the Industrial Revolution did most Americans begin living in one place and earning a living in another. And this, says the inimitable Peter Drucker, "had a great impact on the family. The nuclear family had long been the unit of production. On the farm and in the artisan's workshop, husband, wife, and children worked together. The factory, almost for the first time in history, took worker and work out of the home and moved them into the workplace, leaving family members behind."[5]

Which leads back to our daughter Sophie. She's never heard of Peter Drucker or those two different matrices of order and meaning. She just knew that Mom's and Dad's offices were in the house—and so that must be where offices are. Our family tends to fall on the integrator side of the continuum. Or to relabel Nippert-Eng's categories, we don't *balance* work and family—trade them off against each other. Instead, we're preindustrial. As our offices demonstrate and our daughter understood, we *blend* work and family.

The reason we don't balance is simple. We tried it—and failed miserably. For more than a year, my wife, Jessica, and I had two real jobs and one real child. Each day, we'd leave our house in the morning, deposit our daughter at day care, scramble to our respective downtown offices—and then reverse the process eight or nine hours later. We had what I call a "commuter marriage": Jessica and I lived in the same house and the same city, but our entire lives seemed to revolve around getting to and from work and day care and back again. The mornings were a mad dash to feed, cleanse, and ferry ourselves twenty-five minutes into downtown Washington. The early evenings were a mad dash to retrieve our daughter before the day care center locked her inside, and then return the three of us to the house where we "lived," though I use the term loosely. And the late evenings, of course, were the time to prepare for the next day's wagon train. Ours was a life built around organizing and maintaining a life—not living a life. We tried balancing work and family—and even with one kid, it left us physically, emotionally, and spiritually imbalanced.

Sound familiar? These balancing acts are running Americans ragged. Between 1960 and 1986, the amount of time parents spent with kids shrank by ten hours per week for white households and twelve hours per week for African-American households.[6] The time squeeze I mentioned in Chapter 6 has closed so tight that some parents and children make the ninety minutes they spend strapped into the minivan each day their daily "quality time." Even men—who rarely bear the same domestic burden as women—have grown weary. A 2000 Radcliffe survey found that more than four out of five men in their twenties and thirties said that it was more important to them to have a schedule that permitted time with their family than it was to have a job that paid a lot or offered a professional challenge.[7] The attitudes of this generation of men, the first to be raised by working mothers, nearly mirror the attitudes of women.

That's why the solution for many families, as it was for ours, is to blend. Blending, not balancing, is far more consistent with the free agent work ethic I described in Chapter 4. Blending offers freedom—the liberty to sculpt work boundaries based on your own values rather than the demands of your employer. (Free agents, for instance, generally needn't worry about making "personal" calls at work.) Blending permits authenticity, too. The free agents who talked about putting on disguises or becoming Stepford Workers felt they could be themselves only at home. By blending, they now can bring their full selves to work—rather than leaving their identity suitcase at the office door. And blending allows people to define success on their own terms. To be sure, integration isn't perfect. Sometimes blending turns work into a Roach Motel: You can check in but you can never check out. With the phone, the fax, and e-mail just a few steps away, the potential for overwork is enormous. But blending is catching on. One example: In 1999 Americans took 23 million business trips with their kids—a 200 percent increase from 1987.[8] For many families, the positive-sum game of blending is more satisfying than the zero-sum game of balancing.

When we first married, my wife and I were DINKs (double income, no kids). Then we found ourselves in a commuter marriage. When that didn't work, we became a DINJ couple (double income, no jobs). We're not alone. Dennis Benson, whom I introduced in Chapter 4, runs his Appropriate Solutions microbusiness with his wife, Sandy. Rene Agredano and her husband, Jim Nelson, left jobs in Silicon Valley to become partners in a home-based marketing business in rural Eureka, California. "I got tired being in my car for two to three hours a day, going to a job where I was busting my butt for a living," Nelson told me. And Carole and Geoffrey Howard are veritable veterans. Geoffrey has been a free agent training consultant for twenty-four years, Carole for eighteen. They work together on training projects, sitting side by side in a home office that overlooks woodlands in Warwick, New York. They also maintain a few separate clients so they don't suffocate each other. "We've collaborated on our free agency for twenty years and on our marriage for thirty," Geoffrey told me, "and so far, so good. But we think that means we're entitled to celebrate our fiftieth anniversary this year."

Again, free agent couplehood is nothing new. Before the industrial economy, spouses often worked together. Just as those small shopkeepers lived above the store, my family—with Dad's third-floor office—lives below the store. And thanks to the Internet, Mom and Pop's operation doesn't have to be a mom-and-pop operation. Just ask Julia and Michael Thomas of Washington, D.C. They operate a small Internet venture called Zoomsearch that matches free agent designers with companies seeking creative talent. What's good for the Thomases may be good for their microbusiness. In *The Millionaire Mind*, his study of the habits and attitudes of 638 millionaires, Thomas J. Stanley notes that one of the most common attributes of the very wealthy is not just being self-employed, but being "careful in selecting a spouse."[9]

The blending strategy is also part of a broader cultural trend toward what marketers call "cool fusion," the shift from either/or solutions to both/and solutions. For example, on health care, Americans no longer feel forced to choose either traditional or alternative medicine. Increasingly they choose a little echinacea *and* some antibiotics. Marriages between spouses of different faiths are spawning new traditions such as "Baptist bar mitzvahs." Likewise, fewer Americans are selecting either work or family, but instead choosing both work and family—and then experimenting to find the mix that's right for them. Cool fusion and blending epitomize the My Size Fits Me approach to work and life in Free Agent Nation. They also help illuminate one of the most intense debates of the early twenty-first century.

FAMILY LEAVE AND LEAVING FAMILIES

Since the early 1990s, few issues have colonized a larger region of the national psyche than the conflict between work and family—and middle-class America's attempt to reckon with it. The debate has roared with books like Arlie Hochschild's outstanding 1997 work, *The Time Bind*—and others with titles like *Not Guilty!: The Good News About Working Mothers*, *When Mothers Work*, *A Mother's Place*, and *When Work Doesn't Work Anymore*. Radio shows fight about it. Newspapers write about it. Scholars think about it. Web sites link about it. And everybody, it seems, has a plan to do something about it.

The search for solutions has followed two steps. First we looked to government. What was the first bill signed by the first baby boomer president? The Family and Medical Leave Act, which in 1993 provided employees of certain-sized companies up to twelve weeks of unpaid leave to care for a new child or ailing relative. This law was no doubt well intentioned. I even wrote speeches bugling its many virtues. But in 1999, only 4 percent of the workforce used this government-sanctioned family leave—and the vast majority for less than two weeks. Near the end of his administration, President Clinton proposed expanding family leave by asking states to use unemployment benefits to finance paid leave, but every state legislature that considered the proposal rejected it.[10] Try as it might, government didn't have the answer.

Families next looked to corporations for solutions. Large companies elbowed each other like aging power forwards as they tried to score spots on those magazine lists of family-friendly workplaces. And these efforts, too, were well intentioned. But the results always seemed to diverge a bit from the press release. According to a Gallup Poll, even though nearly three quarters of large companies offer three or more so-called family-friendly benefits—such as child care, elder care, and flex time—41 percent of workers believe that using these benefits harms their career.[11] When two Baruch College professors studied leave policies at a large financial services company, they found that managers who took (unpaid) family leave suffered for it. They were less likely to get promotions or salary increases, and received lower job performance ratings than colleagues who didn't take leave.[12]

So after a full decade of books written, legislation signed, and corporate memos issued, has the work-family conflict eased? Most people would say no. The reason, I think, is that all of these initiatives, whether governmental or corporate, had two fundamental flaws. They imposed One Size Fits All solutions on a My Size Fits Me workforce. And they assumed that people needed help balancing work and family—when what most people really needed were the resources to blend work and family on their own terms.

For a wiser approach, the pundits, politicians, and corporate potentates would have been better off sitting around Lesley Spencer's kitchen table in Austin, Texas, as I did one sunny afternoon in May.

Spencer, thirty-three when we met, passed three important markers on the road that took her to this tidy house in a spanking new subdivision outside Austin. The first came in 1986. She'd graduated from high school in rural Texas, and took a job as a secretary at a pipe and steel company. "I was laid off after a year and a half," she says. "And I was devastated." Her mother was a clerk at Houston Light and Power, her father a plumber who passed away when Spencer was thirteen. Nobody in her family had gone to college. But she and the man she was dating at the time, who was from a poor family and who later became her husband, decided that college was the way to take charge of their lives. So "we both held each other's hands," knitted together a quilt of loans and grants, and enrolled at Southwest Texas State University in San Marcos.

Four years later, Spencer graduated with a journalism degree—summa cum laude, president of her class. And then Spencer came to the second marker: Even with her accomplishments, she couldn't find a job. So she applied to graduate school, won another scholarship, and slapped another coat of polish on her résumé.

When she left graduate school in 1993, she convinced a local golf school to let her run their public relations department. "As soon as I could get them to give me that job, I was going to the top. I was ready." She was two months pregnant when she took the job, which didn't much faze either her or her employer. Fed a steady diet of women's magazines and commercials telling her she could "bring home the bacon, fry it up in the pan, and never, ever let him forget he's a man," Spencer felt invincible. "I was a career girl," she told me, "not a stay-at-home mom. I was going to go back to work. I worked up until the day before my daughter was born."

Then she arrived at marker number three. "As soon as McKenna was born, my world just turned completely around," Spencer said. From the moment she held her daughter, "there was no way I could envision myself leaving her ten hours a day, every day. It was such a surprise to me." Leaving her family behind—again, something Peter Drucker tells us is a very recent practice—didn't seem right. Yet after six weeks of paid leave, she returned to her job.

"I put my daughter in day care and I cried. The day care workers and everyone knew I was crying my eyes out. I cried the whole way to work, got to work, and cried at work. It was just awful."

So having at last found a job she wanted, she quit. She went freelance—doing any kind of public relations, desktop publishing, news release writing, and brochure design work she could land. Spencer made decent money, but after six months, "it was starting to get really challenging, working at home and having a baby." She looked for support groups, but couldn't find any. So she sent a letter to the editor of an Austin family newspaper asking if any other work-at-home parents wanted to start such a group. Spencer got two dozen responses—and had the seedlings of a national organization.

Today her group, Home-Based Working Moms, is a coast-to-coast association with a paid membership of more than one thousand people. Members get regular newsletters, help in marketing their microbusinesses, a listing on the HBWM Web site, discounts on goods and services, and a ready-made support network similar to the F.A.N. Clubs I described in Chapter 7. HBWM is like an old boys' network—except that its free agent members aren't boys and aren't old. And unlike the paid maternity leave her former employer granted her, or the unpaid family leave mandated by law, Spencer's solution—for herself and for her members—doesn't promote balance. It promotes blending—an imperfect, though often easier and more natural strategy for working parents. Home-based women-owned businesses in the U.S. already number six million and provide full-or part-time employment for an estimated 19 million people. And groups like HBWM that support these mamapreneurs have sprouted in the last several years: the National Association of Entrepreneurial Parents, the Women Entrepreneurs Network, Work at Home Moms, and many others.

These groups are often far more effective than the supposedly family-friendly policies of corporations or government. "One of the things that makes our members comfortable," says Spencer, "is that we don't have to hide the fact that we have kids. So if we carry on business and they hear my kids in the background or they come over and the kids are running around, it's what we're used to." While organizations like HBWM encourage blending, they don't prescribe precisely the one right way to do it. They offer a recipe book—but let people discover the right mix for their own lives.

"When I graduated from high school," Spencer told me, "I thought I was headed to be a supermom—the vision you see of the woman in the suit, running to the grocery store with kids around her legs—rush, rush, rush, climbing her way to the top of the career ladder. That's what I envisioned for myself. It sounded glamorous. But now that I'm at home doing it this route, and seeing so many more people interested in going this route, I really think that today's mom is a home-based mom, trying to run her own business. We'll go the direction we want to go at the pace we want to go."

SAY YOU WANT AN EVOLUTION

René Shimada Siegel, who lives and works in Pleasanton, California, running HighTech Connect, one of the matchmakers I mentioned in the previous chapter, says she grew up in what sociologist Nippert-Eng would have dubbed a segmentor household. Her father worked for a government research facility in Albuquerque, but she didn't know much else about his work. "I really didn't hear much about it," she told me over lunch in the aptly named pleasant town where she lives. "I didn't have a sense of what my dad did, what was his livelihood. What did he get passionate about every day when he got in the car? I had no clue." She visited his office only once a year—on Family Day. "They'd put the secure stuff away and open the doors and have popcorn. That was it."

For six years, her own two children saw her at work every day—in a back bedroom above the family garage. (Siegel's microbusiness recently outgrew her home office and she had to rent commercial space.) The office door was usually closed, but never locked. "My son got to see me and hear me during the day and late at night. I think he got an appreciation for what work means to our family."

Free agent kids sometimes don't know that offices can be somewhere besides the third floor. Free agent kids see their parents work. Free agent kids help their parents work. And maybe that's as it should be. "The reunion of work and home," says author Tom Petzinger, "is only a symptom of a much larger condition: the natural affinity of business and family."[13]

Nigel Nicholson, dean of research at the London Business School and a leader in the movement to use evolutionary psychology to understand business, believes that what pushes us to integrate is evolution itself. He says this deep urge explains "the persistent strength of small to midsize family businesses throughout history," and why such enterprises "remain the predominant model the world over, accounting for approximately 60 percent of all employment."[14] The legendary Harvard zoologist E. O. Wilson told the *Wall Street Journal* that he considered this reintegration of work and family "one of the most heartening and healthful trends ever in social evolution and cultural evolution." He makes the same point as Nicholson, namely that blenders are "returning us back to the hunter-gatherer band in a sense—the group that each of us lives with physically a great deal of the time. It is more like how the human species evolved. You can interweave your family and your contacts with business all through the day."[15]

We humans, it seems, are born to blend.

CHAPTER 11

THE CRUX: The industrial economy separated work and family. The free agent economy is rejoining them. Instead of *balancing* work and family—trading them off against each other—free agents are *blending* work and family. This is one reason why both family-friendly corporate policies and government-mandated family leave, though well intentioned, have fallen short. They force people to balance instead of helping them blend and impose One Size Fits All solutions on a My Size Fits Me workforce. In response, free agents are taking matters into their own hands and are returning us to work arrangements perhaps more consonant with human nature and our evolutionary heritage.

THE FACTOID: Small to midsize family businesses account for about 60 percent of all the employment in the world.

THE QUOTE: "Again, free agent couplehood is nothing new. Before the industrial economy, spouses often worked together. Just as those small shopkeepers lived above the store, my family— with Dad's third-floor office—lives below the store. And thanks to the Internet, Mom and Pop's operation doesn't have to be a mom-and-pop operation."

THE WORD: *Commuter marriages.* Couples with children and traditional jobs, whose lives seem to revolve entirely around the morning struggle to get to work, day care, and school— and the evening battle to return home and begin the process again the following day. (Antonym: *DINJ couples*—double income, no jobs)

PART FOUR

Free Agent Woes

12

Roadblocks on Free Agent Avenue: Health Insurance, Taxes, and Zoning

"It's not bad coverage—it will cover me if I ever get run over by a bus."

—*Jeff Feldman (Minneapolis, Minnesota),*
on his self-financed health insurance

It's a gloomy June afternoon, and I'm alone in a place I heard about repeatedly during my television-saturated childhood: beautiful downtown Burbank. What led me to this 100,000-person city in California's San Fernando Valley—past the fish fountains, to the steps of City Hall—was a rumor I'd heard that Burbank puts free agents in jail.

I swing through the doors of the art deco building, and climb to the second-floor clerk's office, where I take my place in line behind two construction workers seeking a building permit and a man dressed like Don Johnson, circa 1984, hoping to open a restaurant.

"Hi," I say more amiably than usual because I'm about to bend the truth. "I'm a writer. I'm considering moving to Burbank. What do I need to do in order to work out of my home?"

The clerk, who resembles a rumpled college dean more than a small-city bureaucrat, reaches for a shelf, and then sets three documents on the counter: a "City Information Guide"; a two-page excerpt of Section 31 of the Burbank Municipal Code; and a form called a "Home Occupation Application."

After fifteen minutes of probing, here's the gist of what he tells me: If I want to write from a home office in Burbank, I first must apply for a home occupation license. The city would examine my application, and then come to my house to inspect the office from which I intended to work. Once the inspector deemed my home office safe for writing and unthreatening to my neighbors, I could begin earning a living, my workspace now officially blessed by the city.

But that was only the beginning. I'd have to pay a special tax. And I'd have to abide by the strictures of Burbank Municipal Code Section 31-672—which, among other things, said: My office couldn't be larger than four hundred square feet or 20 percent of my home's square footage. I couldn't put my home office in a "garage, carport, or any other area required or designated for the parking of vehicles." The only "materials, equipment, and/or tools" I could use to do my work were things used by "a normal household." I couldn't use my home office to repair cars, sell guns, or operate a kennel. And the only folks who could ever work with me in the office were people who lived with me.

That last provision alarmed me.

Pointing to Section 31-672(c), I ask, "Does this mean I can't have a meeting at my house?"

"Yep," says the clerk. "You'd have to go somewhere else."

"Let me get this straight," I say. "Let's say I'm a writer collaborating on a screenplay. If my collaborator comes over and we work on the screenplay together, that's against the law? It's a misdemeanor to have a meeting at your house?"

"Yep," says the clerk.

"Isn't California a 'three strikes and you're out' state?"

"Yep."

Burbank, we have a problem. I hope it's unlikely that a free agent who has three meetings at her house, and gets caught, prosecuted, and convicted each time, goes to jail for the rest of her life. But the mere possibility reflects a wider problem with America's legal, policy, and tax regimes. They were built for a work world that has largely disappeared, and are ill equipped for the new world that has arrived in its stead.

For example, our employment laws presume that most workers have a long-standing, enduring, permanent, stable relationship with a single employer. That means that independent professionals can't unionize; only "employees" can, and only certain ones at that. It means that independent professionals aren't covered by antidiscrimination laws; only (certain) "employees" are. And it means that micropreneurs don't get unemployment insurance; only (certain) employees get help when they're out of work. Meanwhile, our government often presumes that an "employer" is somebody with a large operation and a stableful of help, so it enlists employers to do much of its own work—collecting taxes, distributing health and retirement benefits, and so on. Now, most of these laws worked reasonably well in an economy that had clear borders between employers and employees—and where stability was the norm and churn a strange exception. But applying these laws in a free agent economy is like requiring someone to wear shoes three sizes too small. The ill-fitting footwear often forces some odd and unexpected dance steps. While Part III of this book describes how and why Free Agent Nation works, this chapter and the next discuss what *doesn't* work. In law and policy, what doesn't work is most glaring in three areas—health insurance, taxes, and, as Burbank demonstrates, zoning.

HEALTH SCARE

You couldn't tell by looking at her, but our younger daughter, Eliza, is a COBRA baby. She was conceived and brought into this world by parents who had their eyes on the intricacies of federal health insurance law. When my wife left her job, almost a year after I left mine, we gave up that staple of Organization Man life—employer-provided health insurance. Say what you will about wage slavery thwarting self-actualization, we had a damn good health insurance plan. For example, the total medical costs of our first pregnancy and childbirth topped $10,000—but because of our outstanding coverage, we paid nothing beyond our modest monthly premiums. When we left behind our employers, we left behind their health insurance. But thanks to a law called the Consolidated Omnibus Budget Reconciliation Act of 1985—COBRA—we had the option of hanging on to my wife's health insurance for an additional eighteen months, if we paid the full bill ourselves. After those eighteen months, we'd be on our own. So we knew that if we wanted a second child, the clock—and not just the biological one—was ticking.

I'll spare you the details of precisely what happened next. Let's just say that within that eighteen-month window appeared Eliza Lerner Pink, beloved by her parents, worshipped by her grandparents, and inspired by a little known federal statute.

I'm sure we're not the first parents to plan a family around our health insurance coverage. And I suspect Eliza is not the only COBRA baby toddling around the playground. But what makes this obstetrical tale rich with irony is that, while our daughter was planned, the health insurance system behind that planning was an accident.

If you have a job and get your health insurance through your employer, be thankful. It was never supposed to be this way. During World War II, when prices began soaring, President Roosevelt imposed a wage freeze to check inflation. Since employers couldn't lure new workers with more money, they had to offer some other sweetener—and the substitute they settled on was health insurance. This scenario, health insurance attached to a job, could have remained a clever response to a momentary crisis. But a powerful force intervened: the tax code. Employers received a tax deduction for paying health insurance premiums, and workers were spared income tax on this new fringe benefit—so the temporary arrangement hardened into a permanent fixture of American life.

Were it not for this odd lineup of circumstances, Americans would likely get their health care coverage some other way. No deep moral or economic logic underpins employer-based health insurance. In fact, the U.S. is the only country in the world that so tightly links health care to employment. And it's one reason why, despite our prosperity, the U.S. record on health care coverage is so sickly—especially for soloists, temps, and micropreneurs.

Nearly 43 million Americans lack health insurance, and 60 percent of these uninsured are self-employed or work for small firms.[1] About one in three self-employed workers is uninsured. In places such as Los Angeles, with large numbers of immigrant micropreneurs, the portion reaches 40 percent.[2] And microbusinesses that manage to get insurance often pay three or four times the rates of comparable group insurance for their larger counterparts.

America's health insurance system is seriously and intrinsically flawed. It traps people who'd like to become independent in jobs they don't want because leaving that job would mean losing its medical coverage. It makes the lives of those who are free agents even more precarious, because they have few options and limited bargaining power in the health insurance marketplace. It imposes heavy costs on organizations and requires them to slog through a morass of laws and regulations in order to provide what many people consider a natural right of employment. And it forces families to make sometimes life-and-death medical decisions based on the rules and regulations of a system that emerged by accident and that is out of sync with today's workplace. No wonder that in surveys for the 2000 presidential elections, 72 percent of women said they wanted their "health insurance to be independent of their employment," according to the *New York Times*. "This was not even one of the issues the pollsters had intended to ask about, but it came up repeatedly in the focus groups that preceded the polling."[3]

Dispensing health insurance through an organization makes little sense when our attachments to organizations are weak and often fleeting—and it makes no sense at all for those who simply don't have employers. First came the backlash against HMOs. The next backlash may be against providing health insurance through employers. In Chapter 18, on the future of free agent politics, I'll explore some possible solutions to this health insurance crisis.

1 + 1 = 1099

Remember your first paycheck? You thought twenty hours of bagging groceries at $3 an hour meant you'd earned sixty bucks. But when you tore open your pay envelope, and lowered your eyes down all those rows to the check's bottom line, you discovered you'd really earned only $39.14. Bummer. Then somehow you got used to it. We all did. We stopped looking at the entries that said "FICA" or "State" or whatever—and instead zoomed immediately to the figure at the bottom, taking as a given that you never really got everything you earned.

It wasn't always thus. The Sixteenth Amendment to the Constitution, which permits Congress to levy income taxes, didn't come along until 1913. And for the next three decades, Americans paid their income taxes by writing a check to the U.S. Treasury. But as with employer-provided health insurance, the crisis atmosphere surrounding World War II changed the way America did things and cemented in place a practice begun as a temporary measure.

The person we have to thank for this change in how the government collects taxes was a "pipe-puffing executive at R. H. Macy & Co. named Beardsley Ruml."[4] (And the person I have to thank for discovering Ruml is Amity Shlaes, whose book *The Greedy Hand* engagingly recounts his story.) In 1942, with Pearl Harbor in the background, and the need for revenue compelling, Congress hiked income taxes and increased the number of Americans who had to pay them. The trouble was, the people newly subject to income taxes typically weren't setting aside enough money to pay their taxes—which meant that at year's end, millions of Americans were going to become tax scofflaws and the Treasury's take was going to be less than it needed.

That's where it helped to have a department store executive like Ruml serving on the Federal Reserve Bank of New York's board of directors. As Shlaes tells it, "At Macy's, he had observed that customers didn't like big bills. They preferred making payments bit by bit, in the installment plan, even if they had to pay for the pleasure with interest."[5] So Ruml applied this principle of consumer psychology to the business of tax collection—and devised a scheme in which employers would subtract a small amount from every employee paycheck and send the money to the government. After the initial surprise on the first paycheck, Ruml predicted, taxpayers wouldn't notice. And to get things moving, Ruml suggested offering amnesty to anyone who didn't pay taxes the previous year but who agreed to this new arrangement. With the carrot of amnesty, the invisible stick of withholding, and the implicit message that this was a provisional step needed to defeat Hitler, Ruml changed our lives. We now consider it perfectly normal to take home less than we take in.

Now, withholding isn't a bad system. It's remarkably efficient. It guarantees wide compliance. And it keeps a steady stream of money pumping into government coffers. But withholding's days may be numbered—and so might be the quiescent tax-paying population it helped engender. The reason is simple: Most free agents write checks.

Think of a typical free agent—say, an unincorporated solo illustrator who works from her home. After each assignment, if all goes well, her client sends her a check. But the client doesn't withhold taxes. The client just mails the full amount due. Our free agent illustrator, though, still must pay her federal taxes. So each quarter, she estimates how much she owes, writes a check for that amount, completes a short form, and sends the money to the IRS. And if she's in a state with an income tax, she usually must do the same thing for her state taxes: estimate, write a check, and mail it to the state capital. Instead of someone else withholding her taxes, she receives all the money she's owed—and then hands over a portion of it to the taxing authority. (And woe onto those who try to conceal their earnings. At the beginning of the following year, all her clients send her a Form 1099 revealing to her and to the IRS how much she earned from that client during the previous year.)

This arrangement establishes a very different relationship with taxes than that of a typical wage earner. Since the state estimated taxes and federal estimated taxes are often due on different days, the self-employed free agent often must prepare eight separate tax filings per year. That's an administrative irritation. But more important, it re-creates that first-paycheck tax jolt an average of once every six weeks. Writing a check made payable to the "United States Treasury" or the "Pennsylvania Department of Revenue" doesn't directly change how much a free agent owes. But it has what may be an even more potent impact: It changes the entire *psychology* of taxation. For free agents, unlike most traditional employees, taxes are like they were before Ruml's brilliant scheme. They are *visible*.

And what free agents see often isn't pretty. The tax code is tilted against most independent workers in three significant ways.

First, there's double taxation. Go back to that paycheck for bagging groceries. One reason your bottom line was smaller than your top line is that your employer subtracted 7.65 percent of your wages and gave it to Social Security. Your grocery employer also sent another 7.65 percent of its own funds to Social Security—supposedly to save for your old age, but really to make sure your granddad gets his check next month. The employee chips in half; the employer chips in half. That's how we finance one of the grand bargains of American life.

But think about that free agent illustrator. She's her own *employee*—so she contributes that portion of Social Security taxes. But she's also her own *employer*—so she contributes that share as well. Instead of losing 7.65 percent like the grocery store bagger, she's out twice that amount—15.3 percent. Of course, some economists would say that the traditional employee loses the same amount. If the employer is coughing up 7.65 percent of its own funds for Social Security, that's money that's not going to the employee in the form of higher wages. Alas, while that may be true in theory, there's no evidence that it's true in practice. And this theoretical justification doesn't do much to balm a free agent hit with a 15.3 percent *payroll* tax before *income* taxes even kick in.

The second float in the parade of visible free agent tax horrors is our old nemesis, health insurance. If the grocery store paid the bagger's health insurance premiums, the grocery store would be able to deduct those premiums as a business expense. Fair enough. But if our illustrator is unincorporated and self-employed, and she pays her own health insurance premiums, she *can't* deduct the full amount. There's no defensible reason for this—except that free agents don't yet have an effective political lobby. And something is better than nothing. As recently as 1992, health insurance premiums for the self-employed weren't deductible at all. But under current law, free agent health insurance premiums won't be fully deductible until 2003. As a result, people like me have had to contemplate strange legal gymnastics— such as incorporating, hiring one's spouse, and providing fully paid family health insurance to this "employee"—and then deducting the full premium as a business expense.

Along with double taxation and health insurance deductions comes the third problem: the sheer brain-melting complexity of the tax code. When you're a free agent, you're not just your own boss. You're your own accountant. That's no fun, which is why since 1980 the number of people who've hired somebody else to prepare their returns has climbed 44 percent.[6] Tax complexity, according to a Stanford economist, costs more than $100 billion in compliance, another $100 billion in tax evasion, and yet another $100 billion in "distortions from pursuing tax-advantaged investments." In all, the costs of the federal income tax are "larger than the Defense Department, larger than Social Security, perhaps as large as the combined budgets of the fifty states."[7] Val Oveson, the IRS's national taxpayer advocate, said in his first report to Congress in 1999 that complex tax laws were "the most serious and burdensome problem facing taxpayers."[8] And free agents suffer more than most. Simply trying to do the right thing can be a nightmare. Every dollar you spend is both a potential tax deduction and a potential audit trigger for the IRS. Says one tax lawyer, "If you're self-employed, odds are that you're going to be audited at least once during your taxpaying life."[9]

In short, becoming a free agent means entering a sort of tax hell: You're hit with double taxation. You're not permitted to deduct much of your already towering health insurance premiums. You're forced to navigate a thick and complex tax code—with each decision potentially making you audit bait. And you're reminded of these happy facts as often as eight times a year.

But things could be worse. You could be a free agent in New Jersey.

TWILIGHT ZONING

Neptune, New Jersey, is far from Burbank in both geography and attitude. While few people in the laid-back San Fernando Valley seem especially steamed about draconian zoning ordinances, in Neptune I met a man who'd made reforming these misguided laws his cause.

His name is Chris Hansen, a former Sears manager and door-to-door typewriter ribbon salesman who now runs Advanced Copier and Data Supply, a modest computer supply business on West Sylvania Avenue. Like many entrepreneurs across the country, Hansen began his business from his home. And like many entrepreneurs in New Jersey, Hansen was breaking the law. Even though New Jersey has some 600,000 citizens who work at home, home-based free agents and microbusinesses are illegal in all but a few of the state's 566 municipalities. Some local ordinances impose fines of up to $1,000 a day and ninety days in jail on homeworkers. As a result, many free agents are forced to hide—as Hansen did for many years, unable to join the local chamber of commerce or speak up at town meetings. And that got him mad.

In 1996 he started the Home Based Business Council, so that free agents could come out of hiding. A glib autodidact who says he reads two books a week and enters highlighted passages in a computer database that now has more than ten thousand entries, Hansen says his goal was "to set a new order of things based on the postindustrial age." With little more than a fax machine from which he sends out 150 press releases a week, and a booming voice from which he cites authorities from Arnold Toynbee to Milton Friedman, he nearly succeeded.

Hansen tried to convince the rest of the state that it didn't matter what people did in their own homes—as long as it didn't bother anybody else. "If you can't tell what somebody's doing in their home," he told me in the back room of his store amid boxes of computer supplies, "they should be allowed to do it. Period."

He took his concerns to the New Jersey state legislature. Legislators said to him: "There are a half-million people or more working at home in New Jersey? And it's illegal? We have to fix this." So he helped the lawmakers craft a bill to make home-based businesses legal. But each time legislators pushed the measure, they met with opposition from municipalities, who thought it undercut their power, and from the state bar association, whose members made money helping citizens secure zoning variances. Hansen's bill passed the State Assembly twice, but twice died in the State Senate, most recently in the final days of 1999. The week of that vote, one free agent graphic artist who worked from her home in Wall Township handed out flyers near the State Capitol in Trenton that read, "My name is Kathy Laird and I am a criminal." She listed her crime as "Working at home so I can raise my children."[10]

Zoning, like so much else I've described in this book, is a twentieth-century invention—mostly unknown before and generally not regarded as a legitimate exercise of government authority until a 1926 U.S. Supreme Court decision established its constitutional validity. And at a certain moment in history, it made terrific sense. Some areas would be residential, other areas industrial, and still others commercial. Nothing inherently wrongheaded about that. Most people don't want to raise their kids next to a gigantic smelter. But that same sort of zoning is harder to effectuate—and wreaks much greater havoc—when the border between the personal and the vocational has muddied. Many local laws that aim to maintain a sacrosanct boundary between commerce and community have outlived their usefulness.

"If I'm a professional bugle-blower and you do it for fun, neither one of us should be able to do it out on the street at 3:00 A.M.," Hansen told me. "If this disturbs the neighborhood in any way, the town has the power to set those standards." Otherwise, they ought to butt out. In Los Angeles, a town where it seems half of the population is home-based screenwriters, the city fathers recently tried to require writers and artists working at home to pay $25 for a city permit. The Writers Guild compared this plan to the practices of communist regimes that kept their creative types on a short leash, and lobbied successfully to block the regulation.

In the free agents struggling to break free from these confining laws, Chris Hansen sees both deep meaning and a new movement. "I believe that God made everyone unique for their own unique purpose," he told me after explaining how he had converted to Catholicism upon marrying his wife. "And in this society, we now have the first chance ever for people to realize their own individual uniqueness." But if that chance is thwarted, he says, people may push back harder than ever before—and that has the potential "to create another political party à la Ross Perot." Adds Hansen, "People are saying in this country, my freedom of choice is number one. Nobody is going to dictate to me."

THE BOX

CHAPTER 12

THE CRUX: The United States operates under a thicket of laws designed for a time when most people held full-time, lifelong jobs with a single employer—and free agency was an exotic choice. These laws have outlived their usefulness, and are hampering the economy most in three areas: health insurance, taxes, and zoning. Employer-based health insurance no longer makes sense because fewer of us have employers. This system, which began as a historical accident, is grounded in little economic or moral logic. And it is forcing many independent workers to go without insurance while locking other workers into jobs they don't want because leaving would mean losing their coverage. Meanwhile, the U.S. tax code punishes free agents by making them pay twice the Social Security payroll taxes of other workers, preventing them from fully deducting their health insurance premiums, and costing them time, money, and aggravation because of the sheer brain-melting complexity of the tax law. Finally, local zoning laws presume a clear boundary between work and home, and many impose severe restrictions—including outright prohibition—on home-based micropreneurs.

THE FACTOID: Tax complexity, according to a Stanford economist, costs more than $100 billion in compliance, another $100 billion in tax evasion, and yet another $100 billion in "distortions from pursuing tax-advantaged investments." In all, the costs of the federal income tax are "larger than the Defense Department, larger than Social Security, perhaps as large as the combined budgets of the fifty states."

THE QUOTE: "If you have a job and get your health insurance through your employer, be thankful. It was never supposed to be this way."

THE BOX

Chapter 12 (continued)

THE WORD: *COBRA baby.* A child conceived and born within the eighteen- month period during which employers are required to continue offering health insurance to departed employees, if the employees pay the full bill themselves. Common reproductive practice of free agents.

13

Temp Slaves, Permatemps, and the Rise of Self-Organized Labor

"If it's something we're going to have to live with, then let's have some say in how workers are treated."
—Christine Macias (San Jose, California), on low-paid temps in Silicon Valley

Free agency sucks. That's what many people believe. And for some independent workers, this harsh assessment is an ugly reality. For them, the new landscape of work is hardly the field of dreams others have described in this book. These workers live lives in which freedom and independence flip quickly into anxiety and insecurity. Some discover that they lack the skills, the savvy, and the desire to make it on their own—and like it or not, they're better off inside the corporate cocoon. Others who work as low-paid temps are sometimes treated despicably and considered by their employers barely more human than the office copy machine. Meanwhile, a few unscrupulous employers dangle the promise of "permanent" employment—and its health insurance benefits and stock options—in front of temps for years but never allow them to move from the back of the workplace bus.

As I've made clear so far, I believe free agency is a mostly positive development in American life. But I believe with equal force that free agency is not a *uniformly* positive development. Not everybody in the independent workforce enjoys the freedom, authenticity, accountability, and self-defined success of the free agent work ethic. For those left out, free agency is a bane and Free Agent Nation is a nasty, brutish land. In this chapter, I'll look at what can go wrong with independent work—and how a new labor movement is emerging to make it right.

TEMP SLAVES

Temps, recall from Chapter 2, account for only about 10 percent of the free agent workforce. And within the temp population are two very different varieties of workers. There are high-end temps like the temporary CFOs I discussed in Chapter 10. And there are low-end temps who do boring work for meager pay sometimes in grim conditions. This second variety, the most glaring example of how some workers can suffer under free agency, is what Jeff Kelly of Madison, Wisconsin, calls "temp slaves."

These temps, he says, live on a "never-ending treadmill of low pay, no benefits, no security and no respect." In Kelly's view, the temp worker is nothing but "a body to be sacrificed to the whims and wishes of a corporate mentality gone berserk."[1] Kelly speaks from experience. He worked as an office temp at a Wisconsin insurance firm for an entire year, waiting for a promised full-time job to materialize. It never did. When he got his two weeks' notice that his services were no longer needed, Kelly used the company photocopy machine to produce what became a stunningly successful self-published magazine—or 'zine—called *Temp Slave!*, which gave a name and a voice to disposable workers like himself.

Temp slaves, as the name suggests, are not planning their ascent of Maslow's hierarchy of needs or holding touchy-feely F.A.N. Club meetings to discuss the deeper meaning of *Jerry Maguire*. Far from it. They are among the most disgruntled workers in the U.S. labor force. And they have two main gripes, both of them largely justified.

The Pay Stinks, the Income Is Uncertain, and the Benefits Are Nonexistent

According to AFL-CIO economist Helene Jorgenson, temporary workers aged twenty to thirty-four earn about 16 percent less than traditional employees doing the same work.[2] While other types of free agents—micropreneurs and high-level freelancers—fare quite well in the talent market, temp slaves lack the skills and the leverage to earn more than a pittance. Being a temp slave also generally means going without certain features of employment that salaried workers take for granted. Fifty-five percent of temps, for instance, don't have health insurance.[3] Where employees' companies often match their contributions to retirement plans, most temps have no pensions at all. And if temps don't work, they don't get paid. These low-paid workers suffer most from the irregular incomes that accompany free agency. One twenty-six-year-old man who temped for a variety of companies in New Jersey during the late 1990s (but who asked that I not use his name) told me: "It pays better than working at the mall. It pays better than flipping burgers. But there is a downside. I have no resources to fill in income gaps between assignments."

Most temp slaves harbor intense animus toward their temp agencies, which are their nominal employers and which issue their checks. One reason for the resentment: Temp agencies typically charge a 30 percent markup on workers they place at companies. Suppose Widget World needs a receptionist for a week and goes to Body Shoppers Staffing Agency for a temp. If Body Shoppers finds Sally for the job, it charges Widget World $10 an hour for Sally's services—but pays Sally only $7 per hour. Since Sally doesn't have the bargaining power or connections to find the job on her own, that $3 an hour premium goes into the agency's pocket, not hers. Some temp slaves also claim that this agency relationship prevents them from moving into so-called permanent jobs—because if Widget World hires Sally to a full-time job, it usually must pay Body Shoppers a sizeable portion (around 25 percent) of Sally's first-year salary. So Sally remains a temp, earns less than she is worth, and signals to the permanent employees how easily a temp slave could replace them. In these arrangements, University of Nevada–Las Vegas professor Robert E. Parker sees sinister forces afoot. In *Flesh Peddlers and Warm Bodies*, his critical look at the temporary help industry, he argues that temporary workers "can be a highly sophisticated instrument for employers, part of an overall staffing strategy that facilitates management's control over the labor process and maximizes the potential output of every hour of paid labor."[4]

Temp Slavery Is Boring, Demeaning, and Stigmatizing

The second temp slave complaint is more about meaning than money. Anybody who's been a low-paid temp knows that the work can be mind-numbing—jobs that one former temp called "brain stealers." Some temps sit in windowless rooms in total silence proofreading bank statements. Other temps spend days and weeks relabeling file folders—or making sure the lids on ice cream containers are secured tightly. One study of low-paid temporary industrial workers found that, "In general, temporary workers were assigned the least complex, most repetitious and dispensable jobs on the assembly line."[5] This is not self-actualizing work. This is drudgery.

Temp slaves also frequently report being treated as somehow less than human because of their status in the workplace. Sometimes temps are shunted into dangerous jobs, because companies don't want permanent employees to risk injury and thus jack up worker compensation costs. But most of the mistreatment is less direct. In *Temp Slave!*, one office temp describes the indignity of being forced to wear around his neck all day a large badge that proclaimed "TEMPORARY." Another says, "They know I'm 'The Temp,' so conversations with me are, in a way, forbidden." In his classic 1959 book, *The Presentation of Self in Everyday Life*, sociologist Erving Goffman described what he called the "non-person." These are people "who are sometimes treated in their presence as if they were not there"—children, the elderly, servants, waiters.[6] In the worst workplaces, temp slaves too become non-persons, which doesn't exactly promote the authenticity and self-expression free agents seek.

These gripes—little money and less meaning—have produced two responses among temp slaves. One is predictable, the other more curious. The first response is that the vast majority of temp slaves say they want regular boring jobs with health insurance. Survey data show that most temporary clerical workers—the largest category of temp workers—would prefer a full-time, "permanent" job.[7] The same is true for most low-paid temps in other fields. No surprise there. Nobody in her right mind would relish working with zero autonomy for paltry wages in unpleasant conditions. For this group of workers, the types of unsatisfying jobs many soloists and micropreneurs have fled represent a step *up* the employment food chain.

The second response is more intriguing. Temp slavery has spawned a thriving, often underground, network of 'zines, Web sites, and popular culture expressions of discontent. This is where temp slaves—deprived of the opportunity to express their creativity on the job—let the world know who they really are. Elsewhere in this book, I've tried to show that new ways of working are yielding a new vocabulary of work. Here are some more terms, all with a decidedly less positive bent—courtesy of Temp 24-7, a Web site for disgruntled temps:

- *Floaters*. Vagrant temps who travel endlessly and fruitlessly from one empty desk to another, "covering" for employees who are out of the office.

- *Solitaire confinement*. A lonely assignment in which the temp works alone with only a minimal workload to cope with, prompting marathon sessions of solitaire to fill up the time.

- *Tempons*. Disposable temps inserted into an office to absorb an excess of work, to be casually discarded when finished.

In addition, other *Temp Slave!* style publications have sprung up—'zines with names like *McJob, working for the man, Contingency Crier*, and *Guinea Pig Zero*.[8] Fox Animation has commissioned a feature film called *Guy Futomaki: Ninja Temp*, about "an undercover ninja who works as a temp at an office in order to expose the demon that lives inside the CEO's body." This follows the modest success of movies like 1993's *The Temp* (in which a nutcase secretarial temp tries to climb the corporate ladder by killing off employees) and 1997's *Clockwatchers* (in which four temps scheme against permanent employees who treat them like non-persons). Indeed, temp slavery has produced a rich literature of sabotage and revenge. Consider a worker known by the pseudonym "Temp X" and his widely published "10 Tenets of Temping." Among them: "Work as slowly as possible. This establishes a norm, allowing you to set the pace, not them," and "Pilfer as much as possible—look for new ways to create your own business. Suggestions: office supplies, photocopying, faxing."

In some ways, though, the situation is not as widespread as it seems. As economist Anne Polivka has found, "While some [temporary] workers are involuntarily in such arrangements, as a proportion of the employed, they are relatively few."[9] Some temps are transitional temps, trying to figure out what to do next. Others are "means to an end" temps—artists, actors, or musicians who are temping to finance their true passions. They may not love their work, but they're doing it for purposes other than the work itself. *But the crucial point is this: Most free agents aren't temps— and most temps aren't temp slaves.* This is where some of the fiercest critics of free agency—Richard Sennett in *The Corrosion of Character*, Jeremy Rifkin in *The End of Work*, Naomi Klein in *No Logo*, Jedediah Purdy in *For Common Things*, and Thomas Frank in *One Market Under God*—run aground. They equate suffering temp slaves with all free agents and thus decry the entire new world of work—when, in fact, those temps are a small minority of the population and when most free agents are surprisingly satisfied with their work and lives. These critics are like a doctor who prescribes euthanasia for an otherwise healthy patient with a broken ankle. The solution is to fix the ankle, not to deem the whole body in mortal danger.

Moreover, as unpleasant as temp slavery is, it masks a deeper problem. Cashiers at McDonald's hold traditional, W-2 jobs. But it's hard to argue that they're significantly better off than these temporary workers. Temp slaves are suffering less because they're temps than because they lack the skills and the bargaining power to get a fair deal in the workplace. Here's the reality: The source of inequality in work today is not between who's an employee and who's a free agent—but between who has skills that are in demand and who doesn't, between who can exercise bargaining power in the new talent market and who cannot. That's the central problem—and as we'll see later in this chapter, the one that a reinvigorated labor movement seems poised to address.

PERMATEMPS

One additional variety of suffering temps—workers who have garnered a fair bit of press coverage in recent years—are permatemps. Permatemps are individuals who work full-time for a company, sometimes for years, doing the same work as employees—but who are hired through a temp agency so that the company where the work is done can avoid providing benefits such as health insurance, pensions, and stock options.

The most famous of these permatemps worked at a little company called Microsoft. Many of them worked right beside full-time Microsofties testing the same products, designing the same user interfaces, and editing the same online publications. But their legal employer was the staffing agency through which they worked—not Microsoft—and that created a bizarre workplace caste system. "Real" employees wore blue badges. Permatemps wore orange badges. The orange-badged couldn't use the company gym, attend company parties, play volleyball on certain courts, or work in an office with windows. As *Fast Company*'s Ron Lieber elaborates, "On the Microsoft email system, an

'A' is printed before the name of temps who are assigned through local staffing agencies—a designation that temps say makes their email opinions easier to dismiss. There's more: Temps can't buy discounted software at the company store. In fact, they can't buy it at all, for any price, even if they wrote the instructions inside of the box."[10]

Richard, who asked that I not use his last name, says he worked six and a half years at Microsoft as a permatemp. "I had been promised a full-time job three times. I did between six and ten contracts," he told me. But the job never came through. Sybil Lundy, whom we met in Chapter 2, began at Microsoft as a $10 an hour software tester hired through a temp agency. She moved on to several new projects, but was continually denied a raise—even though she did increasingly complex work. "I don't expect any kind of job security," she told me in a Seattle coffee shop. "My security is just in keeping my personal confidence up, keeping my skills marketable. I don't have the idea that any corporation's going to take care of me." But she still thought it unfair never to get a raise, and when she brought up the subject with her agency and with Microsoft, each blamed the other.

In 1992, eight permatemps filed a lawsuit against Microsoft, claiming the company had illegally denied them and thousands of others that juicy plum of life in Redmond: stock options. Over the next eight years, this class-action lawsuit, and a companion case, wound their way through the legal system. In the end, federal courts handed the permatemps a victory by declaring that Microsoft had broken the law. In late 2000, the company agreed to pay their former temps a $97 million settlement. And stung by the worker revolt, the courtroom defeat, and the hit to its pocketbook, Microsoft has changed some of its personnel policies—imposing a one-year limit on agency-supplied temporary workers and elevating a few thousand temps to permanent status.

Permatemps, of course, are less sympathetic than temp slaves. Many of them earn decent wages—and get benefits from their temp agency or other sources. One Microsoft temp who's done work for the company off and on for ten years says, "It's always been my choice. I value my freedom. I never wanted an umbilical cord tied to Microsoft. I don't think Microsoft owes me anything beyond what they pay me."[11] And had Microsoft stock not soared—and turned option-holding employees into multimillionaires—one wonders whether the permatemps would have felt so aggrieved.

Nonetheless, workers like these do have a legitimate complaint. They look like employees. They walk like employees. They whine like employees. They're making the sacrifices employees make. But they get none of the advantages—fringe benefits and a modicum of stability—of being an employee. That's true of many free agents, but permatemps don't get the advantages of free agency either. They still must traipse to an office and work for a boss. And they suffer from most of free agency's downsides. Permatemps are neither full-fledged employees nor liberated free agents. They have the worst of both work worlds. That's why some of these permatemps didn't just get mad. They got together.

Self-Organized Labor

Directly across the street from the Seattle coffee shop where I met permatemps Sybil and Richard sit the ramshackle offices of the Washington Technology Alliance. Mike Blain and Marcus Courtney, two former Microsoft temps, launched WashTech in 1998 in response to the permatemps contretemps. WashTech isn't really a labor union, though it's funded in part by one (the Communications Workers of America). It doesn't, for instance, negotiate contracts or bargain on workers' behalf. Yet it isn't really *not* a labor union either. Like traditional unions, it advocates for high-tech workers and depends for its strength on recruiting a large membership. WashTech is a hybrid—one of the new varieties of worker organizations that have appeared in the last decade to address free agency's toughest issues. The American union movement has traditionally been called "organized labor." These new groups are what we might call "self-organized labor."

There's no national labor federation setting broad policy or collecting dues. There are few laws granting them specified legal rights or governing how they can recruit members. But these groups are reviving the American labor movement with some updated approaches to worker woes, four in particular that are worth reviewing.

High-Tech Muckrizing

Mike Blain began his career as a reporter for a few small daily newspapers. Then he went to Microsoft, where he temped for a year writing and editing articles for *Encarta*, the company's best-selling CD-ROM encyclopedia. Today, as a leader of WashTech, he's combined those two work experiences to create a new form of worker advocacy. He and partner Courtney rally workers with e-mail. They operate a thorough and encyclopedic Web site that contains all the information any permatemp might need. And thanks to a sophisticated understanding of media old and new, they've managed to attract enough press attention to make pricey public relations firms spin with envy. I call their approach "high-tech muckrizing." It uses the new tools of e-mail, HTML, and wireless communication to electrify the old-fashioned techniques of muckraking and worker organizing.

An example: Until recently if Microsoft temps wanted to see their job evaluations, the company said they had to go to their temp agency. Microsoft claimed it didn't do that sort of thing, because it wasn't technically their employer. But when Blain and Courtney got wind that Microsoft actually did maintain a database tracking the performance of every temp, they sprayed e-mail to temps letting them know there were indeed personnel files they could view—and they bannered news of the supposedly secret database on the WashTech Web site.

Now WashTech is going after the temp agencies, pressing them to reveal how much they charge Microsoft for each temp—and how much less the worker actually receives. Blain says that the agencies hire whomever Microsoft wants them to hire and exact a hefty premium for merely processing paychecks and cordoning off these workers from Microsoft's official head count. Like the muckrakers of the early twentieth century, Courtney and Blain often use incendiary language to describe their foes—referring to agencies variously as "parasites" and "money launderers."

Yet for all their success raising issues, Blain and Courtney have been less successful building a membership. "The high-tech industry has this kind of maverick, pull-yourself-up-by-your-bootstraps, succeed-on-your-own-merits attitude," Courtney says. And, he admits, a portion of Microsoft temps prefer their short-term, impermanent status. He and Blain are finding it a challenge to slap a union label on a My Size Fits Me workforce. Nonetheless, the mere presence of these muckrizers changes the balance of power between giant corporations and once helpless temps.

Voluntary Codes of Conduct

On the other side of the country, Barrie Peterson is also trying to use information and power on behalf of downtrodden temps. Founder of the New Jersey–based Temporary Workers Alliance, Peterson voices several complaints about the temp industry. But the biggest—and the one he's begun taking on—is this: "You have totally inadequate information flow. It's a bunch of smoke and mirrors." If workers knew more about the agencies that place them, Peterson believes, the temp slave and permatemp problems wouldn't disappear—but they would improve.

So borrowing a page from the campaign against sweatshops, he's trying to persuade agencies that it's in their best interest to become good corporate citizens by policing themselves. He has urged all of New Jersey's temp agencies to sign "24 Principles of Fair Conduct," a voluntary code of good behavior. The principles include promises such as providing health insurance, job training, and other benefits; not basing assignments on race or gender (African-Americans make up 11 percent of the total workforce, but 22 percent of temps); getting rid of bait-and-switch advertising that promises a great assignment and delivers an undesirable one; and not requiring companies to pay an additional fee if they hire a temp as a permanent employee. Nearly three dozen agencies in New Jersey have signed the code. As Peterson told me in his office at Seton Hall Law School in Newark, "What we are doing is providing proper labor market information, so that the right choices can be made."

Worker-Owned Temp Agencies

Amy Dean calls low-paid temps the "shock absorbers of the flexible economy." And as the chief executive officer of the South Bay Labor Council, a coalition of 110 Northern California labor unions, she lives and works in the belly of that flexible beast—Silicon Valley. Shortly after she became the leader of this AFL-CIO operation, she started Working Partnerships USA—a group she hopes will be a voice for the low-paid digital nomads who toil in Silicon Valley. This is no easy task. Organized labor's influence has been shrinking steadily over the last two decades, but Dean is optimistic. "We're going to build the next generation of labor organizations," she told me one sunny April afternoon in San Jose.

Among her solutions to the problem of temp slaves and permatemps is a venture called Solutions @ Work, a temp agency that's owned and run by labor unions. The agency offers temps a minimum salary—$10 per hour—as well as job training and health insurance. And since Solutions is not gunning for an IPO or placating shareholders, any profits it earns go back into the agency in the form of job training or higher pay for the temps.

Union-run temp agencies are a short step from the hiring halls run by the Building Trades, Longshoremen, and other unions that provide skilled laborers a place to find work, and employers a place to find skilled labor. And Dean, considered one of organized labor's rising stars, believes that this strategy will become a hugely important role for labor organizations in a free agent economy. "They will broker supply and demand in the labor market," she says. Think of those corporate yentas from Chapter 10—only these wear the union label.

And the result?

"One of two things is going to happen. We will either control a significant portion of the supply of labor because people are getting paid more coming through us. Or we think our competitors [established temp agencies] will bring up the floor, which is awesome, too." It's the newest medicine in the labor movement's cabinet: the ancient elixir of competition.

Build Brand-New Institutions

Sara Horowitz has a larger vision of labor in the free agent economy. And unlike others we've met, who maintain some affiliation with official organized labor, Horowitz has mostly charted her own course. That's surprising, because of all these labor pioneers, she has perhaps the deepest roots in the trade union movement. Her grandfather was vice president of the International Ladies' Garment Workers' Union. Her father was a labor lawyer. Her husband is a labor lawyer, and so is she. When she graduated from Cornell, she went to work as a union organizer at a nursing home. The only time she's been out of the labor movement was a short stint as a public defender—which, she says, "stands you in good stead for just about anything because you get yelled at all the time." Even there, she was a shop steward.

In 1995, Horowitz founded Working Today—perhaps the most innovative labor group in Free Agent Nation. Horowitz isn't trying to create a labor union. She isn't trying to hold off the changes free agency has brought. Instead, she is forming the sort of institution that she believes can best accommodate the needs of independent workers.

Free agents can join Working Today for $25 per year. Membership entitles them to a variety of benefits—access to group health insurance, volume discounts on office supplies and other products, opportunities for training, information about taxes and other free agent headaches, and soon "a portable benefits fund." that will allow free agents to keep their same health insurance and pension plan even as they move from project to project. So far at least, Working Today's approach has captured the imagination and allegiance of independent workers. The group now has some 93,000 members—and foundations are practically falling over themselves to award nonprofit Working Today more money. And Horowitz herself has won accolades—including a MacArthur fellowship, the much coveted "genius grant."

While Horowitz has not affiliated with the union establishment, and while the traditional labor movement has looked askance at what some consider her infidelity to the cause, she is actually trying to take labor back to its roots. Early last century craftsmen banded together to establish base wages in their industries and to form apprenticeship programs for younger workers. They pooled their money in funds to provide sick leave and pensions. But these mutual aid societies didn't tie the arrangement to an employer, they applied it to the worker—whether, as Horowitz puts it, "they were doing stonework for a skyscraper or laying the foundation for a public library." Such worker organizations, based in part on the craft guilds of the Middle Ages, are already in place in industries where free agency is the norm. The Graphic Artists Guild, for example, sets pricing guidelines, provides legal advice, and maintains standards and ethical practices within the profession. And unions like the Screen Actors Guild enlist members by profession, but operate independently from any particular employer. The guild ethic of mutual aid—allowing workers both to band together and to choose their own path—is what will allow everyone to prosper in the free agent economy, Horowitz says.

How will this emerging labor movement pan out? I found a hint of that answer in an unlikely place.

The AFL-CIO-NBA

On our way to Chicago for some free agent interviews, my family and I stopped in Terre Haute, Indiana, where we checked out the town's two main (and perhaps only) attractions.

The first, on Eighth Street, was the home of Eugene V. Debs, the great American union leader who was arrested and jailed in the bloody Pullman Strike of 1894. Debs helped organize the socialist party in America, and ran as the party's candidate for president five times, including once while in prison. His home is a museum now, full of books and other artifacts from his life. The Debs home isn't exactly Graceland. When we arrived one Sunday afternoon in October, we had to knock on the front door for a good five minutes to rouse the curator from her nap.

Less sleepy is Terre Haute's second tourist spot—a much larger building about a mile away called Larry Bird's Home Court Hotel. The basketball legend went to college at Indiana State University in Terre Haute and now owns the town's largest hotel. Inside the hotel is a restaurant—the Boston Garden—that doubles as a Larry Bird shrine, the walls bedecked with three National Basketball Association MVP trophies, many Bird jerseys, several *Sports Illustrated* covers, and a Buick-sized oil painting of the great one that peers down on the steam tables.

This odd combination—an imprisoned socialist and an NBA superstar—offers a hint of how free agent labor woes might resolve themselves. In the NBA today, teams operate under a salary cap—a limit on the total amount they pay their players. But they can violate that salary ceiling to sign veteran players who might declare free agency (the sports variety) and join another team. That wrinkle in the rule, devised in order to allow the Boston Celtics to re-sign Bird one season, became known as the "Larry Bird exception." The NBA players union has battled hard and endured a lock-out to preserve it.

In basketball, as in many other pro sports, players belong to a labor union. But most also have individual agents. Collective bargaining agreements between the club owners and the players union establish the minimum salary and basic benefits. But then players are free to negotiate individual pay packages above that minimum, often *well* above that minimum, usually represented by an agent. The arrangements are similar in the motion picture and television industries. Every union member is guaranteed a minimum compensation for any project, but members "whose market value might exceed union scale [can] negotiate additional compensation through a personal services contract."[12]

This produces a powerfully appealing result and a model for the free agent labor movement: The most talented can go as high as they want, but the least able or most unlucky don't fall below a certain floor. Such a dual system blocks the low road, but allows workers to travel wherever they want on the high road. It combines the justice of Debs and the liberty of Bird. Only in America—and coming soon perhaps to Free Agent Nation.

THE BOX

THE CRUX: Free agency, of course, has a dark side. Some temp workers do mind-numbing tasks for meager pay in awful conditions. Others perform the same work for the same companies as employees, but are classified as temps and denied health insurance and other benefits. While most of this is deplorable, these beleaguered workers account for only a portion of temps—and temps account for only a portion of free agents. What's more, the source of inequality in work today is not between who's an employee and who's a free agent, but between who has skills that are in demand and who doesn't, between who can exercise bargaining power in the new talent market and who cannot. To take on such challenges, several new worker organizations—a "self-organized labor" movement—have emerged to represent these downtrodden workers. The end result will likely follow the path of professional sports: Independent workers will belong to a labor union to secure a floor, but many will have agents to negotiate more lucrative, personalized agreements above that floor.

THE FACTOID: African-Americans make up 11 percent of the total workforce, but 22 percent of temps.

THE QUOTE: "Temp slaves, as the name suggests, are not planning their ascent of Maslow's hierarchy of needs or holding touchy-feely F.A.N. Club meetings to discuss the deeper meaning of *Jerry Maguire*. Far from it. They are among the most disgruntled workers in the U.S. labor force."

THE WORD: *Permatemp.* Somebody who works alongside a traditional employee, doing the same work, but whose employer classifies him as a temp to avoid providing health insurance, a pension, and stock options. (See also, Temp 24-7 definition of permatemp: "A kinder, gentler . . . euphemism for 'indentured servant.' ")

PART FIVE

The Free Agent Future

14

E-tirement: Free Agency and the New Old Age

Jennifer Kramer, sixty-eight, is tapping her foot impatiently. It's 3:45 on Friday afternoon, and the line at Kinko's stretches out the door. Jen settles in for the wait. She checks her v-mail from her handheld screen phone, and absentmindedly hums one of the Beatles tunes that makes her grandchildren snicker.

When developers built a Kinko's here in 2011, many so-called experts laughed. Computer and copy shops belong on college campuses, they said, not in an old folks' home. But Rocky Cliffs wasn't like those assisted living centers of the late twentieth century. It was a ROPEC—a Residential Office Park and E-tirement Center. And ROPECs were growing like kudzu across America. The latest confirmation: On the cover of its twentieth-anniversary issue, Fast Company magazine declared "ROPEC Nation: Get Ready for America's New Age Spots."

ROPECs were part college dormitory, part condo community, and part corporate campus—with an on-ramp to the free agent infrastructure. And older Americans were flocking to them. Instead of heading for Sun City, as their parents had when they turned sixty-five, this first wave of wrinkled, gray-haired baby boomers (the press now called them "baby bubbes"), were reinventing old age. At places like the Rocky Cliffs ROPEC,

*they worked part-time as free agents, took classes at a nearby
college, and hung out with other people formerly known as
"senior citizens." They lived in housing units that resembled
high-end condominiums. They attended weekly job fairs, where
companies desperate for experienced talent practically begged
people like Jen to accept an assignment. They shopped in mod
boutiques, ate at hip restaurants, and paid for their aroma
therapists with Medicare. The combination of autonomy and
community was appealing to many seniors, especially those
making their first foray into free agency.*

*But ROPECs were creaking with growing pains lately, and the
long line at Kinko's was proof. Maybe, as their generation had
done at every other stage of their lives, these baby boomers
had bent a good thing past its breaking point. "This market
analysis was fun," Jen thinks. "But, my gosh, my mother wasn't
working when she was sixty-eight. I need to relax. It's time to
hop into the RV and hit the highway!"*

In the nineteenth century, people worked until they keeled
over. In the twentieth century, people worked until they retired.
In the twenty-first century, people will work—until they slide into
a new, and as yet unnamed, stage of life.

Call it e-tirement.

It's happening already. Remember Grandma Betty from
Chapter 1? Legions of other sixty-plus Americans are becoming
freelancers, micropreneurs, self-employed knowledge workers,
temps, home-based businesspeople, and independent professionals. They're working as part-time, some time, and anytime
free agents—using the Internet as a platform for finding and executing work.

And in the future, their ranks will swell. E-tirement is less incredible than inevitable, a simple product of supply and demand.

To understand the supply side of e-tirement, connect five demographic dots:

1. *Americans are living longer and better.* When President Franklin Roosevelt signed the Social Security Act, and established sixty-five as the standard U.S. retirement age, the average American life expectancy was sixty-three. Today, life expectancy has soared to seventy-six (and medical and genomic advances soon will push it even higher). Says MIT economist and retirement expert Dora Costa, "Age sixty-five may therefore no longer be as appropriate a demarcation of old age as it was in the first half of the twentieth century."[1] After all, more than 80 percent of Americans already survive beyond age sixty-five. And thanks to the baby boomers—America's population pig-in-a-python—by 2040, one out of four Americans will have reached his or her sixty-fifth birthday, giving the United States a demographic profile even older than the current composition of Florida.

2. *Older Americans are ready, willing, and able to work.* While only about one in five sixty-five-to sixty-nine-year-olds works today, a 1999 AARP study found that 80 percent of baby boomers expect to work during their retirement years.[2] Nearly two thirds of working women plan to stay on the job past age sixty-five, according to the Women's Retirement Conference.[3] And what is desirable may become more doable. One factor: Americans over age sixty-five are covered by Medicare. The lack of employer-provided health insurance, which prevents many prospective free agents from taking the leap, won't hold back e-tirees.

3. *But older Americans will want to work on their own terms.* Too many years of working for a boss can take a psychic toll. That's one reason the self-employment rate among people between fifty-five and sixty-four is two and a half times greater than among those between twenty-five and thirty-four. The first boomers turn fifty-five in 2003—and fellow boomers will occupy this self-employment-prone

fifty-five to sixty-four age space continually for the next quarter century. Research by University of Warwick economist David Storey suggests these older independents may be quite successful. Storey found that about 70 percent of new enterprises started by people over age fifty-five survived—in contrast to a 19 percent survival rate for those of their younger counterparts.[4]

4. *Baby boomers are about to inherit a bundle.* The University of Essex's Mark Taylor has found that a windfall (lottery winnings or an inheritance) of as little as $8,000 *doubles* the probability that someone will become self-employed.[5] Get ready for the mother of all windfalls: In the coming decades, baby boomers will inherit more than $10 *trillion* from their parents.[6] Sure, they'll spend some of that bounty on face lifts and relaxed fit swimwear. But there'll be plenty left over to launch a new career as a senior soloist.

5. *Older Americans are jumping into the Net.* Nielsen Media Research and CommerceNet report that people over fifty are the second-fastest-growing group on the Internet. People in the fifty-five to sixty-four age group account for 22 percent of households that are online and will account for 40 percent by 2003, according to Forrester Research. And Internet companies like Third Age and Seniors.com have built thriving memberships of older Americans.

These five demographic forces will produce a huge supply of talented free agent seniors. But what about demand? The demand side of e-tirement springs from one large demographic data point: We're running out of workers. Baby boomers, 76 million strong, make up almost half of today's workforce. But on this generation's heels are much smaller demographic cohorts—in particular, the mere 41 million-member Generation X. If the boomers retire, there won't be enough younger workers to replace them. That's ominous, because more workers create a bigger economy. One reason our economy has always grown is that our workforce has always expanded. But for the past decade or so, fertility rates have been declining. And by 2013, the labor force will actually stop growing. This is an unprecedented demographic event. In its entire history, the U.S. has never confronted the possibility of a flat or shrinking labor force—an economy in which there is plenty of work to do but not enough people to do it.

Enter the e-tirees. At the very moment that millions of 60-somethings and 70-somethings are contemplating free agency, there will be a ferocious demand for their services. They'll be able to customize work to their own preferences—and negotiate arrangements that square with their family commitments and leisure desires.

We've already seen the first stirrings. Walt Fitzgerald, the General Electric Organization Man of Chapter 1, returned to GE intermittently to take on short-term free agent projects for seven years after he retired. Monsanto has established a Retiree Resource Corps in which people who have retired from the company work as temps to plug gaps in Monsanto's operations. One out of six large companies now offers phased retirement as an alternative to full retirement—the most common strategy being to hire back some of these retirees as free agents.[7] And the decades-long trend toward early retirement, fueled by Social Security earnings restrictions and generous big company pensions, has leveled off.[8]

E-tirement may be even bigger overseas than in the U.S. Between now and 2025, Denmark and the U.K. will have zero population growth. Italy, Germany, France, Japan, and Finland will actually have *negative* population growth—that is, they'll have fewer people then than they have today. (Italy, in fact, already has more people over sixty than under twenty.)[9] They'll have no choice but to look for workers, of any age, beyond their own national borders. With improvements in translation software and continued increases in bandwidth, the Internet may turn seniors into international businesspeople selling their services to eager customers abroad, and delivering those services via a worldwide computer network. Some entrepreneur will no doubt launch a "temp-travel" agency—a combined travel agency/temporary staffing firm specializing in "working vacation" tours of Rome, Paris, or Helsinki. Seniors could do a little bit of work for hard-pressed European companies to pay for their holiday.

Nor will e-tirement be reserved for high-end types—virtual CFOs e-mailing spreadsheets from Palm Springs. This, too, is thanks to the Internet. In the fifteenth century, the printing press made older people less valuable because books and pamphlets created a new repository for the stories and knowledge that elders once passed down orally. But in this century, the Internet could make older people *more valuable* by taking even more of the physical effort out of knowledge work. Former secretaries are transforming themselves into virtual assistants, doing business with clients around the world. And workers of every age are already using the Web to post their résumés and land assignments. Among the Internet's many possibilities is to become a hiring hall for older workers.

While demographic supply and demand is the main rocket powering e-tirement, other recent developments serve as rocket boosters. Congress abolished the mandatory retirement age fourteen years ago, making it easier for seniors to continue working past sixty-five. Recent changes in Social Security laws have removed several disincentives for older Americans to work. While most of the boomers' parents had traditional defined benefit pension plans that required them to leave the workforce at a prescribed age, most boomers have 401(k)-style plans that require them to manage their own retirement finances and choose themselves when to leave the workforce.

This shift in how people will work and live after age sixty-five reflects a deeper cultural move from dependence to independence. Boomers are less likely to rely on either the official state or the corporate state to care for them. Indeed, the retirement their parents enjoyed may go down as a historical blip. "Fixed-age retirement and occupational pensions developed alongside bureaucracies and large companies and were spurred on by the belief that older workers were slowing down overall productivity in increasingly competitive markets," writes historian Stanley Parker.[10] Retirement, in that sense, was a synonym for "harmful to the economy." No wonder in 2000 the American Association of Retired Persons scrubbed the R-word from its name, and now goes by the acronym AARP. MIT economist Costa says the committee that drafted the Social Security Act "believed that the increasing size of the elderly population necessitated an old-age security program because modern industry had no need for older workers."[11] But these premises have grown less relevant in the twenty-first century—and may become quaint anachronisms in a few decades. In the industrial economy, an aging back is a liability. In the idea economy, an experienced brain is an asset.

Expect politicians to be especially fond of e-tirement. It could ease the looming Social Security crisis without requiring politically unpalatable choices. E-tirement could weaken resistance to raising the retirement age. And as more people work more years, they will fill federal coffers with more payroll taxes, possibly saving the system from insolvency. In a sense, e-tirement could do for Social Security what a booming economy did for the federal budget deficit. Those cavernous deficits didn't disappear in the late 1990s because government officials made lots of tough choices or called for massive sacrifice (though both Presidents George Bush and Bill Clinton deserve some credit). No, an unexpected economic development—a technology-juiced economic boom—cured the fiscal malady more swiftly than politicians ever imagined. E-tirement could produce a similar, relatively painless fix for Social Security.

But the ultimate explanation for e-tirement is not that conventional retirement will break the bank, but that it may break people's spirit. A few years of shuffleboard may be peachy. But a few decades? Probably not. Howard and Marika Stone, two sixty-somethings from Weehawken, New Jersey, have launched a popular Web site—Too Young to Retire (*www.2young2retire.com*)—which they describe as "an online community of adventurous people who are reshaping traditional ideas about retirement." Another early adopter is Hardy Ballentine, sixty, a free agent bookbinder I talked with in Yellow Springs, Ohio. The former Peace Corps volunteer left traditional work in 1974 to become a full-time stay-at-home father while his wife secured a tenured professorship at a nearby university. Since the 1980s, Ballentine has run a modest micro-business in a workshop at the back of his home. Although he hasn't worked full-time in more than twenty-five years, he told me flatly: "I'll never retire. This is something I'll always do."

The restless and constantly self-actualizing baby boomers will have a tough time simply kicking back. As they begin reckoning with their own mortality, their search for meaning will intensify in ways that Bocci ball and cribbage can't satisfy. Many will seek that meaning through work. Indeed, the greatest beneficiaries may be nonprofit organizations, which will hire free agent seniors who don't want to stop working but who don't want to be fully employed—those who want to do good without sacrificing doing well.

Of course, e-tirement won't be for everyone. Those who have spent their working lives in physical labor—the longshoreman, the firefighter, or the waitress—may be ready, mentally and physically, to retire at age sixty-five. And by a certain age, even more people will simply want to stop working. Recall the words of Moses in Deuteronomy: "I am a hundred and twenty years old this day; I can no more go out and come in." Grandma Betty, too, will likely retire when she reaches 120. But until then, expect her—and soon millions of others—to make retirement an aberration and e-tirement a way of life.

THE BOX

CHAPTER 14

THE CRUX: In the free agent future, fewer people will retire. More will e-tire. Instead of leaving the work world completely at age sixty-five, they'll continue working as free agents—finding and executing work over the Internet. E-tirement is in many ways demographically inevitable, the simple outcome of supply and demand. As the gigantic baby boom generation ages, it will create an enormous cadre of healthy, able, tech-savvy, self-actualizing older Americans. This supply of labor will arrive at precisely the moment that the "working age" population is shrinking, sparking an intense demand for workers.

THE FACTOID: When Franklin Roosevelt established sixty-five as the standard U.S. retirement age, the average American life expectancy was sixty-three. Today, life expectancy is seventy-six and rising.

THE QUOTE: "Get ready for the mother of all windfalls: In the coming decades, baby boomers will inherit more than $10 *trillion* from their parents. Sure, they'll spend some of that bounty on face lifts and relaxed fit swimwear. But there'll be plenty left over to launch a new career as a senior soloist."

THE WORD: *E-tirement.* A new stage in American working life; working as a free agent after age sixty-five—and using the global communications network as the platform for obtaining and completing work.

15

School's Out: Free Agency and the Future of Education

Dear Ms. Roberts:

I am writing to recommend Molly Kwan for an architecture apprenticeship. Molly is an extraordinarily creative and motivated eighteen-year-old who has studied design, drawing, and mathematics with my guidance for the past three years. Since the age of ten, Molly has taken control of her own education, opting to teach herself and to learn by pursuing her interests and seeking the direction and expertise of others. Molly has decided to forgo a formal university architecture degree and instead to learn this craft the same way she's learned throughout her life—by doing, under the guidance of a successful architect like yourself.

*—**Excerpt from letter of recommendation, October 10, 2008***

Here's a riddle of the New Economy:

Whenever students around the world take those tests that measure which country's children know the most, American kids invariably score near the bottom. Whether the subject is math or science or reading, when the international rankings come out,

European and Asian nations finish first while the U.S. pulls up the rear. This, we all know, isn't good.

Yet by almost every measure, the American economy outperforms those very same, far brainier, nations of Asia and Europe. We create greater wealth, deliver more and better goods and services, and positively kick butt on innovation. This, we all know, *is* good.

Now the riddle: If we're so dumb, how come we're so rich?

How can we fare so poorly on international measures of education yet perform so well in an economy that depends on brainpower?

The answer is complex, but within it are clues about the future of education—and how free agency may rock the schoolhouse as profoundly as it has upended the organization.

THE HOMOGENIZING HOPPER

Whenever I walk into a public school, I stagger a bit at the entrance. The moment I step across the threshold, I'm nearly toppled by a wave of nostalgia. Most schools I've visited in the twenty-first century look and feel exactly like the central Ohio public schools I attended in the 1970s. The classrooms are the same size. The desks stand in those same rows. Bulletin boards preview the next national holiday. The hallways even *smell* the same. Sure, some classrooms might have a computer or two. But in most respects, the schools American children attend today seem indistinguishable from the ones their parents and grandparents attended generations earlier.

At first such déjà vu warmed my soul. But then I thought about it. How many other places look and feel exactly as they did twenty, thirty, or forty years ago? Banks don't. Hospitals don't. Grocery stores don't. Maybe the sweet nostalgia I sniffed on those classroom visits was really the odor of stagnation.

Since most other institutions in American society have changed dramatically in the past half-century, the stasis of schools is strange. And it's doubly peculiar because school itself is not something we inherited from antiquity and preserve to honor our ancestors. School as we know it is a modern invention.

Through most of history, people learned from tutors or their close relations. In nineteenth-century America, says education historian David Tyack, "the school was a voluntary and incidental institution."[1] American kids learned the basics from their families—or from the one-room schoolhouse they'd drop into every now and again. Not until the early twentieth century did public schools as we know them—large buildings in which students segregated by age learn from government-certified professionals—become widespread. And not until the 1920s did attending one become compulsory. Think about that last fact a moment. Compared with much of the world, America is a remarkably hands-off land. We don't force people to vote, or to work, or to serve in the military. But we do force young people to go to school for more than a decade. We don't compel parents to love their kids or teach their kids. But we do compel parents to relinquish their kids to this institution for a dozen years, and threaten to jail those who resist.

Compulsory mass schooling is an aberration in history and an aberration in modern society. Yet it was the ideal preparation for the Organization Man economy. It equipped generations of future factory workers and middle managers with the basic skills and knowledge they needed on the job. And the broader lessons it conveyed were equally crucial. Kids learned how to obey rules, follow orders, and respect authority—and the penalties that came with refusal.

This was just the sort of training the old economy demanded. Schools had bells; factories had whistles. Schools had report card grades; offices had pay grades. Pleasing your teacher prepared you for pleasing your boss. And in either place, if you achieved a minimal level of performance, you were promoted. Taylorism, which I discussed in Chapter 1, didn't spend all its time on the job. It also went to class. In the school, as in the workplace, the reigning theory was One Best Way. Organization Kids learned the same things at the same time in the same manner in the same place. Marshall McLuhan once described schools as "the homogenizing hopper into which we toss our integral tots for processing."[2] And schools made factory-style processing practically a religion—through standardized testing, standardized curricula, and standardized clusters of children. (Question: When was the last time *you* spent all day in a room filled exclusively with people born +/–6 months of your own birth date?)

So when we step into the typical school, we're stepping into the past—a place whose architect is Frederick Winslow Taylor and whose tenant is the Organization Man. The one institution in American society that has least accommodated itself to the values and form of the free agent economy is the one institution Americans claim they value most. But it's hard to imagine that this arrangement can last much longer—a One Size Fits All education system cranking out workers for a My Size Fits Me economy. Maybe the answer to the riddle I posed at the start of this chapter is that we're succeeding *in spite of* our education system. But how long can that continue? And imagine how we'd prosper if we began educating our children more like we earn our livings.

Nearly twenty years ago, a landmark government report with the alarming title *A Nation At Risk* declared that American education was "being eroded by a rising tide of mediocrity." That may no longer be true. Instead, American schools are awash in a rising tide of irrelevance.

Don't get me wrong. In innumerable ways, mass public schooling has been a stirring success. Like Taylorism, it has accomplished some remarkable things—assisting throngs of immigrants in learning both English and the American way, helping more Americans become literate, equipping others to succeed beyond their parents' imaginings. In a very large sense, America's schools have been a breathtaking democratic achievement.

But that doesn't mean they ought to be the same as they were when you and I were kids. Parents and the politicians have sensed the need for reform, and have pushed education toward the top of the national agenda. Unfortunately, few of the conventional remedies in the educational medicine cabinet—standardized testing, character training, recertifying teachers—will do much to cure what ails American schools, and may even make things worse. Free agency, though, will force the necessary changes. Look for free agency to accelerate and deepen three incipient movements in teaching and learning—the surging popularity of home schooling, the emerging alternatives to traditional high school, and inventive new approaches to adult learning. These changes will prove as pathbreaking as mass public schooling was a century ago. Together they will unschool American society.

THE HOME SCHOOLING REVOLUTION

"School is like starting life with a twelve-year jail sentence in which bad habits are the only curriculum truly learned. I teach school and win awards. I should know."[3] Those are the words of John Taylor Gatto. In 1991, Gatto was named New York State's Teacher of the Year. Today he has become one of the most forceful voices for one of the most powerful movements in American education—home schooling. In home schooling, kids opt out of traditional school to take control of their own education and to learn with the help of parents, tutors, and peers. Home schooling is free agency for the under-eighteen set. And it's about to break through the surface of our national life.

As recently as 1980, home schooling was illegal in most states. In the early 1980s, no more than fifteen thousand students learned this way. But Christian conservatives, unhappy with schools they considered God-free zones and eager to teach their kids themselves, pressed for changes. Laws fell, and home schooling surged. By 1990, there were as many as 300,000 American home schoolers. By 1993, home schooling was legal in all fifty states. And since then, home schooling has swum into the mainstream—paddled there by secular parents dissatisfied with low-quality, and even dangerous, schools. In the first half of the 1990s, the home schooling population more than doubled. Today some 1.7 million children are home schoolers, their ranks growing as much as 15 percent each year.[4] Factor in turnover, and one in ten American kids under eighteen has gotten part of his or her schooling at home.[5]

Home schooling has become perhaps the largest and most successful education reform movement of the last two decades:

- While barely 3 percent of American schoolchildren are now home schoolers, that represents a surprisingly large dent in the public school monopoly—especially compared with private schools. For every four kids in private school, there's one youngster learning at home. The home schooling population is roughly equal to all the school-age children in Pennsylvania.[6]

- According to the *Wall Street Journal*, "evidence is mounting that home-schooling, once confined to the political and religious fringe, has achieved results not only on par with public education, but in some ways surpassing it."[7] Home-schooled children consistently score higher than traditional students on standardized achievement tests, on average placing in the 80th percentile in all subjects.[8]

- Home-schooled children also perform extremely well on nearly all measures of socialization. One of the great misconceptions about home schooling is that it turns kids into isolated loners. In fact, these children spend more time with adults, more time in their community, and more time with children of varying ages than their traditional school counterparts. Says one researcher, "The conventionally schooled tended to be considerably more aggressive, loud, and competitive than the home educated."[9]

"Home schooling," though, is a bit of a misnomer. Parents don't re-create the classroom in the living room any more than free agents re-create the cubicle in their basement offices. Instead, home schooling makes it easier for children to pursue their own interests in their own way—a My Size Fits Me approach to learning. In part for this reason, some adherents—particularly those who have opted out of traditional schools for reasons other than religion—prefer the term "unschooling."

The similarities to free agency—having an "unjob"—are many. Free agents are independent workers; home schoolers are independent learners. Free agents maintain robust networks and tight connections through F.A.N. Clubs and professional associations; home schoolers have assembled powerful groups—like the three-thousand-family Family Unschoolers Network—to share teaching strategies and materials and to offer advice and support. Free agents often challenge the idea of separating work and family; home schoolers take the same approach to the boundary between school and family. Think of home schooling as Tailorism for the playground crowd.

Perhaps most important, home schooling is almost perfectly consonant with the four values of the free agent work ethic I described in Chapter 4: having freedom, being authentic, putting yourself on the line, and defining your own success.

Take freedom. In the typical school, children often aren't permitted to move unless a bell rings or an adult grants them permission. And except for a limited menu of offerings in high school, they generally can't choose what to study or when to study it. Home schoolers have far greater freedom. They learn more like, well, children. We don't teach little kids how to talk or walk or understand the world. We simply put them in nurturing situations and let them learn on their own. Sure, we impose certain restrictions. ("Don't walk in the middle of the street.") But we don't go crazy. ("Please practice talking for forty-five minutes until a bell rings.") It's the same for home schoolers. Kids can become agents of their own education rather than merely recipients of someone else's noble intentions.

Imagine a five-year-old child whose current passion is building with Legos. Every day she spends up to an hour, maybe more, absorbed in complex construction projects, creating farms, zoos, airplanes, spaceships. Often her friends come over and they work together. No one assigns her this project. No one tells her when and how to do it. And no one will give her creation a grade. Is she learning? Of course. This is how many home schoolers explore their subjects.

Now suppose some well-intentioned adults step in to teach

the child a thing or two about Lego building. Let's say they assign her a daily forty-five-minute Lego period, give her a grade at the end of each session, maybe even offer a reward for an A+ building. And why not bring in some more five-year-olds to teach them the same things about Legos? Why not have them all build their own forty-five-minute Lego buildings at the same time, then give them each a letter grade, with a prize for the best one? My guess: Pretty soon our five-year-old Lego lover would lose her passion. Her buildings would likely become less creative, her learning curve flatter. This is how many conventional schools work—or, I guess, *don't work.*

The well-meaning adults have squelched the child's freedom to play and learn and discover on her own. She's no longer in control. She's no longer having fun. Countless studies, particularly those by University of Rochester psychologist Edward L. Deci, have shown that kids and adults alike—in school, at work, at home—lose the intrinsic motivation and the pure joy derived from learning and working when somebody takes away their sense of autonomy and instead imposes some external system of reward and punishment.[10] It's like the relationship between freedom and security I described in Chapter 5. Freedom isn't a detour from learning. It's the best pathway toward it.

Stay with our Lego lass a moment and think about authenticity—the basic desire people have to be who they are rather than conform to someone else's standard. Our young builder has lost the sense that she is acting according to her own true self. Instead, she's gotten the message. You build Legos for the same reason your employer father does his assignments: because an authority figure tells you to.

Or take accountability. The child is no longer fully accountable for her own Lego creating. Whatever she's produced is by assignment. She did it for the Man, and therefore, in her mind, he gets a lot of the credit. Her creations are no longer truly hers.

And what about those Lego grades? Won't that A+ motivate our girl to keep on building? Perhaps, but not on her own terms. Maybe she liked the B– building better than the A+ creation. Oh well. Now she'll probably bury that feeling and work to measure up—to someone else's standards. Should she take a chance—try building that space shuttle she's been dreaming about? Probably not. Why take that risk when, chances are, it won't make the grade? Self-defined success has no place in this regime. But for many home schoolers, success is something they can define themselves. (This is true even though, as I mentioned, home schoolers score off the charts on conventional measures of success—standardized tests in academic subjects.)

To be sure, some things most kids should learn are not intrinsically fun. There are times in life when we must eat our Brussels sprouts. For those subjects, the punishment-and-reward approach of traditional schooling may be in order. But too often, the sheer thrill of learning a new fact or mastering a tough equation is muted when schools take away a student's sense of control. In home schooling, kids have greater freedom to pursue their passions, less pressure to conform to the wishes of authority figure teachers and *Lord of the Flies* peers—and can put themselves on the line, take risks, and define success on their own terms. As more parents realize that the underlying ethic of home schooling closely resembles the animating values of free agency, home schooling will continue to soar in popularity.

Several other forces will combine to power home schooling into greater prominence. One is simply the movement's initial prominence. As more families choose this option, they will make home schooling more socially acceptable—thereby instilling still more families with the gumption to take this once unconventional route. The home-schooling population has already begun to look like the rest of America. While some 90 percent of home-schoolers are white, the population is becoming more diverse, and may be growing fastest among African-Americans. And the median home school income is roughly the median income for the rest of the country; about 87 percent of home school families have annual household incomes under $75,000.

Recent policy changes—in both the state legislature and the principal's office—will further clear the way. Not only is home schooling now legal in every state, but many public schools have begun accommodating home schoolers by letting them take certain classes or play on school teams. And about two thirds of American colleges now accept transcripts prepared by parents, or portfolios assembled by students, in lieu of an accredited diploma.[11]

Another force is free agency itself. Many home-schooling parents are themselves free agents. And many free agents will become home-schooling parents. Thanks to flexible schedules and personal control, it's easier for free agents than for traditional employees to home-school their children.

Free agents will also become the professionals in this new world of learning. A carpenter might hire herself out to teach carpentry skills to home schoolers. A writer might become a tutor or editor to several home schoolers interested in, say, producing their own literary journal. What's more, the huge cadre of teachers hired to teach the baby boom will soon retire. Perhaps many instead will e-tire—and hire themselves out as itinerant tutors to home schoolers. For many parents, of course, the responsibility and time commitment of home schooling will be daunting. But the wide availability of teachers and tutors might help some parents overcome the concern that they won't be able to handle this awesome undertaking by themselves.

The Internet makes home schooling easier, too. Indeed, home schoolers figured out the Internet well before most Americans. For example, my first Internet connection was a DOS-based Compuserve account I acquired in 1993. Before the wide acceptance of the Internet and the advent of the World Wide Web, the most active discussion groups on Compuserve then were those devoted to home schooling. Using the World Wide Web, home schoolers can do research and find tutors anywhere in the world. There are now even online ventures—for instance, the Christa McAuliffe Academy in Washington State and ChildU.com in Florida—that sell online courses and provide e-teachers for home schoolers.

Physical infrastructure might also accelerate this trend. Public schools must contend with overcrowded classrooms and dilapidated buildings. Almost three fourths of America's public school buildings were built before 1969.[12] School administrations might be more likely to encourage some amount of home schooling if that means less strain on their crowded classrooms and creaky buildings.

I don't want to overstate the case. Home schooling, like free agency, won't be for everyone. Many parents won't have the time or the desire for this approach. And home schooling won't be for all time. Many students will spend a few years in a conventional school and a few years learning at home—just as some workers will migrate between being a free agent and holding a job. But home schooling is perhaps the most robust expression of the free agent way outside the workplace. And for that reason, its continued rise is inevitable.

THE END OF HIGH SCHOOL

One other consequence of the move toward home schooling—and the broader move away from mass institutions and toward individuals—will be something many of us wished for as teenagers: the demise of high school.

It wasn't until the 1920s that high school replaced work as the thing most Americans did in their teens. But today, "American high school is obsolete," says Bard College president Leon Botstein, one of the first to call for its end. He says today's adolescents would be better off pursuing a college degree, jumping directly into the job market, engaging in public service, or taking on a vocational apprenticeship.[13] Even the National Association of Secondary School Principals, which has blasted home schooling, concedes that "high schools continue to go about their business in ways that sometimes bear startling resemblance to the flawed practices of the past."[14]

In the future, expect teens and their families to force an end to high school as we know it. Look for some of these changes to replace and augment traditional high schools with free-agent-style learning—and to unschool the American teenager:

- *A renaissance of apprenticeships.* For centuries, young people learned a craft or profession under the guidance of an experienced master. This method will revive—and not just for trades like plumbing, but for skills like computer programming and graphic design. Imagine a fourteen-year-old taking two or three academic courses each week, and spending the rest of her time apprenticing a commercial artist. As the home schoolers have figured out, traditional high schools tend to separate learning and doing. Free agency makes them indistinguishable.

- *A flowering of teenage entrepreneurship.* Young people may become free agents even before they get their driver's licenses—and teen entrepreneurs (who both earn and learn by doing) will become more common. Indeed, most teens have the two crucial traits of a successful entrepreneur: a fresh way of looking at the world and a passionate intensity for what they do. In San Diego County, 8 percent of high school students already run their own online business.[15] That will increasingly become the norm and perhaps even become a teenage rite of passage.

- *A greater diversity of academic courses.* Only sixteen states offer basic economics in high school.[16] That's hardly a sound foundation for the free agent workplace. Expect a surge of new kinds of "home economics" courses that teach numeracy, accounting, and basic business.

- *A boom in national service.* Some teenagers will seek greater direction than others and may want to spend a few years serving in the military or participating in a domestic service program. Today, many young people don't consider these choices because of the pressure to go directly to college. Getting people out of high school earlier might get them into service sooner. Imagine a sixteen-year-old serving two years in a Civilian Conservation Corps in her neighborhood—before even considering attending college.

- *A backlash against standards.* A high school diploma was once the gold standard of American education. Today, like gold, it has lost most of its usefulness as a benchmark. Yet politicians seem determined to make the diploma meaningful again by erecting all sorts of hurdles kids must leap to attain one—standardized subjects each student must study, standardized tests each student must pass. In some schools, students are already staging sit-ins to protest these tests. This could be American youth's new cause célèbre. ("Hey hey, ho ho. Organization Man testing's got to go.")

Most politicians think the answer to the problems of high schools is to exert more control. The real answer, the free agent answer, is less control. In the free agent future, our teens will learn by less schooling and more doing.

THE UNSCHOOLING OF ADULTS

For much of the twentieth century, the U.S. depended on what I call the "Thanksgiving Turkey Model" of education. We placed kids in the oven of formal education for twelve years, cooked them until they were done, then served them to employers. (A select minority got a final, four-year basting at a place called college.) But this model doesn't work in a world of accelerated cycle times, shrinking company half-lives, and the rapid obsolescence of knowledge and skills. It's easier to articulate than legislate, but in a free agent economy our education system must allow people to learn throughout their lives. When we turn twenty-one, we've still got three fourths of our life to live and learn.

Instead of cooking a nation of Organization People, home schooling and alternatives to high school will create a nation of self-educators, free agent learners, if you will. Adults who were unschooled youths will know how to learn and expect to continue the habit throughout their lives—and not only when someone from the HR department or the "continuing education" mandarins of their profession tell them it's time for training.

For example, how did anybody learn the World Wide Web? In 1993, it barely existed. By 1995, it was the foundation of dozens of new industries and an explosion of wealth. There weren't any college classes in Web programming, HTML coding, or Web page design in those early years. There weren't any university departments devoted to the topic. Yet somehow hundreds of thousands of people managed to learn. How? They taught themselves—working with colleagues, trying new things, and making mistakes. That was the secret to the Web's success. Indeed, imposing formal requirements (required courses or a Web head bar exam) would have snuffed creativity and slowed development. The Web flourished almost entirely through the ethic and practice of self-teaching.

This is not a radical concept. Until the first part of this century, most Americans learned on their own—by reading. Literacy and access to books were an individual's ticket to knowledge. Even today, in my Free Agent Nation online census, "reading" was the most prevalent way free agents said they stayed up-to-date in their field.

In the twenty-first century, access to the Internet and to a network of smart colleagues—much more than access to a fancy college degree—will be the ticket to adult learning. Expect more of us to punch and repunch those tickets throughout our lives.

Look for these early signs:

- *The devaluation of degrees.* As the shelf life of a degree shortens, more students will go to college to acquire particular skills than to bring home an entire sheepskin. People's need for knowledge doesn't respect semesters. They'll want higher education just in time—and if that means leaving the classroom before earning a degree, so be it. Remember: Larry Ellison, Steve Jobs, and Steven Spielberg never finished college.

- *Older students.* Forty percent of college students are now older than twenty-five. According to the *Wall Street Jour-*

nal, "by some projections, the number of students age 35 and older will exceed those 18 and 19 within a few years."[17] Young adults who do forgo a diploma in their early twenties may find a need and desire for college courses in their forties.

- *Free agent teaching.* Distance learning (private ventures like the University of Phoenix, Unext, Ninth House Network, and Hungry Minds University) will help along this self-teaching trend. Today, some five thousand companies are in the online education business. Their $2 billion of revenues are expected to hit $11 billion by 2003.[18] And nontraditional teaching arrangements will abound. One lament of independent scholars—genre-straddling writers like Judith Rich Harris and Anne Hollander—is that they don't have students.[19] Here's a ready supply. More free agent teachers and more free agent students will create tremendous liquidity in the learning market—with the Internet serving as the matchmaker and market maker for this new marketplace of learning.

- *Big trouble for elite colleges.* All this means big trouble in Ivy City. Attending a fancy college serves three purposes in contemporary life: to prolong adolescence, to award a credential that's modestly useful early in one's working life, and to give people a network of friends. Elite colleges have moved slowly to keep up with the emerging free agent economy. In 1998, 78 percent of public four-year colleges offered distance-learning programs, compared with only 19 percent of private schools.[20] Private college costs have soared, faster even than health care costs, for the past twenty years. But have these colleges improved at the same rate? Have they improved at all? What's more, the students who make it to elite colleges are generally those who've proved most adroit at conventional (read: outdated) schooling. That could become a liability rather than an advantage. In his bestseller *The*

Millionaire Mind, Thomas J. Stanley found a dispropor-
tionately large number of millionaires were free agents—
but that the higher somebody's SAT scores, the *less* likely
he or she was to be a financial risk-taker and therefore to
become a free agent.[21]

• *Learning groupies.* The conference industry, already hot,
will continue to catch fire as more people seek gatherings
of like-minded souls to make new connections and learn
new things. One stunningly successful example is *Fast
Company*'s Real Time Conferences—semiannual, phantas-
magoric assemblages of models, mentors, tools, and networking. Notty Bumbo, a free agent medical consultant I
introduced in Chapter 8, said, "I can attend a conference
or seminar, and in essence, there is a sort of Socratic institution there. I can choose the mentor I will pay attention to for the next hour, or two hours, or day—whatever.
I will listen to them at their knee, and also be in a position to ask them questions, challenge their assumptions,
challenge my own assumptions, work within a group
structure to test the ideas." The F.A.N. Clubs I discussed
in Chapter 7, and the many book clubs that already exist,
will become important sources of education—much as
Ben Franklin's Junto educated a generation of colonial
free agents.

The next few decades will be a fascinating, and perhaps revolutionary, time for learning in America. The specifics will surprise us and may defy even my soundest predictions. But the
bottom line of the future of education in Free Agent Nation is
glaringly clear: School's out.

CHAPTER 15

THE CRUX: In the free agent future, a host of changes will unschool American society. Mass compulsory education will give way to a variety of learning alternatives. Home schooling, perhaps the most robust expression of free agent values outside the workplace, will continue to boom. More free agent families will go this route. And more free agents will offer their services as itinerant tutors serving this population. High school as we know it will cease to exist—replaced and augmented by a variety of hands-on options, better attuned to the free agent economy. And the self-teaching ethic learned in youth will continue into adulthood, diminishing the value of college degrees and upping the value of informal, self-directed learning arrangements.

THE FACTOID: Forty percent of college students are now older than twenty-five. Within a few years, the number of thirty-five-plus-year-old college students will exceed the number of eighteen- and nineteen-year-old college students.

THE QUOTE: "So when we step into the typical school, we're stepping into the past—a place whose architect is Frederick Winslow Taylor and whose tenant is the Organization Man. The one institution in American society that has least accommodated itself to the values and form of the free agent economy is the one institution Americans claim they value most."

THE WORD: *Thanksgiving Turkey Model.* The education model that predominated in the twentieth century. Society placed kids in the oven of formal education for twelve years, cooked them until they were done, then served them to employers. A few youngsters also received an additional four-year basting at a place called college.

16

Location, Location . . . Vocation: Free Agency and the Future of Offices, Homes, and Real Estate

FOR SALE: 3BR, 2ofc Victorian. Located in active home-schooling comm. Walking dis. from Starbucks, MailBoxes Etc., Barnes & Noble. In FedEx early delivery region. T-1 capability, Dell server in bsmt, home network—ready. 20 min. from airport. Flexible zoning.

—**Ad in Washington Post** *real estate section,*
June 14, 2009

In the previous fifteen chapters, I've discussed the who, what, when, why, and how of free agency. In this chapter, I'll examine the where: Where will soloists, temps, and micropreneurs do their work in the free agent future? Of course, some might say the "where" question doesn't matter much today. The industrial economy's three building blocks were land, labor, and capital—but in the knowledge economy, we can get by with just the final two. The digital and wireless revolutions have fundamentally rewritten the rules of business, this argument goes. We're virtual. We're mobile. And when being anywhere at all is possible, being anywhere in particular is irrelevant.

There's some truth to this perspective. We do have greater flexibility in where we must be. But all the talk about virtual teaming, holographic teleconferencing, and other ways to overcome the messy reality of skin and bones and bricks and mortar reminds me of those endless predictions of the "paperless office." I'm still waiting—and figure I'll wait a long while more. Similarly, free agency won't obliterate the significance of spaces and places. It won't create, say, "officeless paper." Instead, it will change the "where" of work in some surprising ways. And the place to begin to understand those changes is in the office—my office, in fact, the one I mentioned in Chapter 11.

ELKS LODGES AND PRIVATE IDAHOS

I'm writing this from the third floor of our family's house, which sits on a sleepy street in northwest Washington, D.C., about a mile from the Maryland border. Developers built many of the homes in our neighborhood in the late 1930s to house the federal workers then filling the nation's capital. As in most homes at the time, the builders included a third-floor attic. For home buyers then, the attic wasn't a central feature—just a place to store things unworthy or unwelcome in the rest of the house. But for my wife and me, when we bought this house in 1997, the attic was essential. We needed a home office. And any house that didn't accommodate this desire quickly slid off our list.

This afternoon, as I stare into the computer screen and write this chapter, my wife is in her own second-floor office answering her e-mail. Our house has two offices, two Aeron chairs, three computers, four phone lines—and one car. A few other families near us live this way, too. We're neither oddballs nor trailblazers. We're just swaying to work's new rhythm.

After all, there's nothing inherently necessary or desirable about living in one place and working in another. When most Americans were farmers, most Americans didn't disappear from their homes each morning to work someplace else. The things they needed to do their jobs were generally right there at the homestead. As I explained in Chapter 3, only when those tools became too costly for one person to purchase, too cumbersome for one person to start, and too complicated for one person to operate did Americans leave their dwellings to earn their livings. In those days, the workplace served as a gargantuan toolshed. It housed the tools the company bought and paid you to use. No matter what job you held, traveling to the toolshed was obligatory. The "office" was the "official" place to work.

But as I also explained in Chapter 3, toolshed offices don't make much sense in an economy like today's, where the tools are easy for one person to purchase, house, and operate. For individuals, the arrangement is inefficient and sometimes irritating. "I absolutely love working at home," free agent writer and Web consultant Karen Solomon told me in a dingy coffee shop in San Francisco's Haight-Ashbury neighborhood. "But waking up early and going to an office job is absolutely demeaning. You'll be in an office for eight hours and doing the amount of work you could easily get done on your own in three." For organizations, the toolshed arrangement is inefficient and sometimes expensive. Peter Drucker once famously questioned why any company would pay (in salary and time) to transport a 170-pound body twenty miles downtown when all it needed was the body's three-pound brain. And for the broader society, the arrangement can be just plain wasteful. Office buildings stand empty half the day. Homes stand empty for the other half. And people spend a huge amount of time shuttling back and forth—with cars, trains, and buses chewing roads and spewing pollution.

At some point soon, toolshed offices will go the way of the typewriter—and will be replaced by two different types of offices, more sensible for independent workers. Think of the first variety as your own private Idaho. (The term comes from a B-52's song: "You're living in your own private Idaho, underground like a wild potato.") A private Idaho will be a place very much like the 9 x 15 foot room I clamber up to each morning. It will be the setting for "heads-down" work—tasks for which people need privacy, autonomy, and control. For many workers, this heads-down office will be at home. I, for example, am far too lazy—and I like my three female co-inhabitants far too much—to travel someplace else for my heads-down work. But others may prefer a room of one's own that's not in their home. And arranging that will become increasingly easy thanks to the growth of executive suites (discussed in Chapter 9 and about which more in a moment) and the proliferation of technologies that allow greater control of one's environment. For instance, noise-canceling technology—sound wave machines that cancel out competing sounds—will allow people to carve a quiet, heads-down space even in a hectic setting. And microclimate controls, already on the market, and virtual windows that simulate natural light will allow individuals to fashion and refashion their heads-down space to suit their own needs. Tailorism, the free agent approach to work styles, will be the core design principle of workspaces.

But what a sad world if we spent all our days with our heads lowered, sequestered in our own private Idahos. What a counterproductive world, too. As I've discussed earlier, for both hard-headed and softhearted reasons, free agents need contact, community, and collaboration.

And one place they'll find it is in the second type of office that will emerge. I call this one a Free Agent Elks Lodge. A Free Agent Elks Lodge will be a place to hang out, to chat about last night's (Webcast) sitcom, and to work face-to-face with colleagues on projects that require intense interaction. These places will look a lot more like Kinko's or Starbucks than like the cubicle farms of the 1990s. Free agents will buy memberships much as today they join health clubs. And they will come to these New Age offices to do the very things we say we don't like: to gossip and to be interrupted. Those occasions of inadvertent contact, we'll discover, are crucial for creativity and innovation. When our noggins ache from all that heads-down work, when we can't solve a business problem on our own, or when we're working with a team on a big project, we'll seek a productive place where everybody knows our name and they're always glad we came. (Along those lines, we may see free agents begin buying "time-share" offices, much as yuppies buy time-share beach houses, and establish their own, more exclusive lodges. A group of novelists and journalists in San Francisco has already created such a place, a writers den that they've dubbed The Grotto.) In short, toolshed offices are history. Private Idahos and Free Agent Elks Lodges are the future.

HOME IS WHERE THE MAC IS

These two new office models will reshape the business of real estate. Start with the residential side of the real estate market. Free agency will reconfigure the function and design of the home—similar to the way that television adopted the typical living room and practically birthed the family room. The home office—whether in a third-floor attic, a basement, or an apartment's den or spare bedroom—will become an essential feature rather than a surprise bonus in most American homes. This transition is already underway. In 1998, about one third of American households had a home office, up from barely one in twenty a decade earlier. In new construction, home offices are now standard—and often include separate entrances, soundproofing, and high-speed Internet connections.[1]

Smart Realtors understand. When they sell houses, they now tout offices as major features, several agents told me. Some have even used free agency and home officing to sell not just an individual property, but a particular locale. For example, in her year-end real estate newsletter, which I came across during my free agent journey in the Southwest, New Mexico Realtor Nobel Davis wrote: "We are also seeing an increase in technological commuting where an owner can operate a business from home anywhere—and given the choice, who wouldn't choose Santa Fe?"

The inside of homes will also change as home networking becomes more commonplace—and eventually not much more exotic than home electricity. Your home network will connect all your family's computers to a single printer and Internet connection—and may even wire together a bunch of other appliances, too, from your refrigerator to your living room lights. In the basement, you'll have a server to manage that home network and possibly even run your microbusiness's e-commerce site. But you'll barely know it exists. It will be like your furnace. You'll notice it only when it breaks down.

All these changes will feed a continued boom in the home improvement industry. New free agents will want to add an office for themselves—or for their e-tired parent who's tired of the ROPEC and comes to their kids' house to live and work. As people spend more time at home, they'll put greater strains on the house and need more repairs more often. And if they're going to spend so much time at home, they might want more space or rooms that serve multiple purposes—once again, fueling demand for home improvements. The retrofitting of homes to accommodate free agent lifestyles will be one of the great growth industries of the early twenty-first century.

Another booming industry will be selling all manner of merchandise—furniture, office supplies, telecommunications services—to this growing market of at-home workers. The so-called SOHO (Small Office/Home Office) market is already worth some $20 billion in annual sales. At an array of conferences—the crown jewel of which is Terri Lonier's annual SOHO Summit—companies from Visa to Apple Computer to Herman Miller gather to learn the needs of this new breed of small entrepreneurs. The circulation of the specialized SOHO-centric magazines *Home Office Computing* and *Small Business Computing* already exceeds the combined circulation of *Wired* and *The New Republic*, and is roughly the size of the readership of *Forbes*. I wouldn't be surprised to see marketers next target what I call the "HOHO" market—for His Office/Her Office, though the designation works just as elegantly for same-sex couples—households like mine where two adults both have heads-down offices.

Free agency may even shake up the residential *rental* market. For example, in Seattle I met a free agent design consultant named Tim Celeski who has come up with an innovative office arrangement. He told me that when his office was in his home, he tended to work too much and began resenting his work. Then in 1984, "I found, two blocks away, a mother-in-law house that was on somebody else's property. Ever since then, it has turned out to be a perfect combination." Celeski, in other words, has a home office that's not in *his* home. His studio, which he rents from a couple in their eighties, allows him to create what he calls a "soft separation" between home and work—less segmented than a home uptown and an office downtown, but less integrated than a home upstairs and an office downstairs.

We could see an emerging market in these "Celeski suites." In the past, empty-nest couples sometimes rented rooms to students at nearby colleges. In the future, those empty-nest couples may instead rent spare rooms to neighborhood free agents who won't stay overnight, play loud music, or mess up the kitchen— but just use the space as a place for heads-down work.

In fact, the very phrase "home office" might grow rusty and redundant. Home will become the primary place for heads-down work—so having an office where you live won't be much stranger than having a kitchen where you live. In fact, as more people use their kitchen area not for cooking but mostly for unpacking and eating meals prepared elsewhere, maybe a "home kitchen" will seem odd, and an "office" just another room in the home of every family on the block.

TROPHY TOWERS AND GROWN-UP DORMITORIES

Free agency will likewise turn commercial real estate upside down. Think about your current workplace—or the last large workplace where you labored. Chances are, everybody there had a cubicle or a desk, if not a full-fledged private office. And chances are, many people spent a huge portion of their day . . . somewhere else. That would be ordinary. At any given moment during the workday, 70 percent of desks, offices, or workstations aren't occupied. Factor in weekends and holidays, and the occupancy rate of the typical office hovers around 15 percent.[2]

Today, the typical nonretail commercial space consists of 80 percent offices and cubes and 20 percent meeting rooms. That arrangement forces people to travel in order to perform heads-down work they could easily do somewhere else—and it leaves insufficient room for doing the collaborative work that is the chief reason for people to share the same space. As more individuals declare free agency and fashion their own private Idahos for quiet work, that four-to-one private-space-to-public-space ratio will change. The workplace of the future will likely consist of 20 percent private offices, 20 percent "touch-down" spaces (where people can plug in their laptop, check their e-mail, or make a quick phone call), and 60 percent meeting rooms and other venues for group interaction. With this configuration, some employees of companies would still come into the office every day, but most would have to do so only for a specific purpose. And for free agents working with that company, they'd have ample room to hold a meeting or connect their laptop instead of hastily grabbing the office of someone who happens not to be at her desk.

The Free Agent Elks Lodges I mentioned a moment ago would import similar design principles, but serve independent workers almost exclusively. They would consist of one part collaborative space (whiteboards, meeting nooks, and foosball tables) and one part touch-down space (small desks equipped with electrical outlets, phone plugs, and videoconferencing capabilities). They'd work somewhat like the American Airlines Ambassador Club, the Harvard Club, or the local union hall—and some perhaps would be owned and operated by professional associations or by the worker guilds I discussed in Chapter 13. Free agents might pay some sort of annual membership that would entitle them to visit and use the touch-down spaces. And they could rent conference rooms or common areas for meetings, brainstorming sessions, and presentations. These Free Agent Elks Clubs would be equipped with the hardware and tools of a Kinko's, but have the softer glow of a neighborhood pub.

As with so many aspects of the free agent future, the larval forms have already arrived. In San Francisco, I arranged a few interviews at a place called Circadia. At first, Circadia looks like a hip coffeehouse. Inside are mod oversized chairs, lava lamps, and oddly shaped tables. But look more closely, and you'll see that each table has a phone. And look more closely still and you'll see that each phone has a data port for your computer. And what's that over there? Why, it's "The Green Room," which you can book for $50 an hour to hold a meeting. The Green Room even has a wall-sized computer monitor hooked to the Internet. The menu lists the prices of everything from the drip coffee of the day ($1.35) to the Tapenade Trio ($6.95)—alongside Compaq laptop computers ($9.50 for 90 minutes) and floppy diskettes ($1.00 each). Who owns Circadia? Starbucks, of course, confirming what I argued in Chapter 9—that this apparent coffee company is really in the commercial real estate business.

And those who are indeed in the commercial real estate business—companies like Regus Business Centers, InterOffice, and other executive suites that rent offices and meeting rooms by the month—will begin to look more like your neighborhood Starbucks. These places, too, will morph into cool Free Agent Elks Lodges rather than the antiseptic locales many are today. And just-in-time officing—where free agents can rent an inexpensive office or a conference room and pay by the hour—will continue apace.

Meanwhile, trophy towers like the Chrysler Building in New York or the TransAmerica Building in San Francisco will give way to multipurpose towers that combine office space, residential space, and retail space. A free agent could live in a nice pad on the fifteenth floor, work for a four-person microbusiness on the fourth floor, and shop in a grocery at ground level. Think of it as a grown-up dormitory. Free agents lead integrated lives. They will groove on integrated real estate. Or developers could even turn a trophy tower into one of the ROPECs that I imagined in Chapter 14. Grandma Betty Towers, perhaps?

In the end, how we use land will be crucial to making the best use of labor and capital. Indeed, private Idahos and Free Agent Elks Lodges could make the "where" of work more critical than ever. And with all the changes these wild new free-agent-inspired offices will unleash in residential and commercial properties, we may be forced to update a mantra known to home buyers and sellers everywhere. In twenty-first-century real estate, the three most important words may be: location, location, vocation.

THE BOX

CHAPTER 16

THE CRUX: In the free agent future, the toolshed office—which exists mostly to house the things workers needed to produce wealth—will splinter into two new varieties of offices. One will be private Idahos, places for quiet, heads-down work. The other will be Free Agent Elks Lodges, places for collaboration and community—part friendly pub, part executive suite. These new office varieties, in turn, will reshape both residential and commercial real estate. Home offices will become the standard, altering the design and use of the home and triggering a boom in the home improvement industry. Commercial offices will become predominantly collaborative spaces, and trophy tower office buildings will morph into multipurpose residential, office, and retail spaces for a largely independent workforce.

THE FACTOID: At any given moment during the workday, 70 percent of desks, offices, or workstations aren't occupied. Factor in weekends and holidays, and the occupancy rate of the typical office hovers around 15 percent.

THE QUOTE: "A Free Agent Elks Lodge will be a place to hang out, to chat about last night's (Webcast) sitcom, and to work face-to-face with colleagues on projects that require intense interaction. These places will look a lot more like Kinko's or Starbucks than like the cubicle farms of the 1990s. Free agents will buy memberships much as today they join health clubs. And they will come to these New Age offices to do the very things we say we don't like: to gossip and to be interrupted."

THE WORD: *HOHO.* His Office/Her Office. A descendant of the well-known marketing label SOHO (Small Office/Home Office), this term describes family homes with two offices. Designation also works for same-sex couples.

17

Putting the "I" in IPO: The Path Toward Free Agent Finance

First Badger Bank of Wisconsin
August 16, 2010

(A free agent electrician, JOHN ROBINSON, is sitting before the desk of SNIDELY MISER, a bank loan officer with the charm of Dr. Kevorkian.)

ROBINSON: Good morning. I'm here to see about getting a $50,000 loan for my microbusiness. I'm an electrician. Business has been great. Here are my earnings statements.

MISER: That's very nice, Mr. Robinson. But you're hardly the kind of enterprise to which this fine bank would lend money. You don't even have any employees. I mean, you're just some . . . some dude, I think you call them . . . asking for fifty grand.

ROBINSON: Well, the reason I don't have any employees is that I don't want any. Too much hassle. But check out those earnings statements. I've done more than $200,000 worth of business each year for the past five years. I'm a great electrician, if I do say so myself. Here . . . look at what my customers say about me.

MISER: Let me tell you something about banking, Mr. Robinson. We don't give a rat's ass about what your customers say. Here at First Badger, we lend money to businesses—real businesses.

ROBINSON: But I am a real business. I make more money than you do. I've got the proof. I just want a little capital to buy a new computer, get some new tools, fix up my office, and take a distance learning class. All those things would help me make even more money.

MISER: Mr. Robinson, believe me, you don't look like a business. You look like a guy—a guy with dirty hands. Hey! Don't touch my credenza! We lend money to guys with dirty hands only for important things like boats and cars—not for frivolous indulgences like yours.

ROBINSON: I see.
(rising to
leave)

MISER: If you insist, though, I can check with my boss's boss—see if
(looking   I can't work something out. Of course, I'll need some
at a form)   collateral—the deed to your home, the rights to your
                second-born child, and at least four quarts of plasma . . .

MISER: Mr. Robinson? Mr. Robinson?
(looking up
to see
Robinson's
now empty
chair)

***

Wisconsin Federation of Free Agent Electricians
August 17, 2010

(*Our same electrician, JOHN ROBINSON,*
is at a conference table with MARGARET MOORE,
the federation's chief financial officer)

ROBINSON: Good morning, Margaret. I'm here because I'm trying to raise capital for my business. I need about fifty grand to get a better computer, purchase some better tools, expand my office, and take a great wiring course I found on the Internet.

MOORE: Sounds smart. How've you been doing these days?

ROBINSON: Business is great. All these new home offices that need electrical work are keeping me busy. Look at these earnings statements. I've done more than $200,000 worth of business each year for the past five years.

MOORE: Impressive. It's a little risky lending to one person, but we've got a great program here at the federation. What do you say we float a $50,000 bond in Robinson Electric?

ROBINSON: Cool. Uh, what's that mean?

MOORE: We'll assemble a pool of investors to lend you $50,000. You'll pay it back each month with an interest rate that we settle on once we do a little background work on how good you are—probably about 9 percent.

ROBINSON: Okay. That was easy.

MOORE: Yeah, well, the reason we can do it is that we're doing it for lots of members of the federation. We take all these bonds, bundle them together, and sell them as a package. Investors get a stream of income by lending money to talented people

like you. You get fifty grand at a decent interest rate.
Everybody wins.

ROBINSON: *Wow. Thanks!*

MOORE: *Don't thank me, John. Thank Michael Milken and David*
           Bowie.

ROBINSON: *Huh?*

MOORE: *Never mind.*

Capitalism without capital, Jesse Jackson once said, is just an "ism." Companies need funds to get started, get bigger, or get out of trouble. And when they seek financing, most firms generally have two options. They can borrow—and pay back the lender with interest. Or they can sell a piece of the company—and make the investor a partial owner. The first approach—taking out a loan, issuing a bond, or charging expenses to a credit card—is debt. The second approach—soliciting investments from friends and family, chasing venture capital, or selling shares in a public offering—is equity. Debt and equity are the two main rivers that feed America's multitrillion-dollar sea of capital.

But where does all this money come from in the first place? Most of it originates from tiny tributaries called you and me. As I discussed in Chapter 5, over the past two decades, high finance has become democratized, turning the middle class into the investing class. So when companies float bonds or issue stock to raise capital, Joe Six-Pack and Jane Lunch Bucket—through their pension plan holdings, 401(k)s, and direct individual investments—supply the funds. But as power continues to devolve from the unit of the firm to the unit of the individual, this democratization of finance will intensify. The first stage was expanding the number of people who *invest* in stocks and bonds. The next stage—just a few years away—will be expanding the number of people who *issue* their own stocks and bonds. Freelance computer programmers, home-based brownie companies, self-employed electricians, and all sorts of other free agents will soon go directly to debt and equity markets, much as large companies already do, for the funds they need to finance their small enterprises. Get ready for free agent debt and free agent equity—along with an array of new financial instruments to make them possible.

F.A.N. Bonds

Corporate finance—a world filled with derivatives, hedges, and countless other complicated products—can be stupefyingly arcane. So bear with me while I offer a speedy Cliffs Notes account of the democratization of corporate debt over the last fifty years. If you follow this short setup, you'll better appreciate the punch line that will arrive in a few pages.

In the days of the Organization Man, finance was distinctly undemocratic. Banks back then were an insular, clubby world—peopled mostly by slow-footed, change-resistant men who made low-risk loans to established companies. Large companies could usually borrow money. So could slightly smaller firms that were members of the club. But unknowns, upstarts, and outsiders had a much tougher time convincing commercial bankers to lend them cash.

That wall of resistance cracked a bit in the 1960s and 1970s with the emergence of corporate bonds. Instead of begging the banker for bucks, some companies sought out a wider set of lenders—insurance companies, investment banks, even individuals—and sold them bonds. Bonds are a simple concept. They're essentially a contract that says Company A will borrow money from Bondholder B and pay it back at a specified interest rate over a certain amount of time. The company will use the funds to expand or improve its assets, and pay back the sum out of future earnings. If Company A doesn't repay what it borrowed, it could end up in bankruptcy. For the bondholder (B in our example), bonds paid a higher interest rate than from, say, parking the same money in a savings account. For the bond issuer (A in our example), bonds were a way to raise more funds, more easily than it could get from a bank.

But what really greased this simple concept was that bond-holders began trading bonds much as they did stocks. Today, traders buy and sell about $350 billion in bonds every day—eight times the daily trading amount on NASDAQ and the New York Stock Exchange.[1] And an entire apparatus—you've probably heard of ratings agencies like Moody's and Standard & Poor's—has emerged to help potential lenders evaluate the risk of buying certain bonds. The result has been dramatic: Bond-holders now edge out banks as the biggest lenders to private enterprises.

But traditional corporate bonds still restricted the number and kinds of companies that could raise capital. The person who widened the circle further—and even more radically democratized corporate finance—was that 1980s icon, Michael Milken. While his investment banking counterparts were issuing bonds for relatively safe and steady companies, Milken began investigating "junk bonds." Junk bonds went to enterprises too risky for traditional corporate bonds—the start-ups, the shaky, or the sagging. But because these enterprises were indeed high-risk (that is, they were less likely to repay the money than, say, General Motors), they were also high-yield (you could charge them a higher interest rate). Milken's great discovery was that these supposedly high-risk companies in fact weren't all that much riskier than traditional companies. Since you could exact a higher interest rate, junk bonds could be a very lucrative proposition. And if you bundled them together—and spread the risk over many bonds—you could make a ton of money. He did. He also went to prison after pleading guilty to securities fraud unrelated to his central insight. But Milken remains a hugely important figure, the Henry Higgins of high finance. Almost single-handedly, he turned junk bonds from the low-rent district of corporate finance into a respectable $1 trillion market that has helped finance many innovative companies that might otherwise have gone unfunded.

The next episode in our short history of debt came in 1997 when rock star David Bowie issued a bond . . . in himself. Bowie owns the rights to roughly three hundred songs and twenty-five albums that produce a regular stream of royalties. Using that stash of lucrative music as collateral, he raised $55 million by issuing fifteen-year Bowie Bonds that offered a 7.9 percent rate of return. Moody's assigned the bonds an AAA rating, higher than those issued by the state of New York, and the Prudential Insurance Company of America bought the entire offering.[2] For Prudential, the Bowie Bonds represented a steady and predictable income stream. For Bowie, it was a big wad of cash he could use to diversify his investments or expand into new areas. (If he defaults, Bowie loses the rights to his songs—just as someone who defaults on her home mortgage loses her house.)

Other entertainers have followed Bowie's lead. In a deal orchestrated by a creative New York investment banker named David Pullman, the songwriting team Holland-Dozier-Holland—which crafted some three hundred songs for the Supremes, the Temptations, and others—issued Motown Bonds: $30 million of securities backed by the future royalties of their songs. (Moody's rating: A).[3] And Pullman helped make the hardest working man in show business the hardest working bond on Wall Street. In 1999, James Brown issued bonds that allowed him to borrow $30 million at an interest rate of 8 percent, backed by ninety-eight songs to which the Godfather of Soul owned the rights.[4] "I feel good," indeed.

In other words, over the past fifty years, each newly invented financial instrument has further democratized debt. In the beginning, blue chips borrowed money from country club bankers. Then established companies borrowed money directly from capital markets by issuing corporate bonds. Then shakier companies borrowed money from investors willing to buy high-risk, high-yield junk bonds. Finally, as economic power began shifting from organizations to individuals, celebrities borrowed money by issuing their own bonds securitized by a royalty stream from their collection of works.

The next step seems inevitable. Just as corporate bonds expanded beyond sturdy large companies to riskier upstarts, Bowie Bonds will expand from big stars to little people. We'll go from "junk bonds" (high-risk, high-yield bonds for companies) to "hunk bonds" (low-risk, low-yield bonds for superstars) to "punk bonds" (higher-risk, higher-yield bonds for punks like you and me). (See Table 17.1) These new securities—Free Agent Nation (F.A.N.) Bonds—will become another instrument free agents use to raise capital for their enterprises.

TYPE OF DEBT SECURITY		
	Low-Risk/Low-Yield	**High-Risk/High-Yield**
Companies	Corporate Bonds	Junk Bonds
People	Bowie Bonds	F.A.N. Bonds

Table 17.1

This is less fanciful than it seems. After all, there are already two thriving debt markets for free agents. They're called student loans and credit cards. What is a student loan really but a bond? An individual borrows money to improve or expand an asset—in this case her intellectual capacity, skills, and credentials—and pays back the funds, with interest, out of the earnings that asset produces. Credit cards also operate as a capital market for free agents. How many times have you heard about an independent filmmaker or a garage-based techie bootstrapping for years on MasterCard or Visa? Christine Harmel, a self-described digital yenta I talked with in Manhattan, told me she once ran five microbusinesses off her credit card. And she's not alone. A 1998 Arthur Andersen study found that 47 percent of entrepreneurs had financed their business with credit cards, double the portion in 1993. Credit cards have surpassed commercial loans as the leading financing mechanism for these small operations.[5]

Yet student loans and credit cards are imperfect free agent financial instruments. Student loans have the advantage of relatively low interest rates, but the disadvantage of being extremely restricted. In order to get one, you must behave in a specified way—that is, enroll in a college or graduate school and use the money for that purpose. Even though living in France might be a more effective way to become fluent in French and prepare for a career as a translator than taking a year's worth of language courses at Harvard, you could never get a student loan to hang out in Paris for six months. Credit cards have the advantage of being easy—often too easy—to obtain. But they carry extremely high interest rates—often upward of 18 percent annually. You could use your Discover Card for your six-month European sabbatical, but you'd pay a big premium for the privilege.

F.A.N. Bonds would be easier. They would carry higher interest rates than student loans, but they'd be available to more people and for a broader set of purposes. They'd be more difficult to obtain than a typical consumer credit card, but they'd be less risky for the issuer and therefore would have lower interest rates than a typical American Express Card. Just as David Pullman's investment bank specialized in entertainment bonds, new investment banks could specialize in floating bonds for any of the 33 million free agents who want to raise funds this way. And soon we'd likely see ratings agencies that would evaluate the bond offerings of individual freelancers and microbusinesses—a free agent Standard & Poor's. For instance, an all-star marketing guru—with a fifteen-year record of accomplishment, an MBA from Stanford, and a roster of regular clients—might be an AA-rated F.A.N. Bond. A graphic designer just out of art school who's shown some talent but lacks a track record might receive a BB rating from the new Free Agent S&P's—higher risk, but higher yield.

Still, F.A.N. Bonds would be risky. Most of us don't have an orchard of royalty-producing songs we can use as collateral. That's where another recent financial innovation comes in—securitization. Securitization is the process by which some entity purchases a large number of obligations—auto loans, mortgages, credit card receivables—and packages them together into securities. For example, Fannie Mae, a Washington, D.C., company chartered by Congress but owned by shareholders, has become the largest nonbank financial services company in the world by buying and securitizing home mortgages. It assembles huge pools of these mortgages to sell to large investors who seek a safe and predictable income stream. In terms of assets, Fannie Mae (with assets of $600 billion) is the largest corporation in the world.[6] Sallie Mae—with $44 billion in assets—buys and securitizes student loans. A similar entity—I'd call it Bowie Mae, in honor of the pioneer—could do the same for F.A.N. Bonds. Bowie Mae could buy up F.A.N. Bonds, package them together to spread the risk, and sell the bushels of bonds to investors. These bondholders would be paid off with the cash flow from the interest and principal that comes in each month as the free agents pay off their obligations.

In the alternative, professional associations could assume part of this role. They could team with a bank or other lender, make the loans, bundle them, and sell them to investors. Instead of buying the bonds of an individual graphic designer, investors could spread the risk and essentially bet on the graphic design industry. Groups like the American Bar Association, the National Writers Union, or Working Today could get into the financial services business. Or how about F.A.N. Bond mutual funds? Investors already can choose from about 2,250 different bond mutual funds. Imagine a new fund that consisted of F.A.N. Bonds issued, say, by skilled carpenters, perhaps even members of the same building and trades union. Some portion of these carpenters might default on their F.A.N. Bond obligations, but spread over one thousand or ten thousand talented people, it would be a safe bet. (Who knows? The emerging free agent political movement may even press for making the income on these bonds tax free—just as investors don't pay taxes on the income they receive from municipal and state bonds that finance public improvements.) Another possibility would be convertible securities—in which investors would lend money to an individual entrepreneur (that is, buy a bond) but could convert that bond into stock in that person's first publicly held company.

Whatever the exact form it takes, debt will continue to become more democratic. Corporate debt financing moved from bank borrowing to corporate bonds to junk bonds. Individual debt financing will move from credit cards to Bowie Bonds to F.A.N. Bonds.

INDIVIDUAL PUBLIC OFFERINGS

Equity financing of free agents—say, e-lancers selling stock in themselves—is perhaps less likely than F.A.N. Bonds. But it's still a possibility, because equity, too, has become steadily democratized. Stocks also were once a clubby world. Small stocks couldn't get listed on the major exchanges. But new technologies, new business models, and new financing techniques have increasingly allowed more small firms to raise capital in public equity markets.

Consider venture capital. It used to be a dangerous game played only by a few risk-loving financial cowboys. But in the last decade, venture capital has gone mainstream. Stodgy banks established venture funds, and it seemed as if everybody who wasn't making an independent film with their Visa card wanted to become a VC. In the second half of the 1990s, the flow of venture capital to start-up companies quintupled. By 1999, venture capital investments had topped $48 billion, and they continue to surge even in the aftermath of the 2000 dot-com meltdown. The venture explosion, in turn, propelled companies to seek more funds by offering stock to the public earlier and earlier in their lives, often before they had profits. And it helped give rise to publicly held companies built around a single celebrity—for example, Dick Clark Productions, Tommy Hilfiger, Stan Lee Media, and Martha Stewart Living Omnimedia.[7] The narrative resembles the story of debt: The club broke open, which gave way to "junk equity" (risky venture capital), then "hunk equity" (celebrities with shareholders)—and perhaps next, "punk equity" (equity for the rest of us.)

However, most soloists and microbusinesses will have a much tougher time selling shares in their operation than will a wreath-making empress like Martha Stewart. VCs, for instance, aren't exactly shimmying up the drainpipe and climbing through the window of my third-floor home office begging for a stake in Pink, Inc. Instead, to raise money, free agents tend to hit up the people closest to them. According to Fed chairman Alan Greenspan, "more than two thirds of equity financing for small businesses comes from the owner or family and friends."[8] Yet it's possible to imagine small enterprises raising equity financing much as big companies already do—through a new kind of IPO, an Individual Public Offering.

One model for these free agent IPOs is what's called a direct public offering. Under these arrangements, small companies sell their shares directly to the public without the help of underwriters. In 1998, there were 321 direct public offerings that raised $439 million.[9] DPOs were the technique used by cottage firms like Annie's Homegrown, Inc.—which makes organic, environmentally sensitive macaroni and cheese—and Zap Power Systems, a Northern California company that peddles (but doesn't pedal) electric bicycles. It's a short step from small company DPOs to free agent IPOs. Such micro-offerings are an obvious option for people who want to take their tiny enterprises to the next level. And they're even a possibility for committed soloists. Many boxers already finance their training by selling shares to investors. About one in ten pro fighters have syndicated financial backers, whose investments yield these investors a percentage of the boxer's earnings over a specified time.[10] Soloists willing to forgo some autonomy in exchange for an influx of cash that would allow them to prepare for bouts in their own professions might also go the way of the welterweight. In fact, the pen might prove mightier than the fist. A publicly held author could perhaps sell shares in herself instead of getting a book advance from a single publisher—and give her investors a share of future royalties and perhaps a say in what she writes next.

Again, Individual Public Offerings and free agent equity are less far-fetched than they may seem. Recall from Chapter 3 the shrinking half-life of corporations and the expanding longevity of people. Savvy long-term investors might be better off investing in a promising individual than in an existing company. That person will likely be around for decades, earning income and paying dividends. But the company? Who knows? Along these lines, authors Stan Davis and Chris Meyer have proposed the ingenious idea of "reverse stock options." Instead of talented individuals becoming minority shareholders (via stock options) in the company for which they work, their company would become minority shareholders in them. These individuals would sell their employers an option on some portion of the stock in their one-person corporation. Large companies would thereby bind themselves to high-growth individuals rather than the reverse.[11]

Of course, what really makes stock rock and roll is not that investors can buy shares, but that they can *sell* them—for a profit, in a secondary market. To insure that investors could buy and sell their free agent shares—and to create liquidity and fair pricing—we'd need an exchange. FASDAQ, anyone? Remember: NASDAQ didn't exist until 1971. Before then, small-company shares traded in a haphazard, decentralized way on small regional exchanges and through individual brokerages. Remember, too, that exchanges are simply places for lots of buyers to connect with lots of sellers. The Internet can create those places with relative ease. Just look at the growing impact of Electronic Communications Networks (ECNs) such as Island and Archipelago, electronic marketplaces that match buyers and sellers of NASDAQ-listed company shares more quickly and cheaply than giant securities firms can. Free agent ECNs, making markets for individual equities, may be next.

And to offer investors in free agent equities greater diversification, once again there could be mutual funds. Imagine a Tech Gurus Fund, with shares of the one thousand highest paid publicly held software gurus. Or a PricewaterhouseCoopers Alumni Fund, with stock in former employees of that consulting firm. Or an index fund weighted to include the five hundred best publicly held free agents in a dozen representative fields.

Of course, equity financing won't be for everyone. The overwhelming majority of businesses today aren't publicly held. The overwhelming majority of free agents won't be publicly held either. Most equity financing will go to the upper echelon of free agents. And free agent equities would face some obstacles. Investors might prefer to respond to the shrinking half-life of corporations with something less than the Full Monty—and invest in projects rather than people. (They might buy short-term shares in a particular book instead of long-term shares in a particular author.) And plenty of freedom-loving independent workers might resist giving up control to outsiders. Besides, I'm not so sure I like the idea of some scruffy guy in Montana day trading me or speculating in my daughters. And we'd likely need some sort of regulatory arm—perhaps a free agent division of the SEC, which means free agent equivalents of S-1s and all the other disclosure documents public companies must file.

But at this early stage, the details matter less than the broader point: As power shifts from companies to individuals, so, too, will the financial instruments that provide capital. The democratization of finance has already gripped our lives. For the first time ever, middle-class Americans have more of their wealth in stock equity than home equity. In American living rooms, bulls and bears are more than Chicago sports teams, and Charlie Schwab is at least as famous as Charlie Brown. But just as we've grown comfortable with this reality, financial democratization will broaden its reach.

Pogo, phone your broker. We've met the market. And it is us.

CHAPTER 17

THE CRUX: In the free agent future, individuals will raise capital the same way companies do today. They will borrow money (debt) or sell stakes in their enterprise (equity). This will produce an array of new financial instruments—such as F.A.N. Bonds (see below) and perhaps even Individual Public Offerings.

THE FACTOID: A 1998 Arthur Andersen study found that 47 percent of entrepreneurs had financed their businesses with credit cards, double the portion in 1993. Credit cards have surpassed commercial loans as the leading financing mechanism instrument for small enterprises.

THE QUOTE: "Many boxers already finance their training by selling shares to investors. About one in ten pro fighters have syndicated financial backers, whose investments yield these investors a percentage of the boxer's earnings over a specified time. Soloists willing to forgo some autonomy in exchange for an influx of cash that would allow them to prepare for bouts in their own professions might also go the way of the welterweight."

THE WORD: *F.A.N. Bonds.* A form of debt financing for free agents. A financial instrument more widely available than student loans but with lower interest rates than credit cards. To allow the market to flourish, a corporation, perhaps chartered by Congress but owned by shareholders, would buy F.A.N. Bonds and package them into securities—much as Fannie Mae does for home mortgages. (See also: *Bowie Mae*)

18

A Chip Off the Old Voting Bloc: The New Politics of Free Agency

"I'm a free agent and I vote."

*—popular bumper sticker during the
2016 U.S. presidential campaign*

American election years have started to resemble Chinese New Years: Each one comes with its own living symbol. First came the Year of the Woman, next the Year of the Angry White Male, and then the Year of the Soccer Mom. Beware: The free agent—or to make it official, the Free Agent—is about to enlist in this cavalry of election year icons. As the standoff between Big Business and Big Labor recedes into irrelevance, some election soon will be the Year of the Free Agent.

The arrival of free agent politics, like so much else here in Part V of this book, has the look of inevitability. To see it coming, you don't need a crystal ball. You just need a calculator.

In Chapter 2, I reviewed a welter of statistics about Free Agent Nation. Let me display a few of those numbers again, this time within a political frame. While Democrats pander to labor unions and Republicans flay labor unions, organized labor is becoming much less integral to our economy and our politics. Total union membership has been flat for more than a decade, the membership base is growing older, and each year organized labor represents an ever thinner slice of the overall workforce. In the private sector, union membership has actually declined—to the point where more than nine out of ten private sector workers are *not* members of labor unions. Today, America's 33 million free agents outnumber union members two to one.

Yet for all the dreary news in the house of labor, the outlook isn't much cheerier across the street. The union downswing has not loosed a corresponding upswing in favor of big business (even though *both* parties, their appetites for campaign cash insatiable, continue to pander to this corporate constituency). As Alan Wolfe noted in *One Nation, After All*, his perceptive study of contemporary American values, "If middle class Americans can be described as indifferent to unions, they are also increasingly hostile to corporations."[1] More than twice as many Americans now consider big business a greater threat to the country than big labor, according to a regular Gallup Poll of U.S. attitudes toward institutions.[2] Here, too, the figures favor free agents. The portion of the workforce employed by Fortune 500 companies has been plummeting since the 1970s—and free agents easily outnumber Americans who work for these multinational megacorps.

In other words, the cold war between Big Labor and Big Business is over.

Free agency won.

Yet the two political parties remain like soldiers with greased faces and camouflage clothing in a low-budget World War II movie—stuck on some remote island, continuing to fight a war they don't know has already ended. Most politicians remain obsessed with groups that are old and shrinking while ignoring a group that is young and booming. And when they do cast their eyes toward free agents, Republicans see close-minded, modern-day Babbitts, antagonistic to government and greedy for profit, while Democrats see oppressed "contingent" workers.

Still, tap the number 33 million into a calculator, and any fool can see political potential in that row of zeros. And if you then multiply those 33 million free agents by the dozens of wrongheaded laws and policies I discussed in Chapter 12, it's obvious that some politician somewhere will figure out that free agents are the sleeping giant of American politics.

THE FREE AGENT AGENDA: A NEW ECONOMY DEAL

The New Deal began as a progressive response to a changing economy and the Great Depression, and became one of the great triumphs of twentieth-century America. This set of programs cushioned the pain of deep unemployment, boosted the welfare of millions of poor Americans, and lifted the elderly out of poverty. But grand as its achievements have been, the New Deal approach doesn't fully engage with today's real new economy—free agency. The strands from which the New Deal safety net is woven—the premises about what people need and how economies operate—no longer support the emerging independent workforce. In its place will emerge Free Agent Nation's "New Economy Deal"—a reform agenda keyed to the realities of work and life in the twenty-first century.

Expect four major shifts in the underlying principles of public policies (see also Table 18.1):

- *From security to opportunity.* The New Deal assumed that government's highest responsibility was to shield people from risk. The New Economy Deal will hold that government's responsibility is to help the truly helpless, but to let others manage risk on their own terms. Instead of dangling a false promise of security, the New Economy Deal will offer a real shot at opportunity—and equip all individuals, especially the least well off, with the tools they need to make their own way.

- *From the corporation to the individual.* The New Deal assumed that the large corporation was the most just and efficient mechanism for dispensing benefits such as health insurance and pensions. The New Economy Deal will recognize that fewer Americans work for large corporations, that companies have shrinking half-lives, and that the unit of the *individual* is now the most sensible and moral focus for these benefits.

- *From rights for jobholders to rights for citizens.* The New Deal assumed a clear boundary between employer and employee, and thus awarded special privileges to those on the weaker side of the divide—people who held the "jobs." The New Economy Deal will recognize that the old boundary lines have blurred—and that such rights and benefits ought to belong to an individual not because he's an "employee," but because he's a citizen and a human being.

- *From stability to mobility.* The New Deal assumed that government's role was to promote and maintain stability. The New Economy Deal will hold that government's current duty is to foster a new mobility—to create conditions that allow individuals to move freely and make their own decisions about their work lives.

HOW FREE AGENCY WILL CHANGE POLITICS		
	The New Deal	**The New Economy Deal**
Focus of law, policy, and benefits	*The corporation*	*The individual*
Government's overriding aim	*Security*	*Opportunity*
Goal of workplace policies	*Stability*	*Mobility*
Top concern for labor movement	*Wages and working conditions for employees*	*Benefits and lifelong learning for everyone*

Table 18.1

These recast core principles will produce a free agent agenda that will likely consist of six major components: health insurance, microfinancing, unemployment insurance, taxes, a Temp Workers Bill of Rights, and pensions. (I addressed education, another part of the free agenda, three chapters ago.)

Health Insurance

The eight-hundred-pound gorilla of free agent politics will be health insurance. As I explained in Chapter 12, America's prevailing system of health insurance—getting it from your employer—is a historical accident. This system worked fine for a time, but today it is increasingly leaving behind large numbers of Americans. Even in a strong economy, the number of Americans without health insurance has climbed above 42 million. And most of these uninsured Americans work for a living.[3] The structure is especially outmoded for the growing ranks of people who work, but don't hold a "job," that sturdy construct of the Industrial Age. As Lisa Werner Carr, an independent worker in Dallas, told me, "It's a shame that our cars have to be insured by law but *we* don't."

An employer-based system of health insurance no longer makes sense. A better system, a fairer system, and perhaps a cheaper system would attach health insurance to the person, not the job.

But how to do it? As Bill and Hillary Clinton discovered back in 1994, messing around with health insurance is risky political business. So instead of a massive overhaul, it's most likely that health insurance will end up on the same path as pensions. As I explained in Chapter 5, the first private pensions were defined benefit plans: When a worker retired, the employer sent its erstwhile employee a regular check. Today's pensions are predominantly defined contribution: The employer often helps out by making matching contributions, but the employee is in charge of saving, investing, and later withdrawing her money.

In the reigning system of employer-based health insurance, the employer is still the boss. But the future of health insurance—for free agents and regular employees alike—is to put the individual in charge. Instead of accepting whatever health plan the employer offers, the individual would receive (or pay) a chunk of money, and select the health care coverage right for his family. If he then switched employers, got fired, or declared free agency, it wouldn't matter. The health insurance would belong to him—not to his "job."

If Congress wants a model for such a free agent health insurance system, it should look at its own pay stub and the entry marked "FEHB." That stands for the Federal Employees Health Benefits Program, the health insurance arrangement that covers members of Congress and nine million other federal employees. Here's how it works: Federal employees can choose among a dozen or so plans—from barebones HMOs to expensive fee-for-service insurers. Each person shops around for the best plan at the best price for her particular needs, and is free to switch plans each year if she's not satisfied. To offer its services, each insurer must meet certain minimum standards. And insurers must accept all comers. But because the pool of workers is so huge—nine million, remember—insurers compete eagerly for this business. And while the employer pays a portion of the premium, and deducts the employee's portion of the premium from her paycheck, that's where the employer's involvement ends. The worker is the boss.

Why not let free agents—or anyone else whose employer doesn't provide coverage—buy into an expanded federal plan? Free agents would have to pay their full way (unlike federal employees, whose employer—you and me—pays for the bulk of their premiums). But at least they'd be offered a choice of insurance at reasonable rates.

Of course, poorer Americans would need financial assistance to pay for any form of defined contribution health insurance. So imagine scrapping the One Size Fits All Medicaid program and replacing it with "health stamps" to allow the poor to purchase the medical insurance they need—or providing tax credits so low-income free agents could buy into the federal employee program. These proposals won't be cheap. But here's one way to finance it: How about getting rid of at least a large chunk of what newspapers, think tanks, and a few courageous politicians have called "corporate welfare"—the special-favor subsidies and tax breaks that Congress hands out to large companies with squads of well-connected, Gucci-loafered lobbyists? Pulitzer Prize–winning reporters Donald L. Bartlett and James B. Steele estimate that. "the Federal Government alone shells out $125 billion a year in corporate welfare . . . equivalent to all the income tax paid by 60 million individuals and families."[4] This could be the spark that ignites the free agent political movement: a crusade to boost individual wellness by ending corporate welfare.

The current system contains few incentives for anybody but employers to provide health insurance. That will change. Precisely how remains an open question. (Medical Savings Accounts may expand, for instance, or regulations may loosen to make it easier for independent workers to obtain group coverage through professional associations or worker guilds.) But free agency may be the force that leads to a cure for America's health insurance woes.

Microfinancing

One of the major programs of the New Deal was Aid to Families with Dependent Children—the central component of what became known more generally as "welfare." The welfare system pulled many out of poverty, but it also trapped many others in despair. In 1996, President Clinton ended "welfare as we know it" by limiting how long a person could collect a welfare check. With widespread public support, he decided that the wiser approach was to move people from welfare to work. "Work" in this sense usually meant a job. What about work that isn't a job? The New Economy Deal will have the answer: It will move people from welfare to free agency.

The model for this effort is the extraordinary work of Muhammad Yunnus, who established the Grameen Bank in Bangladesh. This bank makes small loans to small entrepreneurs in some of the poorest places in the world—on its experience that what keeps people in poverty is not bad luck or some character flaw, but a lack of capital and connections. Lending small sums (as little as $50) to Bangladeshi women, Yunnus's "barefoot bank" eventually had two million customers in 35,000 villages. It also has a 97 percent repayment rate, about the same as the repayment rate at Chase Manhattan Bank.[5] One reason: Borrowers are usually organized into peer groups, so if an individual fails to repay, her peers don't get their loans. And Yunnus has objectives larger than simply lending money: "The Grameen loan is not simply cash," he has said. "It becomes a kind of ticket to self-discovery and self-exploration."[6]

U.S. organizations have attempted to mimic Yunnus's approach with modest success. These mircofinancing and microenterprise initiatives are the best bet for moving many poor Americans into a mainstream economy. The women's Self-Employment Project in Chicago, for example, has loaned more than $1 million to fund three hundred businesses. Its repayment rate is 93 percent.[7] At least 341 other programs in forty-six states have awarded $160 million in loans to more than a quarter million people—all in an effort to turn low-income Americans into a new generation of micropreneurs.[8]

Says Lisa Servon, a Rutgers University sociologist who has studied these programs, "Instead of trying to channel poor people into a mainstream economy that is no longer a reality, they teach those with an interest in and inclination for self-employment how to strengthen their entrepreneurial skills and stabilize their business."[9] Self-sufficiency will be the path out of welfare in the future—and a major New Economy Deal microfinancing effort will lay the pavement.

Unemployment Insurance

Unemployment is easy to measure when you have a job. One afternoon, you get a pink piece of paper that tells you not to return the following day. But whether you're unemployed is harder to figure out when you're moving from project to project—or when you're serving many customers and clients instead of one big boss. Indeed, the very notion of "unemployment" may be growing archaic. When you work for yourself, when exactly *are* you unemployed? When business is bad? When your skills have become obsolete? When you don't feel like working?

The New Deal–born unemployment system was designed for a world where most people had jobs with employers, and where losing a job was relatively rare and usually temporary. That world has disappeared—but the unemployment insurance system has barely changed at all. It remains reserved almost exclusively for traditional, full-time employees of large operations who have been on the job a prescribed length of time. As a result, only 36 percent of workers today are even eligible for unemployment insurance.[10]

Free agency is inherently less stable than traditional work. Income arrives in waves rather than on a conveyor belt. So an effective "unemployment" insurance plan for free agents won't presume stability or regularity. It will prepare people for the unique circumstances of their particular harder times. Instead of uniform unemployment insurance, imagine, say, Individual Unemployment Accounts (IUAs). Free agents could save pretax dollars to insure against low tides. The funds could support them when business ebbed, or finance them when they needed to learn new skills. Upon retirement or e-tirement, they could funnel any remaining money into their pension accounts. And to assist low-income independents, government could match a portion of the money they've set aside in their IUAs.

Taxes

For the reasons I laid out in Chapter 12, free agent political leaders also will call for both tax fairness and tax simplicity. Expect the New Economy Deal to eliminate double taxation—whereby unincorporated free agents now pay both shares of the Social Security payroll tax. Also expect this new political movement to lock in a 100 percent tax deduction for the premiums free agents pay for health insurance. And since preparing taxes is a form of torture for many free agents—every dollar they spend is both a potential deduction and a potential audit trigger—expect more calls to simplify our crazy tax code. "Self-employed taxes are a nightmare," Diana Wilson, a free agent Realtor and consultant in central Ohio whom we met in Chapter 8, told me. "Why isn't it simpler? Why do I have to get an accountant?" Good questions. The paperwork involved in keeping records and filing returns already costs American families an additional 10 to 20 percent over what they pay in income taxes, says the Brookings Institution's William Gale.[11] Simpler taxes, or even a national consumption tax, might find their way onto the free agent agenda.

Temp Workers Bill of Rights

As I detailed in Chapter 13, while much of Free Agent Nation is getting ahead, a portion of the independent workforce is getting the shaft. Progressive policies that block the low road will broaden support for a New Economy Deal and quiet well-intentioned but misguided cries to resurrect FDR's New Deal. A Temp Workers Bill of Rights could be in the offing. It might include temp worker "right to know" laws, such as those already on the books in Rhode Island and South Carolina mandating that agencies disclose job descriptions, pay rates, and work schedules for temporary employees. And it would mete out stiffer punishment for unscrupulous companies that misclassify employees as temps, turning them into second-class permatemps.

Pensions

Pensions are more free-agent-friendly than health insurance. Free agents already have a few options—SEP-IRAs and Keogh Plans, for example—for setting aside pretax dollars to save for retirement. But where employers often match some part of their employee's 401(k) contributions, free agents don't have that luxury. For wealthier free agents, that missing match is nothing to weep over. They'll just have to deal with it—or if they can, charge more for their services to make up the difference. But for less-well-off soloists, temps, and micropreneurs, free agent political leaders will likely press for something like Individual Development Accounts (IDAs), the brainchild of Washington University professor Michael Sherraden and similar to the Individual Unemployment Accounts I mentioned earlier. For every dollar a low-income person saves, the government contributes two. Account holders can withdraw the money only to buy a home, pay tuition, or launch a microbusiness. A large swath of the middle class has gotten wealthier through 401(k)s. The best way to expand the middle class is to extent these sorts of wealth-building tools to the rest of America.

A FINAL CAVEAT: JUST-IN-TIME POLITICS

One closing note: Free agents will change not just the political agenda; they'll also alter the practice of politics. People who've declared workplace independence tend to prize their political independence. Just as the number of independent workers has increased, the number of independent voters has been climbing for more than a decade. There's a connection here: In my own, admittedly unscientific, online census of Free Agent Nation, more people identified themselves as Independent than with either major political party.[12] This emerging political force will play politics by a new set of rules—rules inspired by an innovation that has already swept American business. I call it "just-in-time politics."

Over the last fifteen years, American manufacturing rehabilitated itself, in part, through a practice known as just-in-time manufacturing. In earlier days, factories churned out items and stored them in warehouses. If companies miscalculated demand, or if the overall economy weakened, they were stuck with huge inventories of unsold goods. Just-in-time manufacturing called for swift production lines and lean inventories. This reduced costs and allowed the type of customization of products well known to anyone who has bought a computer from Gateway or Dell.

Free agency is, in effect, a form of just-in-time staffing. Companies hire the exact people they need for a particular project—no more, no fewer. The political world will slowly morph toward this form. In an era where there are small inventories of party loyalty, effective politicians will fashion coalitions in much the same way that Dell fashions computers—just-in-time.

Just-in-time politics will operate differently from the warehouse politics of the old economy. In the past, one of the main tasks of politics was to keep a single coalition intact—in a sense, to establish a stable inventory that could satisfy any political demand that arose. This, too, is a legacy of the New Deal. For Democrats, keeping together the New Deal coalition of union members, minorities, and senior citizens was the way to pass legislation and win elections. No more. With party affiliation waning and the once exotic ticket-splitting voter now a common species, the modern challenge is to assemble the available components to satisfy the current political demand, do it in real time, and move on to the next task.

Former President Clinton was a master of just-in-time politics, though he never assigned it that name. Early in his presidency, he passed major deficit reduction with an entirely Democratic coalition. A few months later, he put together a radically different, mostly Republican coalition to expand trade with the North American Free Trade Agreement. He raised the minimum wage by assembling one set of political parts and reformed welfare by cobbling together another—all within the same month in 1996. Most political commentators took the nail-biting finishes of some of those fights as a sign of President Clinton's political weakness. Instead, it was merely evidence of a new kind of politics—and if anything, proof that this president had mastered it. The Beltway commentary about the President's "difficulties" was akin to a securities analyst, who upon learning that Dell carries only five days' worth of inventory, declared such information a sign of the company's weakness rather than what it really was—a new way of doing business and a sign of its strength. Moreover, the elections of 2000, which ended in a near-even party split in the U.S. House and Senate—and a statistical dead heat in the race for President—have produced the ideal conditions for just-in-time coalition to supersede the two-party system.

Free agents understand the just-in-time features of today's economy. They will demand a just-in-time politics. If any party attempts to warehouse them, they will resist. Politicians will have to earn their support issue by issue, candidate by candidate, election by election. The person who rouses and feeds this giant first will become powerful. But don't expect the giant to be satisfied for long.

THE BOX

CHAPTER 18

THE CRUX: In the free agent future, the path to the Oval Office will run through the home office. America's independent workers—the sleeping giant of American politics—will become an electoral force. They will help create a successor to the New Deal built on the new premises of the free agent economy. This New Economy Deal will make the individual rather than the corporation the central mechanism for distributing health insurance and pensions and for protecting worker rights. And it will promote an agenda of simpler taxes, microfinancing for welfare recipients, temp worker rights, and individual accounts for unemployment insurance.

THE FACTOID: More than twice as many Americans now consider big business a greater threat to the country than big labor, according to a Gallup Poll.

THE QUOTE: "Most politicians remain obsessed with groups that are old and shrinking while ignoring a group that is young and booming. And when they do cast their eyes toward free agents, Republicans see close-minded, modern-day Babbitts, antagonistic to government and greedy for profit, while Democrats see oppressed 'contingent' workers."

THE WORD: *Just-in-time politics.* The political version of just-in-time manufacturing. Instead of building one coalition and keeping it together, the modern challenge of politics will be to assemble the available components to satisfy the current political demand, do it in real time, and then move on to the next task.

19

What's Left: Free Agency and the Future of Commerce, Careers, and Community

From the September 3, 2012, Wall Street Journal:

Another Megamerger Pushes Dow Up 3.1 Percent; Corporate Alliance Promises Gas, Coffee, Synergies

By E. Liza Lerner
WALL STREET JOURNAL Staff Reporter

SAN FRANCISCO—DaimlerChryslerCitibankTravelersGeneral-Foods (NYSE: DCCTGF) announced today that it had completed a successful takeover of ExxonMobilMorganStanley-DeanWitterStarbucks (NYSE: EMMDS), producing what is, for the moment at least, the planet's largest company. Pending FTC approval, the combined entity will be known as BigCorp.

Kate Doberman, spokesperson for DaimlerChryslerCitibank-TravelersGeneralFoods, told reporters, "This merger is about new synergies and new distribution channels. At BigCorp., consumers will be able to buy a car, gas it up, and grab a cup of gourmet coffee all in one transaction—while also being able to immediately finance all three purchases."

The merger will result in some 125,000 layoffs over the next eight months, said Doberman, adding, "With this announcement, I am out of a job and will become a free agent. I welcome all business for my new enterprise, Kate Communications, Inc. (FASDAQ: KATE)."

Sausalito, California, Mayor Roger Salazar hailed the move, saying, "Having Kate working full-time from home will add to our ranks of home-based workers. That's good for her family and good for Sausalito."

A change like free agency will sweep through almost every region of our lives. I've tried to examine the areas the free agent winds most likely will touch, but I'm sure I haven't explored all of free agency's ramifications. Questions remain. You've probably got some of your own. If so, I invite you to e-mail me your questions about the future of free agency at *Dan@FreeAgentNation.com*.

In the meantime, though, I can anticipate a few questions. And in this—my final chapter before a short Epilogue—I'll offer some answers. Most questions fall into one of three categories: commerce, careers, and community.

COMMERCE

QUESTION: *Isn't the exact opposite happening? Instead of being free agents, won't we all just work for some mammoth multinational corporation?*

In the last decade, large companies have been coupling like nineteen-year-olds in springtime Fort Lauderdale. Between 1994 and 1999, six of America's fifty largest companies disappeared in mergers, and those fifty companies were involved in more than four thousand separate mergers or acquisitions with a total value of $1.4 trillion.[1] But the breadth of these mergers is less than meets the eye. Most have occurred in industries like oil, autos, and banking—industries that are shrinking or that benefit from economies of scale.

Companies in general—and global companies in particular—aren't going away any time soon. Remember: I said in Chapter 2 that about one out of four American workers is a free agent—which means that about three out of four are employed by organizations. Among these organizations we'll see a hollowing out of the middle. Enterprises that can benefit from economies of scale will grow preposterously large, perhaps approaching the size and scope of nation-states. At the same time, ever more enterprises will grow quite small—as free agent soloists and microbusinesses continue to flourish. But midsize organizations will disappear—or at least, become more ephemeral than they are already. In our new economic ecosystem, we'll have many elephants and plenty of mice, but fewer and fewer species in between.

MIT professors Thomas W. Malone and Robert Laubacher have said that "when it is cheaper to conduct transactions internally, within the bounds of a corporation, organizations grow larger, but when it is cheaper to conduct them externally, with independent entities in the open market, organizations stay small or shrink."[2] I agree. Thanks to the Internet, those external transactions will be easy to find and execute. And thanks to corporate intranets, extremely large players will be able to do more internally. As the legendary economist Ronald Coase told the *Wall Street Journal*, "The ease of contracting out tends to make it possible to have many small businesses. And the existence of many small businesses enables some firms to get bigger."[3] But medium-sized organizations will have to leap to one side of the divide or the other, lest they slip into the abyss as the fault line widens.

Alliances will also flourish—short-term partnerships between companies, say to develop a drug or market a product. And start looking for alliances between free agents—as they organize into buying pools to exert more muscle in the marketplace.

Also, as I've suggested, many of the companies that remain will have increasingly short life spans. That may create a market for investing in projects—as I imagined in Chapter 17. And the shrinking half-lives of corporations could give way to a new variety of business organization, halfway between a company and a project—perhaps a microbusiness chartered for a finite period that disappears as a legal entity after a prescribed length of time. This business form, versions of which are sometimes used in motion pictures and real estate, may become as conventional tomorrow as the corporate form is today. (Curious evolutionary side note: Such business organizations would closely resemble the fluid, shifting tribes and clans of hunter-gatherer societies.)

However things unfold, it could be a remarkable time. Innovation occurs through the constant pairing and rearranging of diverse ideas. Start doing that with people and organizations, and we might see some amazing results. What do you get when you cross an elephant with a mouse? I don't know. But in fifteen years, we might find out.

QUESTION: *How are we going to pay for this—not in terms of affording it, but in terms of actually exchanging money? One virtue of large companies is that they're good at collecting and distributing payments. What will happen when we've got all these one-to-one transactions?*

Both the technology and acceptance of "micropayments"—person-to-person exchanges of funds—are in their wee stages. But expect micropayments to become increasingly easy and widespread. Thanks to new financial services companies such as Billpoint, more individuals will be able to accept credit card payments, which will make selling one's services over the Internet even easier. And young companies like PayPal and PayMe are creating ways for individuals to exchange funds easily between themselves—via e-mail or zapping digital cash to someone's Palm Pilot. These services will become increasingly necessary with the growth of Web-based personal advice markets, an industry that some project will be worth $6 billion by 2005.[4] Online escrow services, in which trusted third parties hold the money while the buyer and seller complete the transaction, will also thrive.

We might even see a rebirth of good old-fashioned barter—where people sell services not for cash, but for other services. ("You fix my computer. I'll fix your car.") Each year, about a quarter million companies already conduct $16 billion worth of barter trade.[5] A free agent lawyer might trade her legal services to a designer in exchange for a new logo for her small firm. Direct barter can be an administrative hassle, so we might see the increased popularity of alternative currencies, including innovations such as Beenz, which aims to be a "universal currency of the web . . . a globally acceptable alternative to money," according to its founders. And within certain geographic communities, we might even see more local currencies—like the "Ithaca dollars" used in Ithaca, New York. Free agents could use local scrip, which already exists in 1,500 cities and towns around the world,[6] as a medium of exchange for buying and selling services.

CAREERS

QUESTION: *What will happen to the "career"? Will it simply be a chaotic careening from one thing to another or will there be some kind of pattern people can follow?*

Careers once were rather uniform: education, followed by work, followed by retirement. But in the free agent future, careers will be as diverse as free agents themselves. For instance, some young people might use a stint in W-2 employment as a form of graduate education—to prepare themselves for the world of free agency. Other free agents might return to a traditional job for a few years to pick up new skills. They'd essentially get paid to learn—and then deploy these fresh skills and new connections in their own operation. Others may follow Theresa Fitzgerald's reverse commute that I described in Chapter 1—and move from high-ranking corporate positions into free agency.

Still others may opt for the opposite approach—and use their experience as free agents to improve their position in the traditional work world. For example, Liz Rogers (a pseudonym for a woman who asked that I not use her real name) was flourishing as a free agent for several years, but didn't like the isolation of working on her own. So when she began looking for a traditional job, she did it on her own terms. She told interviewers she had the talent they were looking for, but was also accustomed to a certain work style. She eventually crafted a deal in which she travels far less than is common in her industry. "No way in a million years at the age of thirty-three would I ever have had the nerve to say 'I'm only traveling two to three days a month' had I not been on my own," she told me one afternoon in Manhattan. Caren Ginsberg, until recently a free agent health care analyst in Washington, D.C., told me that she was able to land a high-paying traditional job largely because her new employer was impressed that she had thrived on her own for a decade.

Even amid a wide diversity of career approaches, we might still see a common career pattern among certain groups. Professionals with families, for instance, might move through four stages: 1) Early Intensity—a period of long hours, perhaps in a conventional job or a start-up company; 2) Parental Pullback—part-time, more limited hours, or free agency when children arrive; 3) Empty Nest Energy—after the kids are gone, a more intense pursuit of the same, or perhaps a different, occupation; 4) E-tirement—which I discussed in Chapter 14.

But again, the path of a career will depend largely on the choices of the individual. Indeed "path"—which implies both a route and a destination—may not even be the right word. The new career will be far less linear and systematic. Certainly the career "ladder" of the Organization Man economy has crumbled. Consultant Cliff Hakim, who wrote a smart 1994 book titled *We Are All Self-Employed*, says that what's replaced the ladder is the lattice.[7] Instead of moving up a ladder, he argues, we'll move across a web.

A better metaphor, I think, is the Lego. We'll have Lego careers. Using a basic set of pieces (skills, connections, and interests), we'll assemble a work arrangement—and then disassemble it when we get bored or discover it's too wobbly to stand. We may experiment with odd combinations or stick with steady structures. But the combinational possibilities will be almost endless. And the way that I fashion and refashion my career may be very different from the way you approach yours—even if our constituent pieces are similar. Ladder careers will be exceedingly rare. Lattice careers will become less typical. But Lego careers, and their infinite possibilities and inherent impermanence, will abound.

QUESTION: *What will happen to managers in a world of free agency? Will they become obsolete?*

Most managers are toast. Think about what the traditional manager does: He conducts surveillance on employees, and filters information from one layer of the organization to the other. Both tasks are obsolete. Surveillance is useless when people are often off-site and working in teams. What's more, having a boss-appointed overseer is offensive to genuine free agents and free-agent-minded employees, who prize freedom and autonomy. Filtering information—middle managers as "human message switches," as former MCI CEO William McGowan once called them—is often unnecessary or irrelevant thanks to computer networks and e-mail. As the writers of *The Cluetrain Manifesto*, the brilliant Web screed that became an equally brilliant book, taught us: "Hyperlinks subvert hierarchy" and "A healthy intranet organizes workers in many meanings of the word. Its effect is more radical than the effect of any union."[8] So much for bosses with bosses.

The few managers that survive will be project managers, those who can take a project from start to finish—and "executive producers," managers who operate like Hollywood producers. The core responsibility of these newfangled business operatives will be assembling the right group of individuals for a particular task. That means tomorrow's managers must be sharp judges of talent. And they must have a wide set of connections both within and without the organization, because the people they'll be "managing" (though the term itself will disappear) will be both free agents and employees. (The particular roof under which the talent is temporarily housed won't matter. What matters to customers and clients are the cars, not the garage.) And this person will have to know a fair bit about everybody's job—perhaps because she's done that job herself. The manager of the future will be a combination of a great party host, a great movie producer, and a great basketball coach—a cross between the late Studio 54 founder Steve Rubell, actor/director/producer Penny Marshall, and Los Angeles Lakers coach Phil Jackson.

COMMUNITY

QUESTION: *With everyone gathered in front of their computers working on their own, won't free agency hurt communities and neighborhoods?*

No. In the 1970s, 1980s, and 1990s, during daylight hours, many communities became what I call "neutron bomb neighborhoods." Since both parents left the home to commute to jobs someplace else, their neighborhood often looked like the aftermath of a neutron bomb: The buildings were standing, but the people were gone. Free agents, though, are reinvigorating such neighborhoods. Free agents tend to be more closely integrated to their surroundings than the traditional worker. They watch kids walk to and from school. They know the local merchants. They might not borrow a cup of sugar from their neighbor, á la June Cleaver, but they might go next door when they're suddenly out of Post-its. And the proliferation of F.A.N. Clubs and other ad hoc groups I discussed in Chapter 7 suggests that free agents will fashion their own groups and connections to replace those they no longer have at the workplace. Human beings are social animals. Free agents need community and connection to survive and thrive.

QUESTION: *Are there particular locales where free agency will be especially big?*

Free agency defies geography. In the course of my travels, I interviewed free agents from Harlem to Silicon Valley and countless stops in between. Anyplace where people have skills that others want to buy will be fertile soil for free agency.

That said, I do think that at least nine U.S. metropolitan areas will continue to be free agent hot spots—places where the free agent ethic is in the air and where the social and physical infrastructure of free agency is on the ground. Those American free agent hot spots, from west to east, are: Seattle, the San Francisco Bay Area, Los Angeles, the Dallas–Ft. Worth metroplex, Minneapolis, Chicago, Washington, D.C. and its environs, New York City, and Miami. Overseas, look for free agency to take earliest hold in London, Stockholm, São Paulo, and Sydney.

QUESTION: *It seems like a lot of women are in this book. Are women powering the free agent movement?*

The data are still somewhat scant, but there's plenty of evidence showing that women are shaping free agency in some powerful ways. For example, the number of women becoming small entrepreneurs is soaring—because for many, the best response to the glass ceiling is to exit through the side door. The number of women-owned small businesses has doubled since 1987. In 1999, women ran 38 percent of all U.S. businesses—9.1 million enterprises in all. Some analysts estimate that women-run businesses—large and small—will comprise 50 percent of all businesses by 2005.[9] And while more men than women now run home-based businesses, women are launching businesses at twice the male rate, and are becoming self-employed at *twelve times* the rate of men.[10] Perhaps most interesting in a connected economy, women now outnumber men online.[11]

Combine this smattering of facts with the four free agent values I described in Chapter 4—having freedom, being authentic, putting yourself on the line, and defining success on your own terms—and the next one hundred years might not be the American Century or the Pacific Century. They just might be the Feminine Century.

During my interviews across America, I suspected that women were becoming the, uh, Founding Fathers of Free Agent Nation. However, that suspicion might have come from men's and women's different interview styles. When I'd ask a woman why she declared free agency, she'd often say something like, "I didn't like my boss. The office politics were bringing me down. I missed my family and felt guilty about not being with them more. And I couldn't be myself and do my best." When I'd ask a man the same question, he'd often say confidently, "I wanted a new challenge." Only after another hour of man-to-man conversation would I frequently hear: "I didn't like my boss. The office politics were bringing me down. I missed my family and felt guilty about not being with them more. And I couldn't be myself and do my best." So one reason for my suspicion could be this: Men and women might share the same motivations for becoming free agents, but women are more forthcoming about expressing the reason.

And yet during my travels, I had an experience that deeply affected my thinking about this issue. In Crested Butte, Colorado, I met a woman named Brenda Laurel, who'd founded a now defunct company that made video games for girls. She described four years of research she'd done, involving one thousand children, that explored the differences between how girls play and how boys play.[12] I can't get those findings out of my mind.

Boys, perhaps not surprisingly, tend to play games like King of the Hill. They gain status within their small community by being number one—the toughest, the strongest, the alpha boy. For instance, Bobby has higher status if he topples Billy and lower status if Billy topples him. The boys who can't beat anybody have the lowest status of all. Girls, though competitive, play by a very different set of rules, Laurel told me. The girl with the highest status in girls' play arrangements isn't the one who can defeat the others; She's the girl who most *connects* with the others, particularly if those connections are reciprocal.

So suppose we have five girls: Maria, Kyesha, Rebecca, Sally, and Barbara. And suppose that Maria connects with—that is, plays with, confides in, trusts—all four other girls. And suppose that three of those girls—Kyesha, Sally, and Barbara—connect with her. Suppose that Kyesha is friends with Rebecca and Rebecca with her. Say that Sally and Rebecca have no connection to each other. And suppose that Rebecca has a one-way connection with Barbara—she confides in Barbara, but Barbara doesn't confide in her. If we were to map these arrangements, our picture of these girls' play relationships would look like this:

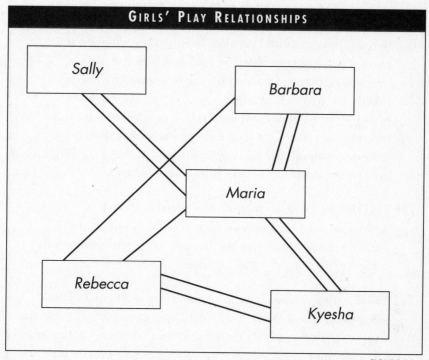

FIGURE 19.1

Maria has the most total connections (seven) and the most reciprocal connections (three). Because she has the broadest and deepest relationships, she's the girl with the highest status.

Look at this diagram again. Then look at Figure 8.4, the Free Agent Org Chart, from Chapter 8, on page 149. Now tell me which gender *you're* betting on in the real new economy.

THE BOX

CHAPTER 19

THE CRUX: In the free agent future, we'll change the way we conduct commerce, guide careers, and build community. Our economic ecosystem will consist of very large enterprises and very small ones—with few in between. Commerce between soloists and tiny businesses will become much easier—thanks to micropayments and possibly barter. The manager as we know it will disappear—to be replaced by a new sort of business operative whose expertise is assembling the right people for particular projects. And rather than deepen isolation, free agency will help revive neighborhoods and communities. Finally, watch for women, rather than men, to define and shape the free agent future—perhaps turning the twenty-first century into the Feminine Century.

THE FACTOID: In 1999, women ran 38 percent of all U.S. businesses—9.1 million enterprises in all. Some analysts estimate that women-run businesses—large and small—will comprise 50 percent of all businesses by 2005.

THE QUOTE: "Enterprises that can benefit from economies of scale will grow preposterously large, perhaps approaching the size and scope of nation-states. At the same time, ever more enterprises will grow quite small—as free agent soloists and microbusinesses continue to flourish. But midsize organizations will disappear— or at least, become more ephemeral than they are already. In our new economic ecosystem, we'll have many elephants and plenty of mice, but fewer and fewer species in between."

THE WORD: *Lego careers.* Instead of climbing a prefabricated ladder, rung by rung, in a predetermined order, careers will have much greater variety. People will assemble and reassemble them much as kids play with Legos. The pieces will be contacts, skills, desires, and available opportunity—and people will build impermanent structures with infinite, idiosyncratic variations.

Epilogue

*"I don't know what the future will bring, but I'm enjoying this.
I feel some kind of satisfaction doing this. After all, I'm
Grandma Betty."*

—Betty Fox (Queens, New York)

Grandma Betty has been acquired.

About a year after Betty Fox and I first met, iGrandparents—a privately held, venture-backed Internet start-up—made her an offer she couldn't refuse.

"They came to my house," Grandma Betty told me in early 2001. "I served coffee and bagels. We had a lovely time. We talked. Then they made a proposal."

The proposal, in short, was this: Grandma Betty would allow her Web site to become part of iGrandparents' site. In exchange, the company would pay her a regular salary, give her some stock options, and offer the technical assistance of engineers at its Philadelphia headquarters.

At first she was wary. She'd already declined two other suitors, because those companies wouldn't guarantee her sufficient freedom. But the men from this company seemed nice enough, she said, and the money was good. So in her gentle way, Betty spelled out her terms. She'd do a deal only on two conditions—that she maintained complete control of her content, and that her Web address (GrandmaBetty.com) remained the same so her loyal followers could find her. The company agreed.

Today her life is much the same as when we originally talked. She still works from her home in Queens. She still operates GrandmaBetty.com all by herself—updating the links and answering senior e-mail. The only difference is the predictable income. "I'm getting paid for what I do," she said. "This is really making life much easier for Grandma Betty."

She says she's both independent and part of a team—that she admires her new partners but that she'd been to their offices only once. "There's nobody telling me anything," she said. "I'm basically on my own. They let me be a free agent."

In *The Organization Man*, William Whyte put it bluntly: "The dice are loaded in favor of the Organization." If you have any doubt that today's game is fixed in a different way, picture the three gung-ho male founders of iGrandparents—flush with venture capital, intent on building an empire—traipsing to Bayside, Queens, to spread cream cheese and sip Sanka in Betty's living room, desperately trying to acquire a one-woman enterprise hatched and nurtured by an out-of-work sixty-eight-year-old.

Today—in good times and bad, at the peak of the boom or the trough of the bust—the dice are loaded in favor of the individual.

That's why I feel good about the future—a future in which more people can assert their independence and guide their economic and personal destiny. It might not be an easy ride. The tempo of work will quicken. The demands of life will escalate. But more people from more backgrounds—whether they're pushed into free agency or whether they leap—will be able to throw off conformity, escape subservience, and live out their true potential. That may not be perfection, but it's certainly progress.

Thirty years ago, Alvin Toffler wrote *Future Shock*, one of the more prescient books of the last fifty years. Toffler wasn't spot-on about everything he foresaw. ("Theories do not have to be 'right' to be enormously useful," he argued.) But that was never his goal. Instead, he hoped to start a conversation—to offer "not the final word," but "the first approximation of the new realities."

You've read my first approximation of the new realities of work and life in the twenty-first century. So pour some Sanka, grab some bagels, and let the conversation continue.

The Official
Free Agent Nation
Resource Guide

What's Inside:

- 10 Steps for Getting Started as a Free Agent
  (including the password for an exclusive
  interactive self-assessment)

- 101 Free Agent Survival Tips

- 10 Sources of Free Agent Health Insurance

- 10 Suggestions for Starting a F.A.N. Club

- 10 Other Books Worth Reading

- Coordinates, Closings & Credits

10 Steps for Getting Started as a Free Agent

"I'd love to work for myself. I just don't know where to begin."

I hear this all the time. That's why I've created, as the first item in the Official Free Agent Nation Resource Guide, this simple 10-step list. Think of it as a starter manual, stripped to its essentials, for launching your free agency.

Follow these steps to freedom:

Step 1. Take a free agent to lunch. Nobody knows more about working independently than your friendly neighborhood soloist, temp, or micropreneur. Call somebody you know who's gone this route. Invite him to lunch. Pick his brain. Get his advice. Then find a few more free agents and do it again. Make sure some of these folks are in your line of work so you can get an even keener sense of what it will be like to work for yourself.

Step 2. Make a list of 5 things you're great at. What do you do exceptionally well? Write code? Fix cars? Devise strategies? Think hard about what you do better than anything else—and better than most other people. Think broadly. Maybe it's something that isn't part of your current work. If you're not sure what you're good at, ask others. Show your list to a few friends, co-workers, and former colleagues to see if they agree.

Step 3. Make a list of 5 things you love to do. What sorts of tasks do you find challenging, engaging, and fulfilling? What would you do if you didn't have to worry about money? Once again, think hard and think broadly.

Step 4. Make a list of where the two lists overlap. No overlap? Go back to Step 2 and try again.

Step 5. Once you have your overlap list, ask yourself: "Will anybody pay me to do any of these things?" If so, you're ready. If not, return to Step 2. This is important. Being a free agent is about more than simply following your bliss. It's about offering something that the marketplace demands. So if what you enjoy, and where you excel, is eating crullers and sitting in a BarcaLounger, you might not be ready (unless, of course, you've spotted want-ads for freelance donut tasters and chair testers).

Step 6. Take the test. Test your mental readiness by taking the Free Agent Nation Aptitude Test and Instinct Collector (FANATIC), an interactive self-assessment for wannabe free agents. You'll find this short profiling tool on the Free Agent Nation Web site. Go to *www.FreeAgentNation.com*. Click where it says "FANATIC." You'll then be asked for a password. The password—exclusively for readers of this edition of *Free Agent Nation*—is **65eap74**. Type in that password, and you'll encounter a series of questions. Once you answer them, you'll get a prediction of how prepared you and your psyche are for free agency.

Step 7. Make (or at least fake) a budget. In traditional jobs, income arrives on a conveyor belt. In free agency, income comes in waves. Sometimes it's high tide. Sometimes it's low tide. Every so often, it's no tide. You need to be ready. And perhaps the best way to prepare is to figure out how much cash you need to live. So come up with a dozen or so categories of what you spend money on. Keep track for a few months. (Use Quicken or other accounting software if it's easier.) You might be surprised . . . or mortified. Also, try to save three months of expenses so you'll have a cushion for when you begin. Equally important for your free agent financial plan: sort out your health insurance options. Determine what kind of health insurance you can get and how much it will cost. For guidance, check out "10 Sources of Free Agent Health Insurance," later in this guide.

Step 8. Talk to your spouse, partner, or close friends. Even if all systems are go, don't press the launch button just yet. This isn't only your decision. Talk seriously—several times—with your spouse or partner. (If you don't have a spouse or partner, talk with your closest friends.) You can't succeed alone. You need support—especially from the people you love. If they're not ready for you to declare independence, the road is going to be rockier and much less fun to travel.

Step 9. Make a list of everybody you know. For a full week, compile a list of everybody you know and everybody you've ever worked with. (Yes, I mean *everybody*—the woman you always see at the grocery store, the jokey guy in accounting.) One of these people—probably the one you least expect—will be the pathway to your first assignment. Put the names and coordinates of these people into a good contact management program.

Step 10. Send out postcards. When you're ready to take off, begin by sending lots of postcards. Let everyone on your contact list know what you're doing, why you're doing it, and how they can reach you (address, phone numbers, fax, e-mail address, Web site). Don't make it an ad. Make it an announcement—even a celebration. And don't use goofy postcards of kittens or postcards left over from your 1979 trip to Kansas City. Design your own simple, yet compelling card. For many free agents, this postcard mailing has led quickly to their first gig.

P.S. Still not ready? Here are four additional tips for the fainthearted:

1. **In your current job, begin *thinking* like a free agent.** Imagine that you're a one-person company that just happens to be on assignment at your current organization. You might not want to leap into Free Agent Nation. But in a working world buzzing with downsizings, rightsizings, and layoffs, you might get pushed. Be ready.

2. **Do some work for a local charity or nonprofit.** Schools, charities, and community groups often need talent—especially free talent. Offer your services. Volunteering isn't only good citizenship. It's also an excellent way to begin building a portfolio of work before you leave your current job.

3. **Dip your toe instead of taking the full plunge.** Begin by moonlighting. In addition to your regular job, try to land a client or customer on the side. Be careful, though. Don't take on too much work. (You'll end up doing poorly at both your day job and your new venture.) And don't use your current office as your base or work for your current company's direct competitors. (If you do, your midnight brainwork might end up creating daytime headaches.) Moonlighting can be tough. But it's often an excellent way to test-drive the Winnebago that is free agency.

4. **Remember: You have a dual passport.** Becoming a free agent—that is, emigrating to Free Agent Nation—doesn't necessarily mean renouncing your citizenship in Corporate America. Instead, more of us will hold dual passports—one in Free Agent Nation, another in Corporate America. Throughout our careers, we'll be able to move smoothly between these two lands.

101 FREE AGENT SURVIVAL TIPS

Here are 101 suggestions for finding more rewarding work, earning more money, and having more fun while you're working for yourself. The tips fall into eight categories:

- Money Matters
- Selling Yourself
- What to Get
- How to Work
- Family Business
- Creativity
- Health and Well-Being (or Protecting Your Asset)
- One Thing To Do in Bed

Begin by reading through all the tips. Then look over the list again and choose one tip to put in place—today. Return to the list once a week, pluck another tip, and enact it in your life.

You probably already do some of the things on this list. If so, kudos. And, of course, *nobody* will ever do *all* these things. I sure don't. I don't think anyone could. (OK, maybe Martha Stewart could, but nobody *I* know.) However, by putting in place one tip per week (with holidays, you've got two years of tips here), your work (and maybe your life) will improve.

Money Matters

1. Get a good accountant. It's worth the money. If you have an accountant and he hasn't been worth the money, get a better one.

2. Keep all your receipts. No matter what it's for, keep every receipt. Toss each one into a folder that you review every week. You'll end up capturing more tax deductions than you'd expect.

3. Diversify. Don't rely on a single client or customer. It's dangerous. If that income stream dries up, it's not much different from being laid off from a traditional job. Whether you're in the stock market, the farmer's market, or the talent market, the principle is the same: don't put all your eggs in one basket.

4. Be brave enough to say no. It's one of the joys of free agency: Turning down work because the client isn't the right fit, the project doesn't square with your values, or the money isn't good. Remember: To the client, a turn-down isn't necessarily a turn-off. It means you're in demand. Warning: This is really scary.

5. Be humble enough to say yes. Sometimes you'll have to do work you don't enjoy or that doesn't rock your world. Why? You'll need the dough. So swallow your pride. Take the money—and run. It's still better than having a real job. Also, consider taking boring or undesirable work if you love the client or the cause. It might pay off in the long term.

6. When possible, charge by the project—not by the hour. Some free agent professionals charge an hourly rate. That's OK. But I recommend charging by the project. Why? You're talent. Do Julia Roberts or Tiger Woods or Yitzhak Perlman charge by the hour? No way. They charge by the performance. They know that buyers care only about the quality of the output, not the duration of the input. If that pricing method is good enough for Julia, Tiger, and Yitzhak, it's good enough for you. Beware: This approach has pitfalls—namely, a client who thinks a particular project is never done. Agree upfront on a project's parameters.

7. Charge enough. Don't sell yourself short. Charge what you're worth. If the prospect won't pay your true value, have the guts to walk away. Another way to look at this: You're not selling time or even services. You're selling solutions to problems. Those solutions are worth something—often a lot—to prospective clients.

8. Don't be shy about getting paid. You earned it. If your client or customer hasn't paid, give a call. Four out of five times a slow payment is due to ineptness rather than bad faith. If you're experiencing that one out of five occurrences, call and call until you find the person who actually writes the check. Take preventive action, too. Spell out the payment terms in your contract.

9. Set aside money for your estimated taxes. Free agents pay their own taxes. Be prepared. Set aside roughly 30% of your revenue. No exceptions. Put it in a money market fund so you can earn some interest. Pay your taxes out of this fund.

10. Save for retirement. You've got an array of choices for saving for retirement. Choose one. For a list of options, look at Nolo Press (*www.nolo.com*) or check with a brokerage firm like Charles Schwab (*www.schwab.com*) or Fidelity (*www.fidelity.com*).

11. Pay yourself first. This is tough when creditors are clawing for payments, but the discipline is important. Set up an automatic withdrawal from your checking account that every month zaps a certain amount into your retirement account.

12. Pay fellow free agents next. You know what it's like not getting paid. Be a good citizen of Free Agent Nation—and pay your comrades fast.

13. Get disability insurance. What's the most important asset of Me, Inc.? You. Insure against calamity and not being able to earn with a disability policy. While you're at it, check your business insurance. If you work from home, your standard home insurance policy probably doesn't provide much coverage for damage, theft, or liability on equipment you use in your business. For more information, check out my favorite insurance site, Insurance.com (*www.insurance.com*).

14. When you're strapped, barter. Let's say you're a designer and you need legal advice. Swap your design services—maybe redo the lawyer's ugly business cards—for her legal services. For more information on exchanging bartered services, contact The National Association of Trade Exchanges (*www.nate.org*) or the International Reciprocal Trade Association (*www.irta.com*).

15. Watch your overhead. Spend money on what you need to earn money. That's it. Treat your business expenses as you treat your investments. If they're not making you money, they're a waste.

16. Celebrate one of the most important holidays in Free Agent Nation: Tax-Mas. Tax-Mas is the week between Christmas and New Year, which makes it the last week of the tax year. Use this week to minimize your taxes. Push income into the new year by asking clients not to pay you until January. Pull expenses—and therefore tax deductions—into the current year by buying new equipment or supplies in December. You can save a ton of money during a week when others are still shaking off their eggnog hangovers.

Selling Yourself

17. Become a brand. I know, I know. Brand You. It sounds so 1997. Tough. It's still true. As Tom Peters says, it's either "Brand You . . . or Canned You."

18. Come up with a brand mantra. Once you've gotten over your distaste for being a brand, distill that brand to its essence. The best technique: Come up with a three-word statement that captures everything your microbusiness represents. It's called a "brand mantra"—and big companies pay lots of money to get it right. For example, Nike's brand mantra is "authentic athletic performance." Disney's is "fun family entertainment." What's yours?

19. Register your name as a domain. Quiz: which of the following seems more credible? An e-mail from *874qz12a@yahoo.com*? Or an e-mail from *Em@EmilyLopez.com*? Many free agents have what Charles Handy calls "byline occupations." So put your name—your byline—on your business. And put your business on the Web. If your name isn't very distinctive and someone has already snapped up the domain, consider appending something about your business—for instance, *www.janebrowndesign.com*. To register your name as a domain, check out Buy Domains (*www.buydomains.com*) or Register.com (*www.register.com*).

20. Look like a business. Don't look like IBM. In your stationery and other materials, don't look like a guy working from a card table in your kitchen. (This is doubly true if you *are* a guy working from a card table in your kitchen.) That said, don't let these concerns conceal the charms of being small, nimble, and creative. Think distinctive boutique, not bland conglomerate.

21. Make cool business cards. Business cards are more important than you may think. If they're memorable, you'll be memorable. On this, as for all your materials, hire a great designer (if you're not a designer yourself). In the free agent economy, design matters. A talented designer is always worth the money. A few microtips: Because many people now use business card scanners, keep your fonts simple. Spelling your e-mail address in Old English letters that form a relief map of Botswana is very difficult for a scanner to read. Also, consider using the back of the card—for your mission statement, a quotation, a cartoon, or your coordinates in another language.

22. Hone your elevator speech. Be able to explain who you are, what you do, and why someone could benefit from your unique talents—in 30 seconds. Then cut your pitch to 15 seconds. Practice it. Sharpen it. Test it on a few friends or family members. Then be ready to use it. You never know who'll be standing beside you on your next elevator ride. Caveat: An elevator speech shouldn't *sound* like an elevator speech. It's really an exercise in being honest, concise, and interesting.

23. Use your .sig file. A signature file (or .sig file) is text that you can automatically place at the bottom of every e-mail you send that lists your phone number, e-mail address, title, and other information. Include your basic coordinates, of course. That'll make it easier for people to contact you. But also include something more inventive—a provocative quotation, a funny line, or your brand mantra—that captures who you are.

24. Listen. Some of the best marketers use a novel technique: They shut up. Let your prospective customer do the talking. Listen—really listen—to what she has to say and how you can help her.

25. Think long-term. You're not trying to make a one-time sale. You're trying to build a long-term relationship. If people feel tricked into hiring you, or buying from you, they won't come back. And that, along with the collateral damage it causes to your reputation, will doom your business.

26. Make a list of ten dream projects or clients. You never know where your work will take you. Creating this list might reveal what you're really seeking in your work. And by building a profile of your ideal clients, you'll be able to recognize them when you encounter them.

27. **ABC.** Always Be Closing. That is, always be ready to seal the deal. Note: this classic advice applies only to people in sales. Reminder: If you're a free agent, you're in sales.

28. **If you have something to say, consider starting a weblog or launching an email newsletter.** On your weblog, you can offer commentary on your profession or industry and provide links to interesting articles and Web sites. If you publish an e-zine, you can provide "news you can use" to readers interested in your topic. Either can be a great way to show off your expertise, enhance your brand, and have a little fun. Caveat: offer real, useful content—and not a sales pitch. For information on 'blogs, check out BlogSpot (*www.blogspot.com*). To set up an e-zine, my favorite service is TalkList (*www.talklist.com*).

29. **Consider a matchmaker or talent agent.** You read about them in Chapter 10. Even though matchmakers and talent agents exact a premium for hooking you up with work, they're a good way to get started and a great supplement to your own marketing efforts. For a list of matchmakers and talent agents, check out the Free Agent Nation Web site (*www.freeagentnation.com*).

30. **You're only as good as your last gig.** *What have you done for me lately?* In the new world of work, everybody is asking that question. You'll have to answer. And answer. And answer. Don't attempt to hustle business based on that amazing work you did during the Eisenhower Administration.

31. **Set your own standard of customer service.** Think about an enterprise whose customer service you admire. Nordstrom? Ritz-Carlton? Your family doctor? The corner drycleaner? Study what they do. Apply those lessons to your own operation. Treat your own clients and customers just as well.

32. **Say thank you.** Never underestimate the power of a handwritten thank-you note. It's easy. It's effective. And your mother will be proud.

33. Keep in touch. Don't forget about former clients or customers. Make a point of contacting them regularly—say every six months—BEFORE you need work. Give them a call. Send them an interesting article. Take them out for coffee. Veteran free agents know it's much easier to get business from former clients than it is to find new ones.

What to Get

34. Get a second phone line. If you work at home, don't use your home line for business. Get a second line, and a separate phone number, dedicated to your business.

35. Get voice mail. Throw away that creaky disco-era answering machine. It makes you look (and sound) low-rent.

36. Get a good contract. Ask a veteran free agent for a copy of his standard contract. Use that contract as your foundation—and shape it to your own needs. That way, you don't have to reinvent the wheel—and you don't have to hire a lawyer. My favorite source for legal and contractual information on independent work, much of it free, is Nolo Press (*www.nolo.com*).

37. Get a good chair. If you're a knowledge worker, you'll do a big portion of your work sitting on your butt. Treat that butt—and the rest of your body—right with a quality chair. This is the one piece of furniture you should spend real money on. (Example: I've worked for five years using an old door supported by two battered file cabinets as my desk—while sitting in pricey, ergonomically correct chair.)

38. Get a whiteboard. Use it for reminders or quotes or lists. Caution: without erasable markers, this item won't do you much good.

39. Get an individual FedEx account. To set one up, all you need is a credit card. Having your own account makes sending overnight packages much easier. And it makes you look like a more legitimate operation. No wonder a few million free agents have them.

40. Get a coach. Coaches, we learned in Chapter 10, are "shrinks without the couches, management consultants without the flow charts, and sympathetic bartenders without the row of shot glasses." If that seems like something you could use, consider a coach. Coaches aren't for everyone, of course. But for many people who work for themselves, coaches are valuable partners. For more information, check out the International Coach Federation (*www.coachfederation.org*) or Coach U. (*www.coachu.com*).

41. Get a back up plan. Most free agents spend many hours on their computers. So be sure to back up your files regularly. I know this sounds obvious. But when was the last time you backed up? If it's been longer than three days, you're asking for trouble. Get a Jazz drive—and keep the disks in a safe place. Or consider an online backup service such as @Backup (*www.backup.com*), Driveway (*www.driveway.com*), or Xdrive (*www.xdrive.com*). Extra protection: Guard your computer from viruses with software such as McAfee Anti-Virus (*www.mcafee.com*) or Norton Utilities (*www.symantec.com/nu/*).

42. Get a great contact manager. Your network is your lifeline. Keep your contacts up to date—and in one place—using contact manager software like Act! Warning: See preceding tip.

43. Get a filing system. Keep files on everything. I follow the advice of time management maven David Allen and group my files into two categories: project files and everything else. Then I add a third category: financial files. No need to get fancy here. Just keep the files in alphabetical order. Hint: You're going to need more file cabinets. For more information about the magic of files, check out David Allen's Web site (*www.davidallen.com*).

44. Get a labeler. I use a battery-operated label-printer to spit out nifty adhesive labels for my file folders. An astonishing number of free agents do the same. No, I don't get it either. And perhaps my affection for my labeler should frighten me (or my wife). But somehow these gizmos work. Find an inexpensive one and start cranking. You'll never go back.

45. Get a virtual assistant. Unlike honchos in the traditional world of work, most free agents don't have a personal assistant. Most of us wouldn't want one either—at least all the time. But sometimes a helper would be a godsend. And now you can find one on the Internet—a virtual assistant. For more information, check out AssistU (*www.assistu.com*), StaffCentrix (*www.staffcentrix.com*), and the International Virtual Assistants Association (*www.ivaa.org*).

46. Get an online postage account or a postal machine. They add the look of legitimacy and make it easier to track postage expenses. Check out Stamps.com (*www.stamps.com*) or Pitney Bowes (*www.pitneybowes.com*).

47. Get a free fax number. You can save money by skipping the fax machine. Instead, consider an online fax service such as eFax (*www.efax.com*) or jConnect (*www.j2.com*). Basic service is usually free. Added services are usually cheaper than an actual fax machine. Another advantage: Online faxes save space in cramped offices.

48. Get some caffeinated peppermints. You read it right. These mints, manufactured by a small Seattle company and called Penguin Caffeinated Peppermints, are spiked with free agents' favorite stimulant. They come in nifty little tins, and three tiny mints deliver the punch of one cola beverage. Think Altoids on steroids. (Coordinates: *www.peppermints.com*.)

49. Get *Jerry Maguire*. It's the ultimate free-agent movie. (If you've forgotten why, look at Chapter 4.) Forget the now-famous line, "Show me the money." The film's real spirit is the words of Maguire colleague and main squeeze Dorothy Boyd (Renee Zellweger): "I care about the job. But mostly I want to be inspired." Rent this movie. Watch it carefully. *Jerry Maguire* is to free agency what *It's a Wonderful Life* is to Christmas.

How to Work

50. Establish an opening ritual. Try to begin your day the same way. If you work at home, maybe take a short walk before you go to your office. Have a cup of tea or read or meditate before starting your work. An opening ritual will ease your mind, body, and soul into the day.

51. Establish a closing ritual. Know when to stop working. Try to end each work day the same way, too. Straighten up your desk. Back up your computer. Make a list of what you need to do tomorrow. Free agent life can often feel like free verse. Sometimes it helps to impose your own punctuation marks.

52. Get used to the three "-ty's." Ambiguity. Uncertainty. Volatility. They're part of free agent life. Projects collapse. Money evaporates. Customers go wiggy. Get over it. That's the way it works.

53. Be yourself. Throw off the gray-flannel straightjacket. Forget the mask. Be who you really are. It's not only liberating. It's good business.

54. Learn. To succeed as a free agent, you must always be learning. Become a learning machine. Ask questions. Take smart people to lunch. Read. Read some more. Listen to audiobooks. Take classes. Go to conferences (which are also great places to network). Added benefit: This makes life more interesting. Yet another benefit: Studies have shown that people who make constant learning part of their lives end up living longer.

55. Tell the truth. To paraphrase Mark Twain (in a slightly different context), this will gratify some people and astonish the rest.

56. Be nice to your FedEx driver. Same goes for the UPS person, your letter carrier, the barrista at Starbucks, and the copy jocks at Kinko's. Why? In some sense, they're your co-workers. More important reason: It's better, smarter, and easier to treat people well.

57. Benchmark. If you're selling services, get in the habit of rating your clients and your gigs. Here's how: After a project ends, ask yourself four questions about it: 1) How much money did I earn? 2) How much did I learn? 3) How many new connections did I make? 4) How much fun did I have? Respond to each question with a rating from 1 (almost zilch) to 10 (a ton). Keep a record for the next time that client calls or the next time you're trying to figure out which assignments to accept.

58. Failing is OK. Not failing is not OK. If you don't flop every so often, you're not trying hard enough.

59. Say "I don't know." Here's a secret: Offering this answer is much more impressive than spreading a thin layer of b.s. Caveat: If this is your only response, you're going to have some problems.

60. Guard your calendar. Make sure your time is focused on your one or two top priorities. Ask yourself: "Is this how I want to be spending my time right now?" Remember: You *are* your calendar. So treat your calendar with respect.

61. Be paranoid. The good times won't last.

62. Don't be paranoid. The bad times won't last.

63. Never say up front that you can beat a deadline. Just turn your work in early and look like a hero. Related advice (which is ancient but unassailable): Underpromise, overdeliver.

64. Be quick. But don't hurry. This one isn't mine. It comes from the legendary UCLA basketball coach John Wooden. Read it again. Think about it. Makes sense, huh?

65. Take it "bird by bird." This one isn't mine either. It comes from the writer Anne Lamott, in her book of the same name. Here's the story that produced the advice: "Thirty years ago, my older brother, who was ten years old at the time, was trying to get a report on birds written that he'd had three months to write. [It] was due the next day. We were out at our family cabin in Bolinas, and he was at the kitchen table close to tears, surrounded by binder paper and pencils and unopened books on birds, immobilized by the hugeness of the task ahead. Then my father sat down beside him, put his arm around my brother's shoulder, and said, 'Bird by bird, buddy. Just take it bird by bird.' " That's the best writing advice I've ever heard—as well as some mighty fine counsel about life in general.

66. Getting bigger is a choice. Getting better is a must. In Free Agent Nation, bigger isn't necessarily better. Better is better.

67. Do your own performance review. When you're a free agent, you don't have an onion-breathed boss herding you into a conference room every six months to tell you how you're doing. But you still need to know. After each assignment, write a paragraph about how you think you did and what you could improve. Even better, whenever possible, ask your client to fill out a short customer satisfaction or performance assessment that you've created.

68. Respond to calls and e-mails quickly. Even if your response is

"I'll get back to you," try to get back to people within 24 hours. They'll appreciate the courtesy. Reality check: sometimes you'll violate this rule.

69. Don't take yourself too seriously. You're not curing cancer or ending world hunger. Note: If you are doing either of these things, disregard this tip.

70. Take advantage of slow periods. When you work for yourself, sometimes you'll be cranking all day, all week, all month. Other times, you might not have much to do at all. Don't squander this downtime worrying about going broke. Instead, use the time to clean your office, take a trip, plant flowers, or have some fun. When the mania begins again, you'll be glad you did.

71. Answer to a small group. Recall the words of Erika Tauber from Chapter 7: "When you have told three or four other people you'll do something, you will do it." Small groups can be sounding boards for ideas and wellsprings of inspiration. For guidance on forming your free agent posse, turn a few pages and read "10 Suggestions for Starting a F.A.N. Club."

72. Volunteer your talents. One reason: It's the right thing to do. Another reason: Especially during slow times, working for charitable causes—a national charity, a local nonprofit, your neighborhood church, synagogue, or mosque—can strengthen your network of contacts and surface new opportunities.

73. Spend 10 minutes today laughing out loud. Turn on Comedy Central, read a funny book, look at photographs of yourself in junior high. Laugh. Fully.

74. Make a "to don't" list. Another gem from the inimitable Tom Peters. Prepare a list that contains all the things you shouldn't waste your time on—useless tasks, unnecessary meetings, worthless phone calls, and so on. Then place it next to your "to do" list—and stick to it.

75. Remember why you became a free agent in the first place. Some days will be hellish. Especially on those days, don't forget why you decided to take control of your life.

76. Do your errands when wage slaves are in their cubicles. It's a small pleasure. But damn it's nice to go grocery shopping at 2 P.M., when the aisles at Safeway are empty enough for drag racing.

77. Be good. Don't forget: The underlying operating system of the free agent economy is the Golden Rule. If you don't know what I'm talking about, look back at Chapter 8.

Family Business

78. Set a boundary. If you're working at home, and you've got the space, find a room with a door that closes. Make that your office—and *only* your office. This will be good for your loved ones and better for your business. Blending work and family can be great. But it has its limits. For guidance on setting boundaries, visit the Turn It Off Web site (*www.turnitoff.com*).

79. Hire your spouse. If you're married, consider hiring your spouse. By making him your employee, you can provide him a retirement savings plan as well as generous health insurance for his (and therefore your) entire family. It's crucial that your spouse actually do some work, that you write a job description, and that you enlist a payrolling service to pay his wages. But once you get the details worked out, you can likely save some money. (Unfortunately, this technique is much more complicated for domestic partners.) As with all such matters, check with your tax consultant first.

80. Practice desktop parenting. If you've got kids, putting a little desk in Mom or Dad's home office is a great way to integrate work and family. Stock it with paper, crayons, scissors, books, even homework—and the two (or more) of you can each work happily for an hour or two. Of course, no sane person would do this all the time (or even lots of the time)—or when facing a deadline. But on late nights or rainy afternoons, it's nice.

81. Give your kids some responsibility. Kids can learn a lot by occasionally doing real work and shadowing their parents. So toss the twins in the car when you have to race over to Kinko's or drop a package at FedEx. Ask your daughter to stamp envelopes. Older kids may even be able to proofread or fix your computer. Make your microbusiness a family business.

82. Put your neighbor to work. A free agent mom offered me this advice, which I'll repeat verbatim: "Do yourself a favor and hire a neighborhood teenager to play with your young children for a few hours a day—or even just a couple of hours a week. They will appreciate the money and you will have a few hours of intense concentration to get your work done! The kids also look forward to a special visitor to play with!"

83. Buzz off. Let me put this delicately: Sometimes your family won't be as excited or worried or obsessed with your work as you are. Remember that. This is particularly true for children. Don't forget: they're kids. They shouldn't be working. You're an adult. You *should* be working. In Free Agent Nation, every day can be Take Your Children to Work Day. But if you carry this too far, the little ones may start organizing their own event: Leave Us the Hell Alone Week.

Creativity

84. Carry a notebook and pen. Thomas Edison did it. Virginia Woolf did it. And so did Charles Darwin. They toted a notebook with them everywhere and wrote down ideas that popped into their heads. Follow their example. Scribble a thought, a question, or an observation that occurs to you in the middle of something else. A surprising product you spot in the grocery store. A beautiful design you see. A great line you hear or read. Page through the notebook periodically. Trust me: This is a fantastic way to spark ideas and to weave creativity into the fabric of your life. Alternative: Keep a microcassette recorder with you—and talk your ideas and observations into it.

85. Take a walk. A change of scenery coupled with some physical movement can often move you past creative blockages.

86. Rediscover your public library. Spend an hour there just looking around. You'll be surprised by how many incredible things you'll find. Get a library card. Use it. Public libraries were offering free info well before the Internet. And they're much better organized.

87. Venture outside your domain. Go to a newsstand. Find 10 magazines that you've never read and never would buy. Buy them. Look for ideas on how to market yourself or new services you can offer. Creativity is about combining ideas from diverse realms—using the unfamiliar to understand the familiar. Example: I once got a great business idea by reading a magazine about cake decorating. (Cake decorating!) Warning: Your spouse or partner may look at you suspiciously, as mine did, when you come home holding copies of *Divorce Magazine*, *Teen Cosmo*, and *Cat Fancier*.

88. Take a nap. Once you get over feeling guilty for "sleeping on the job," you might find that the siesta works wonders for creativity and alertness. Albert Einstein was a napper—and he thought up some pretty good ideas.

89. Read a novel. Sure, reading business books and tech magazines is a fine use of your time. (Besides, it helps people like me feed our families.) But—and let this be our little secret—you can usually learn just as much by reading a good novel: the dynamics of relationships, the habits of the human heart, the demons that drive our behavior. Get the facts—read some fiction.

90. Leave your comfort zone. Try this two-step plan: 1) Think of someone you'd be uncomfortable to call for lunch. 2) Call that person.

91. Get a one-year museum pass. Free agents often get hooked on the narcotic of overwork. Sitting in your office, doing your own thing, it's easy to forget about the outside world. So give yourself a passport to renewal. A one-year membership to a cool museum. Or a gift certificate to a movie theater. Or a year's pass to the local zoo. Free agents cannot live on work alone. Fortunately, there's a two-word solution: get out. Added bonus: this makes a great—and (usually) tax-deductible—gift for fellow free agents.

Health and Well-Being
(Or Protecting Your Asset)

92. Exercise. It's good for you. Seriously. Do it. Vigorous exercise at least every other day will clear your head, help you sleep, and extend your life.

93. Take a "Sabbath." Choose one day during the week when you don't work. Don't go into your office. Don't check your phone messages. Don't answer your e-mail. Respecting your own "Sabbath" will be good for your soul—and better for your business. A crutch for the compulsive: Post a pad of paper or a whiteboard on the outside of your door during your Sabbath. If you can't help yourself and must write down an idea or a to-do item, write it there—to avoid the temptation of entering your office.

94. Eat your fruits and veggies. Sorry to be a nag, but this is really important. Scrap the Cheez Doodles—and instead munch on apples, carrots, grapes, figs, and almonds. While you're at it, drink plenty of plain old water.

95. Watch the ergonomics. Free agency can be a pain. Don't make it worse with a poorly configured workstation. Pay careful attention to how your desk and chair are set up. And make sure you get up and move during the day.

96. Go underground. At least twice this year, spend three or more consecutive days without reading your e-mail, making a business phone call, or checking your voice mail. I call this "going underground"—and in our hyperkinetic, information-drenched world, it helps cleanse the soul and freshen the mind.

97. Sleep. Get enough. You need it.

98. Take a shower. If you work from home several days straight, even the most hygienic among us can, uh, forget. So soap up. You'll feel better. Your family will appreciate it. And showers have been known to be great idea generators.

99. Eat some chocolate. Hey, people tell me this works. It's not a fruit or a veggie, but it probably can't hurt.

100. Get a checkup. Too many people I know have detected potentially horrible problems simply by getting a thorough physical every year or so. If your health insurance makes this somewhat affordable, get a physical exam in next three months. No joke. Take care of yourself.

One Thing To Do In Bed

101. Take the Sunday night test. If you're like 99 percent of the population, you've experienced "Sunday night dread." This ailment begins creeping up your spine around 4:30 on Sunday night and reaches a crescendo around 11 P.M., as you realize you're going to have to go to work the following day. (My own research has shown that Sunday night dread begins forming around third grade and eventually dissipates around age 70.) Most free agents, however, don't suffer this weekly malady. Sure, they contract it occasionally—like a head cold. But it's not a chronic syndrome. So this Sunday night, when you go to sleep, ask yourself: "Am I suffering from Sunday night dread?" If so, you might be doing something wrong. But if you're not getting it—if you're lying there in bed thinking, "You know, I sorta like this. I'm not dreading tomorrow. I'm actually looking forward to it"—then you're probably on the right path.

10 Sources of Free Agent Health Insurance

It's the issue that alternately grips, terrifies, and angers the citizens of Free Agent Nation: health insurance. Finding it. Affording it. Keeping it.

Because getting health insurance through an employer remains the standard method in the United States, many Americans find themselves trapped in jobs they don't want, because leaving would mean losing their health insurance. Meanwhile, people who decide to work for themselves often "go bare" and try to survive without coverage—and free agents who manage to find coverage often pay more to get less.

Alas, there's some good news. As more people become free agents, more insurance companies are waking up and seeing an attractive market. Over the last few years, some new options have emerged and some old options have improved. If you work at it, you will likely be able to find some form of health insurance.

Nonetheless, be wary. Since health insurance is regulated by states, laws vary from place to place. A free agent in Sheboygan won't have the same options as her sister in Schenectady. If you or a family member has a pre-existing condition, insurance will cost a bundle—if you can get it at all. And in general, the system doesn't easily accommodate independent workers. So do your research. Run the numbers. And read the fine print.

Meanwhile, here are ten sources to consider as you begin your search:

1. **Your employed spouse.** If your spouse has a regular job and that wonderful Organization Man perk called employer-provided health insurance, that's often your best option. (Unfortunately, many states and companies still don't extend family health insurance benefits to domestic partners.)
2. **Your former employer.** If you had employer-financed health insurance in your last job, federal law entitles you to keep that coverage for 18 additional months—if you pay for it yourself. Under the Consolidated Omnibus Budget Reconciliation Act (COBRA), you can maintain your coverage provided that you

pay both the employer and employee share of the monthly premium. Getting coverage this way will cost more than when you had a real job. And it won't last beyond those 18 months. But for many free agents—including this free agent (see Chapter 13)—COBRA has offered a helpful bridge.

3. **Labor unions, guilds, and professional associations.** Many of these groups are large enough to negotiate good deals with insurance companies. Figure out which unions, guilds, or associations you're eligible to join. Then see what insurance benefits they offer. Bonus: Being a member of a union or professional association has many other advantages—and the dues are often not substantial. Reality check: Many association plans, for complex legal reasons, don't operate in every state. So you could be a card-carrying member of the Association of Free Agent Gourd Painters, but not be able to get their health insurance plan because you live, say, in Louisiana. Also, be sure to look at Working Today's Portable Benefits Network, an innovative insurance plan for free agents who work in New York's new media industry or who belong to certain professional associations. (For more information, visit the Working Today Web site at *www.workingtoday.org*.) Other organizations to consider: Your local Chamber of Commerce, the National Association of the Self-Employed (*www.nase.org*), and the National Federation of Independent Businesses (*www.nfib.org*). Another possibility: If you're a college graduate, your school's alumni association might offer health insurance.

4. **Group purchasing programs.** In some states—such as California, Texas, and Connecticut—microbusinesses and (often soloists) can form group purchasing pools to command more power in the health insurance marketplace. Small enterprises can band together to negotiate the same sort of more affordable and comprehensive rates that large companies get. The pools vary considerably from state to state—some are government initiatives, others are nonprofits—but if you're eligible, you can usually find better rates than securing insurance on your own.

5. **The open market.** When bargaining for health insurance, it's

better to be part of a group. But it's not mandatory. Many individuals (and families) buy health insurance on the open market much as they would purchase station wagons or
strawberries. These individual policies are usually more expensive than group coverage. But for people with families, it's
often worth the cost. One carrier that many free agents have
used to find open market health insurance is the Blue
Cross/Blue Shield plan in their state (*www.bluecross.com*). But
shop around, because rates and coverage can vary considerably.
And whatever answer you get, ask for a better deal. One more
thing: Be sure to choose a carrier with a very high rating from
A.M. Best (*www.ambest.com*), the insurance rating service.
Also, under the Health Insurance Portability and Accountability Act (HIPAA), certain individuals can't be denied individual
health insurance even if they have pre-existing conditions. This
law is complicated and limited, so investigate fully. One good
source is the federal government's HIPAA Web site
(*www.hcfa.gov/medicaid/hipaa/*).

6. **Online.** One way to assess the market is to visit one of the
    many Web sites that offer quotes on health insurance. On
    most of these services, getting a quote is free. But if you're ul-
    timately interested in a package you're offered, you'll likely
    have to work with an insurance agent. Among the most pop-
    ular of these sites are eHealthInsurance (*www.ehealthinsur-
    ance.com*) and QuoteSmith (*www.quotesmith.com*).

7. **A matchmaker or talent agency.** Free agents who find work
    through a talent agent or matchmaker (see Chapter 10) can some-
    times also obtain health insurance through these intermediaries.
    You become the "employee" of one of these entities—and receive
    certain employee benefits—even as you move from project to proj-
    ect. Another option for free agents, especially microbusinesses, is
    essentially to outsource your H.R. Department by enlisting a Pro-
    fessional Employer Organization (PEO), which provides pay-
    rolling, tax withholding, and health insurance to small enterprises.
    For a list of PEOs, contact the National Association of Profes-
    sional Employer Organizations (*www.napeo.org*).

8. **A high-deductible policy.** If you don't earn much, consider a bare-bones policy that offers catastrophic coverage with a very high deductible. That way, you're covered in the case of a calamity and your monthly premiums won't be outrageously high. This isn't ideal, of course. You'll pay out of pocket for doctor visits and routine medical expenses. But a high deductible policy is usually better than no coverage at all.

9. **Medical Savings Account (MSAs).** This option, created by Congress in the mid-1990s, allows free agents to combine certain high deductible policies with a medical version of an Individual Retirement Account (IRA). Each year, you can contribute pre-tax earnings to your MSA just as you would to an IRA or a 401(k). Then, when you have a medical expense (say, a doctor's visit), you use MSA funds to pay the bill. If you have money left over at the end of the year, the funds stay in your account and earn interest. For people who are healthy and don't have children, MSA's can be extremely cost-effective.

10. **The federal government.** Some free agents might be eligible for government-financed health insurance. If you're over 65, you're probably eligible for Medicare. (People who have certain disabilities are also eligible.) For more information, call 1-800-MEDICARE or visit *www.medicare.gov*. If you have a very low income or a significant disability, you might qualify for Medicaid, a joint federal-state program administered by the state. For information on Medicaid, contact your state insurance office or visit the federal Health Care Finance Administration on the Web (*www.hcfa.gov*).

One last note: free agent health insurance premiums are almost always deductible as a business expense. How much you can deduct, though, depends on a host of factors—including how you've set up your enterprise and when you established your plan. Check with a good tax consultant to ensure that you maximize any savings.

10 SUGGESTIONS FOR STARTING A F.A.N. CLUB

Since the first edition of *Free Agent Nation* appeared, many people who work for themselves, intrigued by what they read in Chapter 7, have emailed me about starting their own Free Agent Nation Club. (F.A.N. Clubs, recall, are clusters of free agents who meet regularly to exchange business advice and personal support.) Independent workers yearn to come together. They're just not sure how to do it.

So I asked a bunch of free agents who'd formed these small groups for their advice on how to get started. They told me that there was no secret formula locked in a safe in Atlanta nor some complicated F.A.N. Club blueprint printed on microfilm and hidden in a safe house. But they did offer several suggestions, which I've assembled here.

1. **Think about what you want to accomplish.** F.A.N. Clubs are as different as free agents themselves. Most combine hard-headed counsel with softhearted sociability, but the exact mix always varies. So figure out what you're seeking. By considering *why* you want to start a F.A.N. Club, you'll get a better sense of *how* to start one. Also, see if any friends or colleagues have formed a F.A.N. Club. Ask if you can visit. Getting a feel for how a few groups operate will help you form your own.

2. **Recruit one pal.** Find a friend or close colleague whom you'd like to be in your group. Congratulations. You two are the nucleus of this amoebic F.A.N. Club. Now each of you should find one more person, whom the other doesn't know, to join your gang. That makes four—and you're on your way.

3. **Balance similarity with diversity.** What happens next can be tricky. You want the members of your F.A.N. Club to share some common ground. But you don't want that ground to go swampy with sameness. So instead of immediately rounding up the usual suspects, work the edges of your respective networks. If you're stuck, consider advertising in a trade publication or making an announcement at a meeting of your professional association or labor union. Most important,

choose people who are strong where you are weak. If you excel at marketing but don't fathom finance, seek someone with head for numbers. Warning: Finding the perfect mix of people is tough. You probably won't get it right at first.

4. **Choose the right meeting locale.** Location matters. Where you hold your gatherings will help shape their form and feel. Many F.A.N. Clubs schedule each meeting at a different member's home. Others snag a room or a large table at a restaurant. More possible venues: a local bookstore, your public library, a coffee shop, your neighborhood community center.

5. **Meet at a regular time.** The F.A.N. Clubs that endure establish a schedule—and then stick to it. For instance, Women Entrepreneurs Homebased in Belmont, Massachusetts meets on the first Monday of every month. Women Independent Consultants in Silicon Valley gathers on the third Thursday of every month. Choose a rhythm that works for your group. Once a week is probably too often, once a year not often enough. Then make sure every member has every F.A.N. Club meeting for the next six months inked into his calendar.

6. **Stick to an agenda.** With F.A.N. Clubs, a little anal-retentiveness can go a long way. Terri Lonier's group, which I discussed in Chapter 7, has a strict agenda. Each person gets 10 minutes to talk. They describe what they're working on, seek advice from the others, and then announce one goal they'll achieve by the next session. Then somebody else gets ten minutes. And so on. At every meeting, one F.A.N.Club member keeps time. Another records each person's goal (so the others can then enforce it) and e-mails a summary to the members after the meeting. The end of the meeting can be more free-wheeling, but adhering to a set format works well for this group—as it does for just about every other F.A.N. Club I've encountered.

7. **Eat.** I don't know why, but F.A.N. Club meetings tend to work better when there's food. Consider scheduling your meetings around a meal. Or make each meeting a potluck. Or ask whoever is hosting that particular meeting to cook for the rest of

the group. Also, many F.A.N. Clubs benefit by consuming food for thought. Consider assigning an article for everyone to read and discuss. Organize a meeting around a particular book. Or invite a guest to make a presentation about a cool topic or teach the members some new business technique.

8. **Consider meeting by telephone.** Convening human bodies in real space can be a hassle. That's why many F.A.N. Clubs meet by telephone, often using a "bridge line." These telephonic pow-wows have another advantage: You can assemble people from far-flung locales who couldn't meet at the corner donut shop.

9. **Remember that groups evolve (and sometimes devolve).** Sometimes people don't get along. Sometimes one member doesn't operate on the same emotional frequency as the others. Sometimes groups just don't gel. That's life. If your group disintegrates, don't despair. Try again when you're ready. Also, if your group isn't doing the trick for you—or, heck, even if it is—consider a specialty group that's more intensely devoted to a particular profession. For instance, many writers meet with a group of other writers to critique each other's work. Same goes for photographers and other artists. Computer programmers, carpenters, and coaches could do the same.

10. **Invite me.** If your F.A.N. Club meets within 50 miles of Washington, D.C., I'd be happy to come to a meeting— if you'd like to have me, of course. Just send me an e-mail: *Dan@FreeAgentNation.com.* And if you meet by telephone, the offer holds. I'll happily participate in a telegathering, too. I'm a big believer in these small groups—and I'm willing to do my small part to help them succeed. (I also like hanging out with cool people and hearing their stories.) So if you're game, take me up on this challenge. I dare you.

10 OTHER BOOKS WORTH READING

Bird By Bird: Some Instructions on Writing and Life by **Anne Lamott** (New York, NY: Anchor Books, 1994). Don't fret about finishing the whole thing. Just take it bird by bird.

Flow: The Psychology of Optimal Experience by **Mihaly Csikszentmihalyi**. (New York: HarperPerennial, 1991). This book examines the concept of "flow"—those transcendent moments when you're completely absorbed in an activity. One of the most illuminating books I've read.

Growing a Business by **Paul Hawken** (New York: Fireside, 1988). One of the first (and still one of the best) books to celebrate micro entrepreneurship as an economic force and a socially useful way of life.

Life Makeovers: 52 Practical and Inspiring Ways to Improve Your Life One Week at a Time by **Cheryl Richardson** (New York: Broadway, 2000). A slim and handy resource guide from one of America's best-known coaches.

The Organization Man by **William H. Whyte, Jr.** (Garden City, NY: Doubleday Anchor Books, 1956). Read this classic and beautiful piece of business sociology to see how much (though not everything) has changed.

The Project50, The Brand You50, **and the rest of the** *Reinventing Work* **series by Tom Peters** (New York: Alfred A. Knopf, 1999). Uberguru Peters has produced a series of short, inventively designed books packed with advice, inspiration, and humor. Lots of fun and dozens of great takeaways. Also visit his Web site (*www.tompeters.com*).

Self-Reliance and Other Essays by **Ralph Waldo Emerson**. (New York: Dover, 1993). Emerson's essay on self-reliance is the ultimate manifesto on independence and integrity. If you like this, you'll also enjoy two classic American tales: *The Autobiography of Benjamin Franklin* and *Narrative of the Life of Frederick Douglas, An American Slave: Written by Himself.*

What Color Is Your Parachute?: A Practical Manual for Job-Hunters and Career Changers by **Richard Nelson Bolles** (Berkeley: Ten Speed Press, 2001). The only career guide that has stood the test of time. Also check out one of my newer favorites, *Whistle While You Work: Heeding Your Life's Calling* by **Richard J. Leider and David A. Shapiro** (San Francisco: Berrett-Koehler, 2001).

Working for Yourself: Laws & Taxes for Independent Contractors, Freelancers, and Consultants by **Stephen Fishman** (Berkeley: Nolo Press, 2000). An essential handbook for running your own operation. Several of Nolo's other books are great, as is its Web site (*www.nolo.com*).

Working Solo: The Real Guide to Financial Success with Your Own Business by **Terri Lonier** (New York: John Wiley & Sons, 1998). Shrewd advice from one of the leaders of the Small Office/Home Office movement. Her companion book, *Working Solo Sourcebook: Essential Resources for Independent Entrepreneurs*, as well as her Web site (*www.workingsolo.com*), are also excellent.

COORDINATES, CLOSINGS & CREDITS

For more information, visit the Free Agent Nation Web site:
www.FreeAgentNation.com

To reach Dan Pink by e-mail:
Dan@FreeAgentNation.com

Thanks to those who offered guidance, tips, and inspiration to *The Official Free Agent Nation Resource Guide:* Brian Ardinger, Jacqueline Barton, Andrea Berman, Kate Binder, Marian Josefosky Brasher, Isabel Burk, Don Burrows, Frank Byrne, George Campbell, Karen Childress, Sara Cormeny, Geoffrey Day, Robert Gerrish, Gil Gordon, Dawn Falbe, Dean Felton, Howard Highsmith, Jackie Huba, Sara Jalali, Paula Johnson, John Kador, Craig Kempf, Anne Lamott, J.A. Lerner, Simon Maddox, Jeff Mandell, Michael Mastin, Carol McArdle, Michele Payn-Knoper, Tom Peters, Daniel Pryfogle, Nadine Reicher, John Satterfield, Eric Schnure, John Shreve, Halley Suitt, Mark Twain, Esme Vos, James Weissman, Lee Welles, Lena West, Pete Williams, John Wooden, Jeff Zbar, and Renee Zuckerbrot.

Notes

CHAPTER 1:
BYE, BYE, ORGANIZATION GUY

[1] William H. Whyte, Jr., *The Organization Man* (Garden City: Doubleday Achor, 1956), p. 3.

[2] Ibid.

[3] Ibid., p. 6

[4] Ibid., p. 76

[5] Ibid., p. 21

[6] Barbara Rudolph, *Disconnected: How Six People from AT&T Discovered the New Meaning of Work in a Downsized Corporate America* (New York: Free Press, 1998), p. 63.

[7] Jessiva Reaves, "Hey Boss! Our Temp Is Protesting Out Front!," *Time Daily* (August 31, 2000); Frank Swoboda, "Temporary Workers Win Benefits Ruling," *Washington Post* (August 31, 2000).

[8] I am indebted to Joel Kortin and David Freedman, whose article "Why Every Business Will Be Like Show Business," *Inc.* (March 1995), first got me thinking about this shift.

[9] Allan Kozinn, "Who Makes the Music with Whom Is the Work of Hidden Hands," *New York Times* (January 2, 1995).

[10] Tom Peters, "The Wow Project," *Fast Company* (May 1999).

[11] David Blanchflower and Andrew Oswald, "Measuring Latent Entrepreneurship Across Nations" (January 2000). *www.dartmouth.edu/~blnchflr/papers/entrepleague.pdf.*

[12] Gene Koretz, "U.S. Labor Gets Flexible," *Business Week* (January 15, 1996); James Aley, "The Temp Biz Boom: Why It's Good," *Fortune* (October 16, 1995).

[13] Kim Clark, "The Myth of the Free-Agent Nation," *Fortune* (June 8, 1998).

CHAPTER 2:
HOW MANY ARE THERE? THE NUMBERS AND NUANCES OF FREE AGENCY

[1] "Contingent and Alternative Employment Arrangements, February 1997," U.S. Department of Labor press release No. 97-422 (December 2, 1997).

[2] Bureau of Labor Statistics 1999 Annual Performance Plan; "Commodity Programs: Impact of Support Provisions on Selected Commodity," report of the General Accounting Office (February 21, 1997).

[3] Carol Leonetti Dannhauser, "Who's in the Home Office?" *American Demographics* (June 1999).

[4] Walter Scott, *Ivanhoe*, Volume 2, Chapter 4, p. 296; Eric Partridge, *A Dictionary of Slang and Unconventional English* (New York: Macmillan, 1961), p. 300; Jonathan Green, *The Cassell Dictionary of Slang* (Cassell Academic, 1999), p. 446.

[5] Kathleen O'Brien, "Calling the Shots: Not Just Athletes Are Free Agents," *New York Times* (October 18, 2000); Paul D. Reynolds and Sammis White, *The Entrepreneurial Process* (Westport, Conn.: Quorum, 1998), p. 5, as reported in Andrew Zacharakis, Paul D. Reynolds, and William D. Bygrave, "The Global Entrepreneurship Assessment: 1999 Executive Report," p. 1; William J. Dennis, Jr., "Self-Employment: When Nothing Else Is Available?" *Journal of Labor Research* (Volume XVII, Number 4, Fall 1996).

[6] Daniela Deane, "Take a Number," *Washington Post* (June 19, 1999), citing Harvard University's Joint Center for Housing Studies report, "Improving America's Housing" (March 1999).

[7] "Aquent Study Reveals 1 in 4 Americans Is an Independent Professional," press release from Aquent Partners (August 18, 1999), based on a telephone survey of one thousand members of the U.S. workforce conducted by the firm Penn, Schoen, and Berland.

[8] Michele Himmelberg, "The End of Loyalty: Growing Free-Agent Economy Means Everyone's a CEO," *Pittsburgh Post-Gazatte* (August 4, 1999).

[9] Anne E. Polivka, "Into Contingent and Alternative Employment: By Choice?" *Monthly Labor Review* (October 1996).

[10] Ibid.

[11] "Aquent Study Reveals 1 in 4 Americans Is an Independent Professional."

[12] Bureau of Labor Statistics, "Employment Situation Summary" (January 5, 2001).

[13] Merrill Goozner, "Longtime Temps Want Some Perks; Now Some Are Suing Companies for Benefits," *Chicago Tribune* (June 22, 1999).

[14] Sharon R. Cohany, "Workers in Alternative Employment Arrangements," *Monthly Labor Review* (October 1, 1996).

[15] Anne Polivka, "Into Contingent and Alternative Employment."

[16] Gene Koretz, "U.S. Labor Gets Flexible."

[17] Rosabeth Moss Kanter, "Nice Work if You Can Get it: The Software Industry As a Model for Tomorrow's Jobs," *The American Prospect* (Fall 1995).

[18] James Aley, "Where the Jobs Are," *Fortune* (September 18, 1995); Merrill Goozner, "Longtime Temps Want Some Perks."

[19] Brian J. Bohling, "The New Nomads: The Future of Our Changing Workforce" (published by CDI Corp.), p. 6.

[20] Timothy W. Brogan, "Staffing Services Annual Update," report by the National Association of Temporary Staffing Services.

[21] Don Lee and Nancy Cleeland, "State's Boom Brings More Job Insecurity, Study Says," *Los Angeles Times* (May 25, 1999).

[22] Brian Bohling, *The New Nomads,* p. 12.

[23] "Behind Temps' Higher Wages," *Washington Post* (November 10, 1996); James Aley, "The Temp Biz Boom: Why It's Good," *Fortune* (October 16, 1995).

[24] *http://www.guru.com/channel/webbiz/portrait/P58.jhtml;* Randy Komisar with Kent Linebeck, *The Monk and the Riddle: The Education of a Silicon Valley Entrepreneur* (Boston: Harvard Business School Press, 2000).

[25] Bill Meyers, "It's a Small-Business World," *USA Today* (July 30, 1999); John Case, "The Wonderland Economy," *Inc.* (May 15, 1995).

[26] Erik Byrnjolfsson, Thomas W. Malone, Vijay Gurbaxani, and Ajit

Kambil, "Does Information Technology Lead to Smaller Firms?" *Management Science* (December 1994).

27 Rich Binsacca, "Avoiding Overload," *Civil Engineering* (January 1, 2000).

28 Peter Gosselin, "More Employees Taking Entrepreneurial Outlook," *Los Angeles Times* (January 9, 2000); Kevin Kelly, "The Roaring Zeros," *Wired* (September 1999), p. 152.

29 Study by the National Federation of Independent Businesses and Wells Fargo Bank (February 3, 1999).

30 Bill Meyers, "It's a Small-Business World."

31 Thomas Petzinger, Jr., "So Long, Supply and Demand," *Wall Street Journal* (January 1, 2000).

32 Jagdish N. Sheth and Rajendra S. Sisodia, "Outsourcing Comes Home," *Wall Street Journal* (June 28, 1999).

33 Patricia Winters Lauro, "Advertising: Office Retailers Battle for Dominance in a Growing Market," *New York Times* (February 1, 1999).

34 *http://www.aahbb.org/; http://www.hboa.com/executive_summary.htm.*

35 *http.//www.idc.com.*

36 1998 Wirthlin Worldwide study, reported in Carol Leonetti Dannhauser, "Who's in the Home Office?"

37 IDC/Link, 1998, as reported in *Home Office Computing.*

38 *American Demographics* (April 1999), p. 58.

39 "Most Home-Based Workers Are Men, Have Traditional Jobs," *Ohio State University Research News* (March 31, 1999).

40 "What's Brewing at Home," *Home Office Computing* (July 1998), citing a survey of four thousand business owners by the Independent Insurance Agents of America.

41 Susan J. Wells, "For Stay-Home Workers, Speed Bumps on the Telecommute," *New York Times* (August 17, 1997); June Langoff, "The Big Picture," *Telecommute Magazine* (February 1999); Gil Gordon Associates (*http://www.gilgordon.com*).

42 Evan I. Schwartz, "Career Sites Gain Rapidly, Along with Job Hopping," *New York Times* (October 4, 1999).

43 The California Work and Health Survey (1998), principal investigators, Edward Yelin, Ph.D., and Laura Trupin, M.P.H., of the Institute for Health Policy Studies and Department of Medicine at the University of California, San Francisco, released Sepember 7, 1998; Erik Brady and Mel Antonen, "Baseball's

Shifting Loyalties: The Startling Impact of Free Agency," *USA Today* (July 2–5, 1998).

44 Kim Clark, "Why It Pays to QUIT," *U.S.News & World Report* (November 1, 1999).

45 Elena Cabral, "Building Safety Nets for the New Work Force," Ford Foundation Report (Spring/Summer 1999).

46 Working Today Web site *(www.workingtoday.org)*; Ken Hudson, "No Shortage of Non-standard Jobs," Briefing Paper, Economic Policy Institute (December 1999): General Accounting Office, "Contingent Workers: Incomes and Benefits Tend to Lag Behind Those in the Rest of the Workforce," report No. HEHS-00-76 (June 30, 2000).

47 Lorraine Woellert, "A New Safety Net for the New Economy," *Business Week* (February 28, 2000).

48 Michelle Conlin, "And Now, the Just-in-Time Employee," *Business Week* (August 28, 2000).

49 Bureau of National Affairs, Inc., Washington, D.C., *Union Membership and Earnings Data Book: Compilations from the Current Population Survey* (1999 edition) (copyright by BNA PLUS), authored by Barry Hirsch and David Macpherson of Florida State University; Internet site: *http://www.bna.com/bnaplus/databook.html.*

50 America Online quarterly reports (1991–2000).

51 Robert J. Samuelson, "We Aren't All Free Agents," *Newsweek* (June 14, 1999).

52 Steven G. Allen, Robert L. Clark, and Sylvester J. Schieber, "Has Job Security Vanished in Large Corporations?" NBER working paper No. W6966 (February 1999).

53 Kenneth Howe, "Workplace Revolution in California; Only One in Three Holds Traditional Job, Study Finds," *San Francisco Chronicle* (September 6, 1999), citing the 1999 California Work and Health Survey from the University of California, San Francisco.

CHAPTER 3:
HOW DID IT HAPPEN?: THE FOUR INGREDIENTS OF FREE AGENCY

1 Carol J. Loomis, "Dinosaurs? Three Firms in Decline," *Fortune* (May 3, 1993).

2 Thomas A. Stewart, "A New Way to Think About Employees," *Fortune* (April 13, 1998).

[3] Diane Coyle, *The Weightless World, Strategies for Managing the Digital Economy* (Cambridge: MIT Press, 1998), p. 5.

[4] Adam Clayton Powell II, speech at Dynamic Visions Conference, Santa Clara, California (February 20, 2000).

[5] Thomas J. Petzinger, Jr., *The New Pioneers: The Men and Women Who Are Transforming the Workplace and the Marketplace* (New York: Simon & Schuster, 1999), p. 61.

[6] Margaret Webb Pressler, "Leesburg Housewife Makes a Click Profit," *Washington Post* (August 29, 1999).

[7] Christopher Farrell, "The Human Factor," *Business Week* (August 31, 1998).

[8] George F. Will, "Richer, Freer, Healthier—and Entitled," *Washington Post* (January 18, 1996); Robert J. Samuelson, *The Good Life and Its Discontents* (New York: Vintage, 1997), p. 7.

[9] David G. Myers, "The Disconnect Between Wealth and Well-Being: It's Not the Economy, Stupid," Edge Online (January 2000) (*http://www.edge.org/3rd_culture/story/54.html*).

[10] David Whitman, *The Optimism Gap: The I'm OK—They're Not Syndrome and the Myth of American Decline* (New York: Walker, 1998), p. 104 (emphasis added).

[11] *Statistical Abstract of the United States 1998*, chart No. 14, "Resident Population, by Age and Sex: 1980 to 1997."

[12] Kevin Kelly, *New Rules for the New Economy: 10 Radical Strategies for a Connected World,* (New York: Viking, 1998), p. 109; Louis Richman, "How Jobs Die and Are Born," *Fortune* (July 26, 1993).

[13] Gene Koretz, "Where the New Jobs Are," *Business Week* (May 31, 1999).

CHAPTER 4:
THE NEW WORK ETHIC

[1] Abraham H. Maslow, "A Theory of Human Motivation," *Psychological Review* (Volume 50, 1943), pp. 370–96; Abraham H. Maslow, *Motivation and Personality* (New York: Harper and Bros, 1954); other psychologists—most prominently, William James—have offered similar theories of motivation and development, although with fewer and somewhat different levels.

[2] Abraham H. Maslow, *Maslow on Management* (New York: John Wiley & Sons, 1999), p. 116.

[3] Max Weber, *The Protestant Ethic and the Spirit of Capitalism* (London: HarperCollinsAcademic; first published 1930).

[4] Ibid., p. 181

[5] Amy Saltzman, "You, Inc.," *U.S. News & World Report* (October 28, 1996).

[6] Diane Crispell, "The Lure of the Entrepreneur," *American Demographics* (February 1998).

[7] Mihaly Csikszentmihalyi, *Flow: The Psychology of Optimal Experience* (New York: HarperPerennial, 1990), p. 143; Johns Hopkins University study, cited in "Emerging Work Trends," Monster Talent Market (*http://content.talentmarket.monster.com/employer/newsTrends/worktrends.stm*).

[8] "Study Shows Employees Doubt the Integrity of Their Company's Leaders," report by Walker Information and the Hudson Institute (September 30, 1999).

[9] "Workplace Ethics Dilemma," *USA Today* (February 15, 1999).

[10] Robert D. Hisrich, "Ethics of Business Managers vs. Entrepreneurs," summarized in "Study Shows Entrepreneurs Place More Emphasis on Ethics Than Do Business Managers," *Business Week* (May 19, 1998).

[11] Janet Kornblum, "Guy-Site Bosses Take Team Spirit Seriously," *USA Today* (March 1, 2000).

[12] Dave Arnott, *Corporate Cults: The Insidious Lure of the All-Consuming Organization* (New York: AMACOM, 2000).

[13] William Whyte, *The Organization Man,* p. 34.

[14] Lisa Guernsey, "Surfing the Web: The New Ticket to a Pink Slip," *New York Times* (December 16, 1999).

[15] Jube Shiver, Jr., "Workers Lament Loss of E-mail Privacy on Job," *Los Angeles Times* (October 11, 1999).

[16] Maura Kelly, "Your Boss May Be Monitoring Your E-mail," *Salon* (December 8, 1999).

[17] Charles Handy, *The Age of Unreason* (Boston: Harvard Business School Press, 1990), p. 258.

[18] Alfie Kohn, "In Pursuit of Affluence, at a High Price," *New York Times* (February 2, 1999).

[19] Thomas J. Stanley and William D. Danko, *The Millionaire Next Door: The Surprising Secrets of America's Wealthy* (Marietta, Georgia: Longstreet Press, 1996), pp. 8, 227.

[20] "Why We Labor: 'American Dream' Alive and Well," *PR Newswire*

(September 3, 1999), citing "The New Self-Employed Middle Class: Fighting for the American Dream."

[21] Reported in "Upward Mobility Increases," *American Demographics* (November 1999).

[22] Nancy Rivera Brooks, "Workers Place More Value on Training, Flexibility Than Pay, Surveys Show," *Los Angeles Times* (May 2, 1999).

[23] David G. Blanchflower and Andrew J. Oswald, "Well-Being, Insecurity, and the Decline of American Job Satifaction" (April 1999), working paper presented at Cornell University conference (*http://www.dartmouth.edu/~blnchflr/papers.JobSat.pdf*); see also, David F. Blanchflower and Andrew J. Oswald, "What Makes an Entrepreneur?" *Journal of Labor Economics* (Volume 16, Number 1 1998).

[24] Jonathan A. Gardner and Andrew J. Oswald, "The Determinants of Job Satisfaction in Britain," University of Warwick, Department of Economics working paper (March 1999); Richard Donkin, "Happiness at Work," *Financial Times* (March 5, 1999).

[25] Cherry Norton, "Happiest People in the World Are Women, Self-Employed, Well-Educated—and Danes," *The Independent—London* (January 1, 2000).

[26] Rolf Jensen, *The Dream Society* (New York: McGraw-Hill, 1999), p. 116; Michael Schrage, *Serious Play* (Boston: Harvard Business School Press, 1999); Diane Ackerman, *Deep Play* (New York: Vintage, 2000).

[27] "Suburban Legend," *I.D. Magazine* (January/February 2000), p. 69.

[28] Sue Sellenbarger, "The Tomorrow Trap," *Wall Street Journal* (December 16, 1999).

CHAPTER 5:
THE NEW EMPLOYMENT CONTRACT

[1] Robert D. Hershey, Jr., "Survey Says 78.7 Million Own Stocks in United States," *New York Times* (October 22, 1999).

[2] Edward Wyatt, "Share of Household Wealth in Stocks Is at 50-Year High," *New York Times* (February 11, 1998).

[3] Paul A. Gigot, "This Isn't What Marx Meant by Das Kapital," *Wall Street Journal* (March 19, 1999).

[4] Michelle Singletary, "Investments for the Masses," *Washington Post* (March 14, 1999), p. H2, citing a study by Boston-based MFS Investment Management.

[5] William Whyte, *The Organization Man,* p. 75.

[6] Beth Belton, "Tech Advances Raise Job Insecurity," *USA Today* (February 17, 1999).

[7] Ibid.

[8] "Overworked and Overpaid: The American Manager," *The Economist* (January 30, 1999); Patrick Barta, "In Current Expansion, as Business Booms, So, Too, Do Layoffs," *Wall Street Journal* (March 13, 2000).

[9] "Dot-com Job Cuts Hit Record in December," Reuters (December 27, 2000).

[10] Ellen Schultz, "Stocks Swing Wildly, but Many Retirees Aren't Fazed at All," *Wall Street Journal* (October 30, 1997), p. A1.

[11] Susan J. Wells, "Pay Is Rising, Thanks to Sweeteners in a Tight Labor Market," *New York Times* (August 30, 1998).

[12] Paul Starobin, "A World of Risk," *National Journal* (July 10, 1999).

[13] Michael Mandel, *The High-Risk Society* (New York: Random House, 1996), p. 138.

[14] Sharon R. Cohany, "Workers in Alternative Employment Arrangements," *Monthly Labor Review* (Volume 119, October 1, 1996).

[15] Charles F. Manski and John D. Straub, "Worker Perceptions of Job Insecurity in the Mid-1990s: Evidence from the Survey of Economic Expectations," NBER working paper No. W6908, January 1999 (emphasis added).

[16] Brian J. Bohling, "The New Nomads: The Future of Our Changing Workforce" (published by CDI Corp.), p. 15

[17] Quoted in D. Quinn Mills, *The IBM Lesson: The Profitable Art of Full Employment* (New York: Times Books, 1989), p. 16.

[18] Alan M. Webber, "Danger: Toxic Company," *Fast Company* (November 1998).

[19] "Labor Letter," *Wall Street Journal* (February 15, 1999).

[20] Virginia Postrel, "Nostalgia's Illusions," *New York Times* (January 17, 1999).

[21] William Whyte, *The Organization Man,* p. 231.

[22] Tom Peters, *The Brand You 50* (New York: Alfred A Knopf, 1999), p. 108.

[23] AnnaLee Saxenian, *Regional Advantage: Culture and Competition in*

Silicon Valley and Route 128 (Boston: Harvard University Press, 1994).

[24] EPIC/MRA national workforce study, sponsored by Kelly Services (October 25, 1999).

CHAPTER 6:
THE NEW TIME CLOCK

[1] Juliet B. Schor, *The Overworked American: The Unexpected Decline of Leisure* (New York: Basic Books, 1992), p. 29.

[2] "Overtime and the American Worker," a study by Cornell University, New York State School of Industrial Relations, and Institute for Workplace Studies (December 1999), p. 3.

[3] John P. Robinson and Geoffrey Godbey, *Time for Life: The Surprising Way Americans Use Their Time*, 2nd edition (State College: Pennsylvania State University Press, 1997).

[4] Jodi Wilgoren, "With Labor Day Comes More Labor, Less Play," *Los Angeles Times* (September 7, 1999).

[5] Gene Koretz, "Who's Stressed Out at Work," *Business Week* (April 12, 1999).

[6] "Eligible Benefits," *American Demographics* (March 2000).

[7] *Work Trends: America's Attitudes About Work, Employers, and Government,* national survey conducted quarterly by the John J. Heldrich Center for Workforce Development at Rutgers University and the Center for Survey Research and Analysis at the University of Connecticut (March 18, 1999).

[8] "A Third of Workday Spent on Computer," *Washington Post* (February 17, 2000).

[9] James B. Maas, *Power Sleep: The Revolutionary Program That Prepares Your Mind for Peak Performance* (New York: Villard, 1998), p. 11.

[10] Herman Kahn and Anthony J. Weiner, *The Year 2000: A Framework for Speculation on the Next Thirty-three Years,* (New York: Macmillan, 1967), pp. 125–27. Nancy Gibbs, "How America Has Run Out of Time," *Time* (April 24, 1989).

[11] Stephen S. Roach, "Working Better or Just Harder?" *New York Times* (February 14, 2000).

[12] "Overtime and the American Worker," p. 3.

[13] Amy Saltzman, "When Less Is More," *U.S. News & World Report* (October 27, 1997).

[14] Scott Clark, "Like to Surf on Saturday? Report Says You're Not Alone," *Web Developer News* (February 11, 2000).

[15] Cindy Aron, "On Vacation, the Rest Is Work," *Washington Post* (June 13, 1999).

[16] Juliet Schor, *The Overworked American*, p. 32.

CHAPTER 7:
SMALL GROUPS, BIG IMPACT:
REINVENTING TOGETHERNESS IN FREE AGENT NATION

[1] Robert Wuthnow, *Sharing the Journey, Support Groups and America's New Quest for Community* (New York: Free Press, 1994), p. 4.

[2] "The membership figures listed below are based on reports to the General Service Office as of January 1, 2000, plus an average allowance for groups that have not reported their membership," according to the Alcoholics Anonymous fact file (*http://www.alcoholics-anonymous.org/em24doc4.html*).

[3] Eileen Daspin, "The Tyranny of the Book Group Spawns a New Niche for Therapists," *Wall Street Journal* (January 15, 1999).

[4] Robert Wuthnow, *Sharing the Journey*, pp. 45–46; Steven Waldman, "Getting Religion," *Washington Monthly* (July 1999); Wade Clark Roof, *Spiritual Marketplace: Baby Boomers and the Remaking of American Religion* (Princeton: Princeton University Press, 1999).

[5] *Autobiography of Benjamin Franklin*, rocket eBook edition, p. 230.

[6] Ibid., p. 231.

[7] Ibid., p. 235.

[8] "These libraries have improved the general conversation of the Americans, made the common tradesmen and farmers as intelligent as most gentlemen from other countries, and perhaps have contributed in some degree to the stand so generally made throughout the colonies in defense of their privileges." (*Autobiography of Benjamin Franklin*, p. 273.)

[9] Esmond Wright, *Franklin of Philadelphia* (Cambridge: The Belknap Press of Harvard University Press, 1986), pp. 37–38.

[10] Napoleon Hill, *Think and Grow Rich* (New York: Ballantine, 1960), p. 77.

[11] Ibid., p. 169.

[12] Katharine Mieszkowski, "The Ex-Files," *Fast Company* (September 1999).

CHAPTER 8:
GETTING HORIZONTAL:
THE FREE AGENT ORG CHART AND OPERATING SYSTEM

[1] David Stamps, "Off the Charts," *Training Magazine* (October 1997).

[2] Barry Wellman, "Physical Place and CyberPlace: The Rise of Networked Individualism," *International Journal of Urban and Regional Research,* special issue on "Networks, Class, and Place," edited by Talja Blokland and Mike Savage; see also, "From Little Boxes to Ramified Networks: A Paradigm Shift" (April 2, 1998), available at *http://www.candesign.utoronto.ca/wk11text.html#wellman.*

[3] Mark Granovetter, *Getting a Job: A Study of Contacts and Careers,* 2nd edition (Chicago: University of Chicago Press, 1995), pp. 7–11.

[4] Ibid., p. 14.

[5] Ibid., p. 53.

[6] Ibid., p. 54.

[7] Alexandra Maryanski and Jonathan H. Turner, *The Social Cage: Human Nature and the Evolution of Society* (Stanford: Stanford University Press, 1992), pp. vii, 90, 170.

[8] Ibid., p. 162.

[9] Francis Fukuyama, *Trust: The Social Virtues and the Creation of Capitalism* (London: Hamish Hamilton, 1995), p. 14.

[10] UCLA anthropologist Karen Stephenson, quoted in Richard Donkin, "Office Networks: Tending the Grapevine," *Financial Times* (November 6, 1998).

[11] Diego Gambetta, "Can We Trust Trust?" in *Trust: Making and Breaking Cooperative Relations,* ed. Diego Gambetta (Oxford: Blackwell, 1988), p. 221.

[12] Quoted in Robert B. Cialdini, *Influence: The Psychology of Persuasion* (New York: William Morrow, 1993), p. 18.

[13] Lee Dugatkin, *Cheating Monkeys and Citizen Bees: The Nature of Cooperation in Animals and Humans* (New York: Free Press, 1999); Laura Tangley, "Law of the Jungle: Altruism," *U.S. News & World Report* (February 15, 1999).

[14] Robert Cialdini, *Influence,* p. 18.

[15] Alexis de Tocqueville, *Democracy in America,* Volume I (Project Guttenberg Etext), transl. by Henry Reeve, p. 1028. This book was originally published in 1835.

CHAPTER 9:
THE FREE AGENT INFRASTRUCTURE

[1] Ray Oldenburg, *The Great Good Place: Cafés, Coffee Shops, Community Centers, Beauty Parlors, General Stores, Bars, Hangouts, and How They Get You Through the Day* (New York: Paragon House, 1991).

[2] Howard Schultz and Dori Jones Yang, *Pour Your Heart into It: How Starbucks Built a Company One Cup at a Time* (New York: Hyperion, 1997), p. 121.

[3] Chuck Salter, "Office of the Future," *Fast Company* (April 2000).

[4] Executive Suite Association (*http://www.officebusinesscenters.com/news.html*).

[5] Amy Gilroy and Ray Boggs, "Home Offices on the Internet," IDC research report No. W18331 (March 22, 1999); "SOHO Market Overview: Small Businesses with Fewer Than 10 Employees and Home-Based Businesses," IDC research report No. W17680 (April 8, 1999).

[6] International Data Corporation study (January 11, 1999); "Hitting the 'Home' Key," *Kiplinger's Personal Finance Magazine* (May 1999).

[7] "Small Domains," *Business 2.0* (September 26, 2000).

[8] Carol Leonetti Dannhauser, "Who's in the Home Office?" *American Demographics* (June 1999).

[9] Patricia Winters Lauro, "Advertising: Office Retailers Battle for Dominance in a Growing Market," *New York Times* (February 1, 1999).

[10] About MBE (*http://www.mbe.com/aboutmbe/newtrans/overviewus.cfm*).

CHAPTER 10:
MATCHMAKERS, AGENTS, AND COACHES

[1] Charles Fishman, "The War for Talent," *Fast Company* (August 1998).

[2] "This Temp's No Slacker," *Smart Money* (October 1999).

[3] Report from Staffing Industry Analysts (May 17, 2000), available at *http://www.sireport.com/pressreleases/forecastrelease.html*.

[4] Jane Applegate, "U.S. Civilian Labor Force Out in Full Force, Freelancing," *Arizona Republic* (April 4, 2000).

[5] Charlene Li, "The Career Networks," *The Forrester Report* (February 2000), p. 8.

[6] Allan Kennedy and Terry Deal, *The New Corporate Cultures: Revitalizing the American Workplace After Downsizing, Mergers, and Reengineering* (New York: Perseus, 1999).

CHAPTER 11:
FREE AGENT FAMILIES

[1] Christena Nippert-Eng, *Home and Work* (Chicago: University of Chicago Press, 1996).

[2] Ibid., p. 48.

[3] Ibid., p. 22.

[4] Ibid.

[5] Peter F. Drucker, "Beyond the Information Revolution," *Atlantic Monthly* (October, 1998).

[6] Arlie Russell Hochschild, *The Time Bind: When Work Becomes Home and Home Becomes Work* (New York: Henry Holt, 1997), citing economist Victor Fuchs.

[7] Kristin Downey Grimsley, "Family a Priority for Young Workers," *Washington Post* (May 3, 2000).

[8] Alison Stein Wellner, "The End of Leisure," *American Demographics* (July 2000).

[9] Thomas J. Stanley, *The Millionaire Mind* (Kansas City: Andrews McMeel, 2000), p. 393.

[10] Deborah Charles, "Clinton Wants $20 Million for Family Leave Plan," Reuters (February 12, 2000); Dale Russakoff, "Push for Paid Parental Leave Falls Flat in States," *Washington Post* (August 1, 2000).

[11] "Wary of Benefits," *USA Today* (April 23, 1998).

[12] Gene Koretz, "Hazardous to Your Career," *Business Week* (January 17, 2000).

[13] Thomas Petzinger, *The New Pioneers*, p. 218.

[14] Nigel Nicholson, "How Hardwired Is Human Behavior?" *Harvard Business Review* (July–August 1998), p. 144.

[15] "Talking About Tomorrow: Edward O. Wilson," *Wall Street Journal* (January 1, 2000).

CHAPTER 12:
ROADBLOCKS ON FREE AGENT AVENUE:
HEALTH INSURANCE, TAXES, AND ZONING

[1] Employment Benefit Research Institute, "The Working Uninsured: Who They Are, How They Have Changed, and the Consequences of Being Uninsured," EBRI issue brief No. 224 (August 31, 2000).

[2] Don Lee, "An Anemic Rate of Health Coverage," *Los Angeles Times* (July 4, 1999).

[3] Bob Herbert, "Focus on Women," *New York Times* (September 28, 2000).

[4] Amity Shlaes, *The Greedy Hand: How Taxes Drive Americans Crazy and What You Can Do About It* (New York: Random House, 1999), p. 3.

[5] Ibid., p. 4.

[6] Howard Gleckman, "A Simple Plan for Simpler Tax Returns," *Business Week* (May 10, 1999).

[7] Robert E. Hall and Alvin Rabushka, *The Flat Tax*, 2nd edition (Stanford: Hoover Institution Press, 1995), pp. 2, 19.

[8] *Wall Street Journal* (January 20, 1999).

[9] Frederick Daily, quoted in Sandra Block, "Audit Red Flags You Don't Want to Wave," *USA Today* (April 11, 2000).

[10] "Legalizing Home Businesses," *Newark Star-Ledger* (December 13, 1999).

CHAPTER 13: TEMP SLAVES, PERMATEMPS, AND THE RISE OF SELF-
ORGANIZED LABOR

[1] Jeff Kelly (ed.), *The Best of Temp Slave!* (Madison, Wisconsin: Garrett County Press, 1997), p. xiii.

[2] Helene Jorgenson and Hans Riemer, "Permatemps: Young Workers As Permanent Second Class Employees," *The American Prospect* (August 14, 2000).

[3] Ellen Neuborne, "Temporary Workers Feeling Shortchanged," *USA Today* (April 11, 1997).

[4] Robert E. Parker, *Flesh Peddlers and Warm Bodies: The Temporary Help Industry and Its Workers* (New Brunswick: Rutgers University Press, 1994), p. 153.

[5] Jackie Zalewski, "Here Today, Gone Tomorrow: Outsourcing

Electronics Production Jobs and Its Alienating Effects on Temporary Workers," paper presented at the American Sociological Association Conference, Washington, D.C. (August 2000).

[6] Erving Goffman, *The Presentation of Self in Everyday Life* (Garden City: Doubleday Anchor 1959), pp. 151–52.

[7] Robert Parker, *Flesh Peddlers and Warm Bodies,* p. 114.

[8] Katharine Mieszkowski, "Don't Wanna Be Your (Temp) Slave!," *Fast Company* (September 1998).

[9] Anne E. Polivka, "Into Contingent and Alternative Employment," pp. 55, 64.

[10] Ron Lieber, "The Permatemps Contretemps," *Fast Company* (August 2000).

[11] Kristin Downey Grimsley, "Revenge of the Temps," *Washington Post* (January 16, 2000).

[12] Alan Paul and Archie Kleingartner, "Flexible Production and the Transformation of Industrial Relations in the Motion Picture and Television Industry," *Industrial and Labor Relations Review*, Volume 47, Number 4 (July 1994).

CHAPTER 14:
E-TIREMENT: FREE AGENCY AND THE NEW OLD AGE

[1] Dora L. Costa, *The Evolution of Retirement: An American Economic History, 1880–1999* (Chicago: University of Chicago Press, 1998), pp. 191–92.

[2] Patrice Apodaca, "Who Will Replace Retiring Boomers?" *Los Angeles Times* (June 8, 1998).

[3] David Beck, "Most Working Women Will Postpone Retirement," *Human Resource Management News* (December 18–24, 2000).

[4] "A Full Life," *The Economist* (September 4, 1999).

[5] Mark Taylor, "Self-Employment and Windfall Gains in Britain: Evidence from Panel Data" (ESRC Research Centre on Micro-Social Change, University of Essex, England, paper presented at Canadian International Conference on Self-Employment (September 24–26, 1998).

[6] "Opening the Gates," *USA Today* (August 24, 1999).

7 "Phased Retirement," report by Watson Wyatt Worldwide (September 13, 1999), pp. 3, 10.

8 "The New Faces of Retirement," *New York Times* (January 3, 1999).

9 World Bank: 1998, World Development Indicators: 1998, World Bank, Washington, D.C.; Douglas J. Besharov and Keith W. Smith, "Getting Old Ain't What It Used to Be," *Washington Post* (August 1, 1999).

10 Stanley Parker, *Work and Retirement* (London, Boston: Allen & Unwin, 1982), p. 29.

11 Dora Costa, *The Evolution of Retirement*, p. 4.

CHAPTER 15:
SCHOOL'S OUT: FREE AGENCY AND THE FUTURE OF EDUCATION

1 David B. Tyack, *The One Best System: A History of American Urban Education* (Boston: Harvard University Press, 1974), p. 16.

2 Marshall McLuhan, "Cervantes Confronted Typographic Man in the Figure of Don Quixote," *The Gutenberg Galaxy* (Toronto: University of Toronto Press, 1962).

3 John Taylor Gatto, *Dumbing Us Down: The Hidden Curriculum of Compulsory Schooling* (Gabriola Island, British Columbia: New Society Publishers, 1992).

4 Patricia M. Lines, "Homeschoolers: Estimating Numbers and Growth," National Institute on Student Achievement, Curriculum, and Assessment, Office of Educational Research and Improvement, U.S. Department of Education (Web edition, Spring 1999); David Wagner, "No Place (To Learn) Like Home School," *Insight on the News* (December 8, 1997); David S. Gutterson, "No Longer a Fringe Movement," *Newsweek* (October 5, 1998).

5 Steffan Heuer, "Putting the Home in Homework," *Grok* (October 2000).

6 Brian D. Ray, "Home Schooling on the Threshold: A Survey of Research at the Dawn of the New Millennium" (Salem, Oregon: NHERI Publications, 1999).

7 Daniel Golden, "Class of Their Own: Home-Schooled Pupils Are Making Colleges Sit Up and Take Notice," *Wall Street Journal* (February 11, 2000).

8 Jay Mathews, "A Home Run for Home Schooling," *Washington Post*

(March 24, 1999); Jeannie Ralston, "When Home Is the Classroom," *Parenting* (May 2000).

[9] Brian Ray, "Home Schooling on the Threshold."

[10] Edward L. Deci, *Why We Do What We Do: Understanding Self-Motivation* (New York: Penguin, 1995).

[11] Daniel Golden, "Class of Their Own."

[12] "Rebuilding America's Schools," *Washington Post* (April 25, 2000).

[13] Leon Botstein, *Jefferson's Children: Education and the Promise of American Culture* (New York: Doubleday, 1997).

[14] Peter Applebome, "Alma Maters: Two Words Behind the Massacre," *New York Times* (May 2, 1999).

[15] Sharon Nash, "Teenage Entrepreneurs," *PC Magazine* (May 9, 2000).

[16] Mary Lord, "It's Never Too Soon for Econ 101," *U.S. News & World Report* (June 14, 1999).

[17] Yochi J. Dreazen, "Student, Teach Thyself," *Wall Street Journal* (January 1, 2000).

[18] Bob Cohn, "The ABC's of E-Learning," *Grok* (October 2000).

[19] Janny Scott, "For Thinkers Who Want to Be Free, Independence Is Worth the Cost," *New York Times* (May 8, 1999).

[20] Pamela Mendels, "Government Study Shows a Boom in Distance Education," *New York Times* (January 12, 2000).

[21] Thomas Stanley, *The Millionaire Mind*, p. 169.

CHAPTER 16:
LOCATION, LOCATION . . . VOCATION:
FREE AGENCY AND THE FUTURE OF OFFICES, HOMES, AND REAL ESTATE

[1] Carol Dannhauser, "Who's in the Home Office?"

[2] Martha Groves, "The New Nomads of Corporate America," *Los Angeles Times* (March 17, 1995).

CHAPTER 17:
PUTTING THE "I" IN IPO: THE PATH TOWARD FREE AGENT FINANCE

[1] Ianthe Jeanne Dugan, "Online Trading's New Battleground: Bonds," *Washington Post* (February 15, 2000).

[2] Tim Carvell, "Ziggy Gold Dust," *Entertainment Weekly* (April 4, 1997).

[3] Alice Rawsthron and Jeremy Grant, "Motown Writers Issue $30m Bond Against Royalties," *Financial Times* (August 5, 1998).

[4] Bonnie Azab Powell, "Trading Faces," *Red Herring* (November 1999); Ken Kurson, "The Godfather Sells Some Soul," *Worth* (July/August 1999).

[5] Jack Neff, "Financing Your Firm with Credit Cards," *How* (June 1999); Daniel M. Gold, "For Small Businesses, Credit Cards Are Handy," *New York Times* (January 10, 1999).

[6] *http://www.fanniemae.org/markets/mbssecurities/productinfo/ mbs/mbs.html*; Patrick Barta, "As Agencies' Portfolios Swell, Worry on Risks Also Rises," *Wall Street Journal* (April 25, 2000).

[7] Peter Kafka, "Celebrity by the Share," *Forbes* (March 20, 2000).

[8] Remarks by chairman Alan Greenspan, Federal Reserve System Research Conference on Business Access to Capital and Credit, Arlington, Virginia (March 9, 1999).

[9] Paulette Thomas, "Direct Public Offerings Propel Start-ups to Next Level," *Wall Street Journal* (June 29, 1999).

[10] Mark Pittman, Bloomberg News, "Portfolio with a Punch," *Fort Lauderdale Sun-Sentinel* (January 31, 2000).

[11] Stan Davis and Christopher Meyer, *Future Wealth* (Boston: Harvard Business School Press, 2000) p. 111–12.

CHAPTER 18:
A CHIP OFF THE OLD VOTING BLOC:
THE NEW POLITICS OF FREE AGENCY

[1] Alan Wolfe, *One Nation, After All* (New York: Viking, 1998), p. 236.

[2] David S. Broder and Richard Morin, "Struggle Over New Standards; Impeachment Reveals Nation's Changing Standards," *Washington Post* (December 27, 1998); Gerald F. Seib and Bryan Gruley, "Public Backlash Against Big Mergers Isn't Likely Yet," *Wall Street Journal* (April 14, 1998); also, the Star/Eagleton Poll, a regular survey of New Jersey residents found that only 16 percent of those polled said they had a lot of confidence in large corporations (and only 14 percent had a lot of confidence in labor unions), in David Wald, "In GOP We Don't Trust, Jerseyans

Say Poll Finds Most Confidence in Church, Schools," *Newark Star-Ledger* (February 14, 1999).

3 "Employed but Uninsured: A State-by-State Analysis of the Number of Low-Income Working Parents Who Lack Health Insurance," report by Center on Budget and Policy Priorities (February 9, 1999).

4 Donald L. Bartlett and James B. Steele, "What Corporate Welfare Costs," *Time* (November 9, 1998).

5 David Bornstein, "The Barefoot Bank with Cheek," *Atlantic Monthly* (December 1995).

6 Ibid.

7 Ibid.

8 Lisa J. Servon, "Micro Loans Yielding Big Dividends," *Newark Star-Ledger* (March 26, 2000).

9 Ibid., p. 11.

10 Lorraine Woellert, "A New Safety Net for the New Economy," *Business Week* (February 28, 2000).

11 William Gale, "Make It Less Complicated to Pay Taxes," *Los Angeles Times* (February 21, 2000).

12 Gerald F. Seib, "Independents Day," *Wall Street Journal* (January 11, 2000); *http://www.freeagentnation.com/census*.

CHAPTER 19:
WHAT'S LEFT: FREE AGENCY AND THE FUTURE OF COMMERCE, CAREERS, AND COMMUNITY

1 Laura Holson, "The Deal Still Rules," *New York Times* (February 14, 1999).

2 Thomas W. Malone and Robert J. Laubacher, "The Dawn of the E-Lance Economy," *Harvard Business Review*, September/October 1998, p. 147.

3 Interview with Ronald Coase, *Wall Street Journal* (January 1, 2000), p. R36.

4 Leslie Walker, "Tapping Expertise on the Net," *Washington Post* (May 4, 2000).

5 G. Patrick Pawling, "Back to Barter," *The Industry Standard* (December 27, 1999–January 3, 2000).

[6] "Print Your Own Money," *Yes! A Journal of Positive Futures* (Spring 1999).

[7] Cliff Hakim, *We Are All Self-Employed* (San Francisco: Berrett-Kohler, 1994).

[8] Rick Levine, Christopher Locke, Doc Searls, and David Weinberger, *The Cluetrain Manifesto: The End of Business as Usual* (New York: Perseus, 2000), pp. xii, xv.

[9] *NFWBO News* (Number 2, 1999), p. 1; "What's Behind the Surge in Women Entrepreneurs," *Business Week Frontier* (July 15, 1999).

[10] Eleena de Lisser and Dan Morris, "More Men Work at Home Than Women, Study Shows," *Wall Street Journal* (May 18, 1999); "What's Behind the Surge in Women Entrepreneurs"; Terry Costlow, "Women Fight Gender Gap With Self-Employment," *CMP Tech Web* (August 9, 2000).

[11] Linda Himmelstein, "I Am Cyber-Woman. Hear Me Roar," *Business Week* (November 15, 1999).

[12] Conversation with author at the Fourth Digital Storytelling Festival, Crested Butte, Colorado (September 18, 1998); see also, Karen Kaplan, "In Software, It's Still a Boy's World," *Los Angeles Times* (June 28, 1999); Elaine Appleton, "Little Games People Play: Computers v. Gender," *National Post* (March 31, 1999); Elizabeth Weise, "Purple Moon Fades; Girls-Oriented Venture Eclipsed by Bigger Rivals," *Chicago Sun-Times* (February 25, 1999); Dean Takahashi, "Purple Moon Tried, Failed to Topple the (Doll) House That Barbie Built," *Wall Street Journal* (February 22, 1999); Jon Carroll, "Under a Purple Moon," *San Francisco Chronicle* (June 9, 1997).

Appendix:
Results of the Free Agent
Nation Online Census

To supplement my many interviews with independent workers, I conducted an informal and unscientific survey on my Web site (*www.FreeAgentNation.com*) of 1,143 free agents. The census asked thirteen questions that fell into three rough categories: demographics, behavior, and attitudes. Because the survey was not based on a random sample—anybody who visited the site could complete the census—the results, in formal terms, have little or no statistical validity. But they do represent an interesting, if unscientific, numerical snapshot of American free agents. I've laid out the main findings below.

DEMOGRAPHICS

The free agents in the online census tended to reflect America's overall age and gender mix. As for geographic distribution, California was overrepresented—as is customary for the state that so often incubates social trends. The free agents in this survey were much whiter and better educated than the general population—perhaps because the survey was conducted online, where whites and the college-educated are overrepresented. Income skewed slightly higher than the typical U.S. income pattern.

Age
Average age: 42
Oldest: 81
Youngest: 14

Gender
Female: 51 percent
Male: 47 percent
No answer: 2 percent

Marital Status
Married: 56 percent
Single: 30 percent
Domestic partnership: 4 percent

Geographic Distribution
State with the most free agents: California
Other states in the top ten for free agents: Texas, New York,
    Florida, Illinois, Massachusetts, New Jersey, Pennsylvania,
    Washington, Colorado
State with the fewest free agents: Idaho

Race
White: 83 percent
African-American: 5 percent
Hispanic: 2 percent
Asian-American: 2 percent
Other: 8 percent

Education (highest level of formal education completed)
Didn't finish high school: 1 percent
High school graduate: 3 percent
Some college: 20 percent
Graduate of two-year college: 6 percent
Graduate of four-year college: 39 percent
Graduate of professional or graduate school: 31 percent

Income (how much income earned last year from free agency)
0–$15,000: 21 percent
$15–30,000: 11 percent

$30–50,000: 12 percent
$50–100,000: 18 percent
$100,000+: 12 percent
No answer: 26 percent

Political Affiliation
Independent: 37 percent
Democrat: 35 percent
Republican: 18 percent
Other party: 5 percent
No answer: 5 percent

BEHAVIOR

In these questions, I tried to get a more systematic idea of the products and services free agents use. Free agents in this survey were major users of computers, e-mail, and the Web—no great surprise perhaps for a survey conducted online. These free agents also read much more than the overall population, reflecting both independent workers' need for self-education and the tilt toward better-educated respondents in an online survey. The most intriguing findings concern health insurance—particularly the large numbers of free agents who go without it or depend on a spouse's coverage.

"In the past month, where did you do the bulk of your work?"
In my home: 61 percent
Outside my home: 39 percent

"In the past month, which of the following services have you used in doing your work?"
Large office supply store (examples: Staples, Office Depot, Office Max): 76 percent
Overnight delivery service (examples: Federal Express, U.S. Post Office Express Mail): 60 percent
Retail photocopying and office store (example: Kinko's): 58 percent

A separate location for the delivery of mail and packages (examples: Mail Boxes, Etc., Mailboxes USA): 17 percent

A staffing agency to find work (examples: Manpower, Kelly Services): 11 percent

__In the last month, for my work, I've . . .__
Sent or received e-mail: 96 percent
Used the World Wide Web: 91 percent
Sent or received a fax in my home: 73 percent
Used a phone line in my home in addition to the one I use for my residence: 69 percent
Used a cellular phone: 62 percent
Purchased something online: 62 percent
Used a laptop computer: 47 percent
Set up or maintained my own Web site: 38 percent

__"Yesterday, did you happen to do any of the following?"__
Visited a Web site: 83 percent
Read all or part of a daily newspaper: 74 percent
Watched all or part of a television show: 71 percent
Read all or part of a magazine: 67 percent
Read all or part of a book: 59 percent

ATTITUDES

The large majority of these free agents became independent out of a desire for freedom. And most of them plan to remain independent so they can continue enjoying that freedom. But the census respondents also revealed that freedom has a price—most prominently unstable incomes and lack of health insurance.

__"The main reason I became a free agent was that I . . ."__
Wanted greater independence and freedom: 74 percent
Got tired of traditional work: 58 percent
Wanted to make more money: 36 percent
Wanted to spend more time with my family: 26 percent
Was downsized, laid off, or fired: 21 percent
Have always been a free agent: 11 percent

(Note: Respondents were permitted more than one answer to this question.)

"As far as leaving free agency for a traditional job is concerned . . ."
I'd like to: 10 percent
It's possible, but I haven't decided: 34 percent
It's pretty unlikely: 35 percent
No way: 21 percent

In response to the open-ended question "The best part about being a free agent is . . . ," the overwhelming top answer was freedom, independence, and control of life.

In response to the open-ended question "The worst part about being a free agent is . . . ," the top three answers were:
1. Lack of health insurance and other benefits
2. Unstable income, difficulty with cash flow
3. Difficulty marketing one's products or services

Acknowledgments

Working for yourself doesn't mean working by yourself. That's both a point of this book and the key to its existence. Many people helped convert my 1,001 hazy ideas into 315 concrete pages.

My deepest thanks go to the hundreds of free agents across America who opened their homes, their lives, and their hearts to me and my tape recorder. It's fashionable nowadays to be pessimistic about the future. But after a year of talking to these amazing people, I've found it hard to be anything but dizzily optimistic.

Rafe Sagalyn—free agent and literary agent—was monumentally helpful in the making of *Free Agent Nation*. I cannot imagine a more skilled advocate or more astute adviser. Thanks also to the Sagalyn Literary Agency's band of merry pranksters—Ethan Kline, Dan Fois, and Claire Smith.

At Warner Books, executive editor Rick Horgan had the irritating habit of almost always being right. He kept the manuscript focused on the big picture and helped untangle several knots into which I'd tied myself. He also put up with more delays than a Soviet commuter. Thanks, too, Eric Wechter for his careful attention to the manuscript.

Alan Webber and Bill Taylor, founding editors of *Fast Company*, gave me the freedom to explore free agency and a powerful launching pad for these ideas. Alan also taught me the importance of making and delivering a promise to the reader, perhaps the most crucial lesson I've learned as a writer.

Several friends and colleagues read portions of this book and improved it with their comments and criticisms: Jeff Adelman, Dennis Benson, Jack Donahue, Todd Lappin, Jon Orszag, Leslie Pink, Eric Schnure, Marc Tetel, Frank Wilkinson, and the incomparable Renee Zuckerbrot. Much as I'd like to blame them, they're not responsible for any errors of fact or judgment that remain. Several other people, free agents all, handled additional tough tasks. Megan Cytron and Christian Perez of the Alpha 60 Design Shop designed and built the Free Agent Nation Web site. Alice Wonsowski transcribed most of the interview tapes. Joel Velasco found facts and crunched numbers.

My parents—Bebe Lavin and Paul Pink—taught me to think for myself and to work for myself, two qualities I hope are reflected in this book. My in-laws—Liz and Alan Lerner—welcomed my wife and our two daughters when my incessant crankiness drove this trio to escape from Free Agent Nation.

Sophie and Eliza, aka the Pink Sisters, remained scrumptious and amazing throughout the reporting and writing of their father's first book. Sophie reminded me that while "some Moms and Dads work at night, and some Moms and Dads work during the day, you work in the daytime *and* at nighttime." Eliza brought me my shoes—whether I needed them or not.

And in the end, as well as in the beginning and the middle, there is Jessica Anne Lerner—my beautiful, brainy wife. Jessica read every word of this book—and tens of thousands of additional words that, thanks to her keen judgment, you'll never see. She discussed every idea, sharpened every argument, tolerated every idiosyncrasy, soothed every fear—and did it all with such grace that it staggers me to think of it now. She is a merciless editor, a merciful companion, and the love of my life.

Index

About the Author

Daniel H. Pink is author of *Free Agent Nation*, the provocative and acclaimed *Washington Post* bestseller about the rise of people who work for themselves. His articles on business, economic transformation, and the future have appeared in *Fast Company*, the *New York Times*, *New Republic*, and *Slate*, among others. He's also provided analysis of business and social trends on dozens of television and radio broadcasts—including ABC's "World News Tonight," CNBC's "Power Lunch," and NPR's "Morning Edition." A former White House speechwriter, Pink lives in Washington, D.C. with his wife and their three children. He invites readers to email him at dan@freeagentnation.com.

ALSO AVAILABLE FROM WARNER BOOKS

DIGITAL ABORIGINAL
The Direction of Business Now:
Instinctive, Nomadic, and Ever-Changing
by Mikela Tarlow with Philip Tarlow

Once people moved freely in a world strung together not by roads or wires but by impressions and stories. Here two noted authors show how today's technology-driven information blurs old borderlines and that in many ways we live in an era very much like that of our aboriginal ancestors. In this brilliant, forward-thinking book, they urge business managers to re-imagine strategies and customers and help managers and entrepreneurs enter this modern age with a clearer vision of new markets, new products, and new rewards on the digital frontier.

"A road map to the treasures of our primal past, which are now signposts of our future. We serve ourselves well by heeding [the Tarlows]."
— Isisara Bey, vice president, Corporate Affairs, Sony Music

BLUR
The Speed of Change in the Connected Economy
by Stan Davis and Christopher Meyer

Customized products, interactive buyers and sellers, 24-hour-a-day customer service, Web sites, e-mail, beepers, cell phones, overnight delivery. Today real-time responsiveness is standard, distance has disappeared, and change happens so fast it's only a blur. A company can either profit in this new economic world or be destroyed by it. This dynamic, groundbreaking guide reveals who the hottest innovators are today, shows you what tomorrow's winners will need, and gives you fifty ways to blur your business right now.

"Fast, smart, and useful—a decoder ring that any business person can use to make sense of the world of work today."
— Alan Webber, founding editor, *Fast Company*